Beyond Presidentialism and Parliamentarism

Beyond Presidentialism and Parliamentarism

Democratic Design and the Separation of Powers

STEFFEN GANGHOF

UNIVERSITY PRESS

Great Clarendon Street, Oxford, OX2 6DP,
United Kingdom

Oxford University Press is a department of the University of Oxford.
It furthers the University's objective of excellence in research, scholarship,
and education by publishing worldwide. Oxford is a registered trade mark of
Oxford University Press in the UK and in certain other countries

Impression: 1

Published in the United States of America by Oxford University Press
198 Madison Avenue, New York, NY 10016, United States of America

British Library Cataloguing in Publication Data
Data available

Library of Congress Control Number: 2021939831
Data available

ISBN 978–0–19–289714–5

DOI: 10.1093/oso/9780192897145.001.0001

Printed and bound by
CPI Group (UK) Ltd, Croydon, CR0 4YY

Acknowledgments

I am grateful to many people for helping me to improve and complete this book.

My biggest debt is to two of my former team members at the University of Potsdam. Sebastian Eppner is not only the co-author of Chapter 7, but his help in gathering, managing, and analyzing the data for this book was indispensable. It was always a joy to work and publish with him. Alexander Pörschke organized the gathering of the information on the Australian states and shared with me his data on legislative success rates and divisions. I profited greatly from their advice and expertise on many issues.

Many colleagues provided comments on one or several draft chapters or discussed individual arguments with me. The list includes, but is not limited to Joachim Behnke, Flemming Juul Christiansen, David Clune, Tiago Ribeiro dos Santos, Chris Edelson, Bonnie Field, Jessica Fortin-Rittberger, Anna Fruhstorfer, Gareth Griffith, Katja Heeß, Michael Koß, Philip Manow, Anthony McGann, Armin Schäfer, Campbell Sharman, Fritz W. Scharpf, Rodney Smith, Jared Sonnicksen, Christian Stecker, Dag Tanneberg, Mahir Tokatlı, Michelangelo Vercesi, Daniel Viehoff, Albert Weale, Simone Wegmann, and James L. Wilson. Special thanks go to J.D. Mussell, who provided very helpful feedback on all chapters, and to Matthew Shugart, who commented on most chapters and whose own work has been a major inspiration for this book. I am also grateful to three anonymous readers for Oxford University Press and for the comments on an earlier version of Chapter 7 received from the participants at a meeting of the Berlin–Brandenburg research network on political behavior in July 2018 at the Free University of Berlin.

Many Australian colleagues and interviewees generously helped me to better understand Australian politics. I thank Anika Gauja and Rodney Smith for their hospitality and David Clune and Gareth Griffith for their continuous feedback and encouragement. I am also grateful to the editors of the *Australian Journal of Political Science*, who provided the space for a symposium on semi-parliamentary government, and to the late Robert Elgie, Rodney Smith, Marija Taflaga, and Albert Weale for participating in it. Their critical but constructive comments helped me in developing my arguments. Parts of the book draw on the lead article for this symposium (Ganghof et al. 2018), as well as two other open-access articles (Ganghof 2016a, 2018a). I thank the editors and reviewers at these journals for their service and input.

The University of Potsdam and the German Research Foundation provided the resources to hire dedicated research assistants who helped to assemble and document the data for this book. The list includes Malica Christ, Fabio Ellger, Leon Gärtner, Lilly Hock, Marlene Jugl, Carolin Kaddatz, Yannick Krodel, Johannes Kuhn, Christian Lange, Christian Probst, Petra Rollfing, Aaron Schünemann, and Sophie Stadlinger. Denise Al-Gaddooa Christoph Koch and Mona Noé also provided excellent assistance in preparing the manuscript for publication. Thanks also go to Henryke Brade for her help in preparing the index.

The financial support of the Volkswagen Foundation's Opus Magnum program helped me to complete this book and to publish it in an open-access version. I would like to thank the Foundation and its anonymous referees for their trust in the project and Aiko Wagner for his excellent job as a substitute professor during my leave of absence. I am also grateful to my editor, Dominic Byatt, most of all for his enthusiasm about this project, and to everyone involved in the production process, especially Fiona Barry, Roopa Vineetha Nelson, Vicki Sunter, and Olivia Wells.

Last but not least, I thank my family and friends for their love and support.

S.G.
Berlin
April 2021

Contents

List of Figures

List of Tables

List of Abbreviations (Countries and Subnational Units)

Note: Further abbreviations are explained where they appear.
Country and subnational (in alphabetical order)

Country	**Code**
Australia	AUS
Austria	AUT
Belgium	BEL
Canada	CAN
Denmark	DNK
Finland	FIN
France	FRA
Germany	DEU
Greece	GRC
Iceland	ISL
Ireland	IRL
Israel	ISR
Italy	ITA
Japan	JPN
Luxembourg	LUX
Netherlands	NLD
New South Wales (Australia)	NSW
New Zealand	NZL
Norway	NOR
Portugal	PRT
Queensland (Australia)	QLD
South Australia (Australia)	SA
Spain	ESP
Sweden	SWE
Switzerland	CHE
Tasmania (Australia)	TAS
United Kingdom	GBR
Victoria (Australia)	VIC
Western (Australia)	WA

1
The road not taken

This book argues that, in a democracy, a constitutional separation of powers between the executive and the assembly may be a good thing, but the constitutional concentration of executive power in a single human being—what I call executive personalism—is not.

This thesis may seem plausible, perhaps too plausible to be interesting. Yet almost the entire democratic world is dominated by only three types of constitutions, all of which fail to disentangle the separation of powers from executive personalism: On the one hand, parliamentary constitutions reject both, while, on the other hand, their presidential and semi-presidential counterparts embrace both. And even though these three types of constitutions are fairly old (the youngest was invented in 1919), there has been surprisingly little academic thinking about strategies to decouple the separation of powers from executive personalism. I argue that this decoupling is desirable and explore one widely neglected strategy, which I call, for want of a better term, semi-parliamentary government (Ganghof 2018a). Semi-parliamentarism achieves powers separation without executive personalism.

Executive personalism and the locus of powers separation

I use "executive personalism" to describe the extent to which constitutional rules (a) vest executive power in a single human being; who (b) is democratically authorized directly by the voters; and (c) who cannot be dismissed for political reasons by any collective and representative entity, such as an assembly or a political party. To the extent that these conditions hold, executive power is personalized by the constitution. Executive personalism thus understood is, in an important sense, a historical overhang from monarchy (Colomer 2013; Nelson 2014; Scheuerman 2005). Or, as Prakash (2020: 24) suggests for the United States of America, it is itself a form of "limited monarchy"; we just do not recognize this "because we have been fooled by the myths about the Founding and misled by our stereotypes of what makes a king."

Beyond Presidentialism and Parliamentarism. Steffen Ganghof, Oxford University Press.
 DOI: 10.1093/oso/9780192897145.003.0001

The concept of executive personalism says nothing about how much power the chief executive has. In principle, this power may be heavily constrained by the constitutional checks and balances of a separation-of-powers system, as well as informally by political parties and public opinion. Executive personalism must, nevertheless, be conceptually distinguished from the separation of powers. The latter does not require the former. Moreover, executive personalism seems to have a causal tendency, under a broad range of background conditions, to strengthen presidential power and undermine and erode formal and informal constraints on the executive (e.g. Ginsberg 2016: 38–52; Posner 2016; Prakash 2020; Samuels and Shugart 2010).

Whether or not the separation of powers becomes connected to executive personalism depends on its precise location between the two branches. Under parliamentary government, the executive is selected by the assembly and can also be dismissed by it for purely political reasons—there is a fusion of powers between the executive and the assembly majority. In a single chain of delegation, voters elect one collective agent, the assembly, which then selects a prime minister and cabinet as agents of the assembly (Strøm 2000). Under presidentialism and semi-presidentialism, voters also popularly elect, for a fixed term, a second agent: the president. The separation of powers thus becomes entangled with executive personalism. The difference between presidentialism and semi-presidentialism is the location of powers separation. Under presidentialism, the president essentially *is* the executive, so that power is separated between the executive and the legislature. Under semi-presidentialism, there is also a prime minister and cabinet responsible to the assembly, so that the locus of powers separation is shifted into the executive: One part (the president) is separated from the assembly, while the other part (the prime minister and cabinet) is fused with it.

The semi-parliamentary separation of powers

Semi-parliamentarism decouples powers separation from executive personalism by shifting its locus *into the assembly*. Imagine an assembly that is divided into two parts. This can be two separate chambers or a committee embedded within a single chamber. The important point is that both parts are directly elected, so that voters have two agents with robust democratic legitimacy. Let us imagine that these two agents are given two partly different tasks. One of them has the task of selecting and dismissing the prime minister and cabinet, as under parliamentarism. It is a chamber or committee of confidence, whose majority is fused with the government. The other has the tasks of representing voters in the deliberative and legislative process and controlling the government. It is a chamber of legislation and control, which does not participate in the selection and dismissal of the cabinet.[1] Since one part of the assembly is separated from the executive, there is a separation of powers; and since the other is also a collective entity, rather than a fixed-term president, there can be no executive personalism. I contend that this constitutional structure is not only a distinct form of bicameralism (or quasi-bicameralism) but also a distinct form of government (Ganghof 2014). It can achieve the potential benefits of powers separation, while avoiding the perils of executive personalism.

Does semi-parliamentary government already exist? Only to some extent. A few democratic constitutions with bicameral assemblies approximate semi-parliamentarism, but they have not been purposefully designed with a semi-parliamentary blueprint in mind. Their development has been path-dependent, perhaps even "accidental" (Smith 2018a). Moreover, semi-parliamentarism could be implemented in a variety of ways, many of which have never been tried in the real world.

This book therefore takes a two-pronged approach to exploring semi-parliamentarism. On the one hand, it comparatively analyzes the cases that most closely approximate an ideal-type of semi-parliamentary government. These cases are the Australian Commonwealth and Japan, but especially the Australian states of New South Wales, South Australia, Tasmania, Victoria, and Western Australia (Ganghof 2018a). These democratic systems can be classified as semi-parliamentary because they have bicameral parliaments in which both chambers (a) are directly elected and (b) possess robust veto power over ordinary legislation, but (c) where only one of them selects and dismisses the prime minister and cabinet.[2] Using data from 1975 to 2018, I compare patterns of party systems, cabinet formation, legislative coalition-building, and constitutional reform in these cases to those in 21 parliamentary and semi-presidential democracies, as well as Switzerland's assembly-independent system.

On the other hand, my interest does not lie in the intricacies of Australian and Japanese politics. Rather than getting drawn too deeply into the specifics of the cases, the book also explores optimized and new semi-parliamentary

[1] Obviously, the vote of no confidence cannot be an instrument of control for this chamber, but the confidence relationship between executive and assembly often tends to strengthen the former; it tends to create executive dominance. This point is further discussed in Chapter 3.

[2] Chapter 3 elaborates on the operational and ideal-typical definitions of semi-parliamentarism, on their relation to the concept of "symmetrical" bicameralism, and on the notion of robust veto power.

designs, some of which do not require fully fledged bicameralism. Understanding these constitutional options is important to gauge semi-parliamentarism's potential as an alternative to the presidential version of the separation of powers.

In comparing semi-parliamentarism to other forms of government, especially to parliamentarism and presidentialism, the book develops four main themes:

1. Semi-parliamentarism is superior to presidentialism. It can balance different visions of democracy, while avoiding executive personalism.
2. To compare semi-parliamentarism to pure parliamentarism, we have to revise our understanding of what the competing visions of democracy are.
3. Semi-parliamentary bicameralism achieves an effective and stable form of horizontal political control and accountability that is not necessarily supermajoritarian.
4. There is no meaningful way in which presidentialism or parliamentarism is inherently more democratic than semi-parliamentarism.

Why semi-parliamentarism is superior to presidentialism

For a long time, the political science debate about forms of government was organized around Juan Linz's (1990a, 1990b, 1994) famous critique of presidentialism. He argued that the presidential constitution has inherent flaws, which help to explain the instability of democracies, especially in Latin America. Linz's arguments did not systematically distinguish between the flaws associated with the separation of powers (e.g. the problem of inter-branch deadlock) and those due to executive personalism (e.g. the problem of holding presidents accountable). However, when scholars defended presidentialism by highlighting its potential advantages, these concerned the separation of powers, not executive personalism (Cheibub 2006, 2007; Mainwaring and Shugart 1997; Shugart and Carey 1992). Even when authors seem to argue for executive personalism directly (Calabresi 2001), many of their arguments merely justify the separation of powers (Chapter 9).

The central advantage of presidentialism lies in its potential for balancing different visions of democracy. A perennial debate surrounding parliamentary systems is whether electoral systems ought to give voters a clear choice between two political forces (as in the so-called Westminster model) or whether they should focus on representing voters fairly in the legislative deliberation and decision process (Lijphart 1984; Powell 2000; Rosenbluth and Shapiro 2018). Under the presidential separation of powers, both goals are attainable at the same time: "Majoritarian" presidential elections can provide a clear choice, while "proportional" legislative elections can achieve fair representation. Moreover, powers separation can also liberate the assembly from the task of keeping the government in office. As a result, the assembly can potentially achieve greater independence in deliberating and deciding on individual pieces of legislation and in controlling the government. One implication of this independence is that majority coalitions can form in a flexible, issue-specific manner—which some theorists see as more egalitarian and, thus, inherently more democratic than the formation of a fixed veto player coalition (Ganghof 2015a, b; Ward and Weale 2010).

I contend that semi-parliamentary government can achieve these potential advantages of presidentialism just as well if not better. What enables citizens to vote for a clear political direction under presidentialism is not executive personalism but a majoritarian electoral system that narrows the competition down to a few—ideally two—alternatives. This can also be achieved by a majoritarian electoral system for the chamber or committee of confidence.[3] And just as the entire assembly is more independent from the executive under presidentialism, so is the chamber of legislation and control under semi-parliamentarism. This is sufficient to reap the benefits of a more independent legislature.

My argument even goes further. Executive personalism is not only unnecessary to achieve the benefits of the separation of powers, but it also has negative consequences. Direct effects include the weakening of political parties' programmatic and representational capacities (Samuels and Shugart 2010) and the potentially increased risk of an authoritarian takeover by the incumbent president (Linz 1994; Svolik 2015). Indirect effects result from the efforts to contain the dangers of executive personalism through constitutional features such as the impossibility of presidential re-election (Baturo and Elgie 2019) and assembly dissolution. These features undermine some of the alleged advantages of the separation of powers (e.g. electoral accountability) and exacerbate some of its dangers (e.g. unresolvable legislative deadlock). An adequate understanding of how semi-parliamentarism achieves the benefits of

[3] Using electoral plurality or majority rule in *single-seat districts* does not guarantee two-party systems. However, Chapter 8 shows how the chamber or committee of confidence could be elected in a single, jurisdiction-wide district and how local and regional representation could be shifted into the more separated chamber of legislation and control.

powers separation without the perils of executive personalism undermines any instrumentalist case for presidentialism.

Rethinking the visions of democracy

Whether the semi-parliamentary separation of powers is superior to pure parliamentarism, is less clear. To compare these two systems, I explore empirically how they can balance competing models or visions of democracy—what I call normative balancing.

I also propose a new way of thinking about these visions. In political science, it is common to contrast a "majoritarian" model of democracy with a "consensual" or "proportional" one (Lijphart 2012; Powell 2000). Since democracy is fundamentally built on the idea of majority rule, I do not find this approach plausible. Instead, I conceptualize the competing visions as being equally majoritarian. They agree that majorities ought to rule, but differ in how these majorities ought to be formed.[4] Their core disagreement is about how much the process of majority formation needs to be simplified, which is why I call them *simple and complex majoritarianism* (Ganghof 2015a). Proponents of simple majoritarianism are skeptical about voters' cognitive abilities and parties' coordinative capabilities and therefore want to greatly simplify the democratic process (Rosenbluth and Shapiro 2018; see also Carey and Hix 2011; Cunow et al. 2021). Proponents of complex majoritarianism, by contrast, are principally concerned with expanding voters' options. Proportional electoral systems are not preferred because they lead to proportional or consensual government (they do not) but because they offer more choice to voters along multiple dimensions of disagreement and conflict (McGann 2013; Przeworski 2003; Rodden 2020).

From this perspective, it is natural to extend the vision of complex majoritarianism to the idea that legislative proposals should be deliberated and voted on in a flexible, issue-specific manner. Since many issues will be considered by the government between every election and different sets of parties and citizens will form the majority on different issues, Powell (2000: 256, n. 9) considers it "important that the policy-making coalition not be locked into place by the immediate election outcome." In the idealized world of social choice theory, the normative standard of complex majoritarianism might be the issue-specific

[4] Of course, there is also an important debate on the limits of majority rule and whether institutions such as federalism derogate from democracy (see, e.g. Abizadeh 2021). This is not a debate I am concerned with in this book. I discuss bicameralism as a way to institutionalize a particular form of majority rule rather than to limit it.

median, rather than some global median in a one-dimensional conflict space (Ward and Weale 2010).

When we understand the two competing visions of democracy in this way, we can see that they are inherently difficult to reconcile in a pure parliamentary system. Voters elect only one agent, the assembly, whose two main tasks are partially in tension: selecting a government and keeping it in office, on the one hand; passing individual pieces of legislation, on the other. This tension leads to unavoidable trade-offs between competing goals—in the design of the assembly's electoral system and of the confidence relationship between executive and legislature.

Semi-parliamentary government gives us additional options for normative balancing. Since the government originates from one part of the assembly but not the other, voters can elect two different agents under different electoral rules. And because the government survives separately from one part of the assembly, this part is free to form legislative majorities in a flexible, issue-specific manner.

The reconceptualization of the two visions of democracy also implies a different interpretation of cases like Switzerland, which does not have a pure parliamentary system either. The Swiss cabinet is elected by the assembly but serves a fixed term; it cannot be voted out of office. I argue that because this feature is underemphasized in prominent studies, Swiss politics often appears as more "consensual" than it actually is (Lijphart 2012). While Switzerland is technically governed by "oversized" cabinets, these are not like their counterparts under parliamentarism (Ganghof 2010). In a parliamentary system, the parties in an oversized cabinet are veto players: If they are outvoted against their will, the government ends (Tsebelis 2002). By contrast, Swiss cabinet parties can each be outvoted on any particular issue, and they often form *minimal-winning* coalitions on controversial issues. Switzerland is, in many ways, a good example of complex majoritarianism, and the separation of powers between the executive and the assembly is a crucial reason for that.

Since it is assembly-based, semi-parliamentarism could also balance competing visions of majority formation at more fundamental levels. First, it can balance party-based and individualist visions of democratic representation. This is the case in the Australian state of Tasmania, where one chamber is dominated by parties and the other by independents (Sharman 2013). Second, it could balance elections and sortition as competing methods of democratic legitimation (Abizadeh 2020). Finally, it could balance "democratic" and "epistocratic" forms of representation (Brennan 2016).[5] While I do not explore these possibilities in much detail, Chapter 3 highlights semi-parliamentarism's more general potential for normative balancing.

Stable, effective, and majoritarian bicameralism

Semi-parliamentarism is a form of "symmetrical" or "strong" bicameralism (Lijphart 1984), which raises two worries: (a) that it is in practice incompatible with the principles of a parliamentary system; and (b) that it is inevitably supermajoritarian or "conservative" in the sense of protecting the status quo. I argue that both worries are largely unfounded.

Presidentialism and bicameralism have historically been justified as defensive shields against the rise of tyranny (Hamilton et al. 1987; Montesquieu 1977). They separate constitutional powers so as to provide horizontal accountability and control. The problem with presidentialism, though, is that its separation of powers comes packaged with executive personalism. As a result, there has been an important debate about "new" forms of powers separation which centers on two closely connected questions. One is whether bicameralism can be an effective and stable alternative to presidentialism (Ackerman 2000). The other is the extent to which it is desirable to shift the function of review and control from more narrowly political institutions to the judiciary (Bellamy 2007; Waldron 1999, 2006). This is a debate about the relative merits of different types of veto points in a democracy (Watkins and Lemieux 2015). My analysis speaks to this debate by pinpointing the conditions under which the combination of bicameralism and parliamentarism (in the first chamber) can provide effective and stable forms of review, control, and accountability.

Ackerman (2000) worries about presidentialism's executive personalism, but is also skeptical about bicameralism as an effective and stable mechanism of political control and accountability. He therefore embraces a "juricentric separation of powers" (Albert 2010: 22), which he calls constrained parliamentarism. It is a parliamentary system in which the judiciary plays a central role in monitoring the actions of the fused executive and legislative departments. These actions are constrained by a written constitution, an enshrined bill of rights, and an independent judiciary endowed with the power of constitutional review.

[5] The distinction between democracy and epistocracy, the rule of the knowledgeable (Estlund 2008), can be understood as a continuum, rather than as a dichotomy, and *representative* democracy can be seen as a sort of compromise on this continuum (Landa and Pevnick 2020b).

Ackerman's skepticism about bicameralism is shared by much of the literature in political science, which has long been puzzled about the workability and stability of "strong" forms of bicameralism (Lijphart 1984) in otherwise parliamentary systems of government. Many authors have postulated a basic incompatibility between parliamentarism and strong bicameralism. According to Lijphart (1984: 101–104), this incompatibility could only be overcome if politicians build cabinets that control majorities in both chambers. Yet, if this leads to the formation of "oversized" and/or ideologically heterogeneous cabinets, it may not only re-establish executive dominance but also be "unworkable" in practice (Sartori 1997: 186). Ackerman (2000: 673–80) contends that strong bicameralism *requires* a presidential system, rather than being an alternative to it (see also Calabresi 2001: 87).

Other authors, by contrast, are more sanguine about the potential of bicameralism and more concerned about the political power of courts (e.g. Waldron 2006, 2012). Gardbaum (2014) concurs with Ackerman by suggesting that the growth of strong judicial review has partly been caused by a lost faith in "political accountability as an effective and sufficient check on government action" (Gardbaum 2014: 618). He highlights the Australian experience as an important exception and speculates that strong and effective bicameralism helps to explain why the country has resisted the constitutionalization and judicialization of rights.

This important debate falls short in one crucial way. Both sides fail to pinpoint the conditions under which bicameralism can be an effective and stable tool of horizontal political control and accountability. I show that, to understand these conditions, we have to go beyond the prominent concepts of "symmetrical" or "strong" bicameralism (Lijphart 1984: 96–101). These concepts were developed within a particular theory and deliberately neglected how second chambers relate to the executive. For a second chamber to be classified as "symmetrical" or "strong," it does not matter whether it has the right to a no-confidence vote against the cabinet, whether it participates in the cabinet's investiture, whether it can veto the budget, or whether it can be dissolved under certain circumstances. I argue that once these and other design features are systematically considered in comparative perspective, we can understand why well-designed, semi-parliamentary bicameralism can be effective and stable. Its design reduces second chambers' effect on cabinet formation—most notably by denying them participation in the vote of confidence procedures—while allowing for the flexible, issue-specific formation of legislative majorities.

The last point is also important for understanding why bicameralism is not necessarily supermajoritarian, despite what much of the political science literature suggests (McGann 2006: 184; Przeworski 2010: 143–144, n. 10; Tsebelis and Money 1997: 216–217). This literature has long recognized the possibility that the second chamber is "absorbed" by the first; for example, because its partisan composition is identical (Tsebelis 2002). Yet, the reverse may also be true: If the first chamber is dominated by a single majority party that is located in the center of the policy space and builds issue-specific coalitions in the second, it is effectively absorbed by these coalitions. Moreover, given the democratic legitimacy of the second chamber under semi-parliamentarism, it becomes plausible to weaken the veto power of the *first chamber* (Chapter 8). Semi-parliamentary bicameralism does not necessarily imply a rejection of majority rule, but it can institutionalize a particular form of it.

Why semi-parliamentarism is not less democratic

All the arguments advanced so far concern the causal consequences of political institutions. Yet many normative theorists insist that political institutions may also have some kind of "procedural" value which is entirely independent of causal consequences and which can render one set of institutions inherently more democratic than another. Strikingly, while the normative literature has advanced this type of argument for many aspects of institutional design (electoral systems, decision-making rules, judicial review, and so on), it has been virtually silent about forms of government. In the political science and public law literatures, however, we can find two proceduralist conjectures that need to be addressed. Based on a discussion of how proceduralist arguments can be meaningful, I find both of them wanting.

The first conjecture is that presidentialism is inherently more democratic than parliamentarism—and semi-parliamentarism for that matter—in virtue of the direct election of the chief executive (Arato 2000; Calabresi 2001: 67; Lijphart 1992b: 13; von Mettenheim 1997). This conjecture neglects that, in a representative democracy, procedural equality has two dimensions: horizontal and vertical (Dworkin 2000). While the direct election of a president can reasonably be seen as reducing vertical inequality, the indirect selection and deselection of a prime minister by a fairly elected assembly can reasonably be seen as reducing horizontal inequality (McGann 2006). Hence, a purely proceduralist comparison of presidentialism and parliamentarism remains inconclusive. As part of this discussion, I also highlight the lack of interest that proceduralist arguments for presidentialism have shown in the direct recall of presidents (but see Pérez-Liñán 2020). This is striking because the power to revoke an agent's authority is arguably the most fundamental power of any principal.

The second conjecture is that parliamentarism is inherently more egalitarian than semi-parliamentarism in virtue of giving all assembly members equal formal power over the cabinet (Meinel 2019: 212; see also Meinel 2021: Chapter 7). I reject this idea because our concern must be with the equal treatment, not of assembly members, but of citizens. When this point is accepted, there is actually an important sense in which semi-parliamentarism is procedurally superior to parliamentarism, everything else being equal. Most parliamentary systems establish legal or implicit thresholds of *representation* such that the voters of below-threshold parties are purposefully denied any representation. By contrast, semi-parliamentarism establishes a legal or implicit threshold of *confidence authority* such that parties whose vote share is below the threshold are denied participation in the no-confidence procedure. Therefore, when we compare the two forms of government while holding the respective thresholds constant, semi-parliamentarism treats voters *more* equally. If, say, Germany replaced its 5% threshold of representation with a 5% threshold of confidence authority, the voters of below-threshold parties would be denied fewer participation rights. They would be equally represented in parliamentary deliberation, legislative voting, and controlling the government. Their unequal treatment by the democratic procedures would become more visible but less severe.

Chapter overview

To develop in detail the four themes summarized, Chapter 2 begins by elaborating on the distinction between the separation of powers and executive personalism. Prevalent typologies in political science tend to conflate these two dimensions because they limit themselves to dichotomies or trichotomies. The chapter distinguishes six basic forms of government and shows how each represents a specific combination of powers separation and executive personalism. It also shows that semi-parliamentary government is unique in achieving powers separation without any executive personalism.

Chapter 3 specifies the concept of semi-parliamentary government. It provides ideal-typical and operational definitions and gives an overview of the semi-parliamentary cases analyzed in this book. I also highlight the blind spots of existing typologies to explain why the new concept is needed. Finally, the chapter distinguishes different types of normative balancing that semi-parliamentarism may help to achieve.

Chapter 4 explains the normative approach of this book and clarifies the distinction between instrumentalist and proceduralist evaluations of political institutions. It defends a minimalist form of proceduralism, which highlights the comparative evaluation of institutional schemes, as well as the potential conflict between horizontal and vertical equality. Based on these conceptual clarifications, I reject the alleged procedural superiority of presidentialism over parliamentarism and of parliamentarism over semi-parliamentarism.

Chapter 5 elaborates on the distinction between simple and complex majoritarianism and explores how and to what extent parliamentary systems can balance these two visions of democracy. I operationalize each vision in terms of three specific goals and use the resulting empirical measures to create a two-dimensional map of democratic patterns in 22 democracies in the period 1993–2018. The results reveal the conflict between the two visions and show that their most demanding goals cannot be reconciled under pure parliamentarism. Voters cannot make a clear choice between competing cabinet alternatives ("identifiability"), while also being fairly represented in issue-specific legislative decision-making ("legislative flexibility").

Chapter 6 applies the framework developed in Chapter 5 to the semi-parliamentary cases. It explains how semi-parliamentarism can balance simple and complex majoritarianism, compares the institutional designs of the seven cases, and positions them on the two-dimensional map of democratic patterns. The analysis shows how the separation of powers can help to balance the two visions in ways that are unavailable under pure parliamentarism. In particular, semi-parliamentarism can help to reconcile identifiability and legislative flexibility. I complement the two-dimensional mapping of democracies with comparative analyses of legislative coalition-building in Australia, as well as legislative success rates under different forms of government. The chapter also discusses challenges to my argument and sketches the broader implications for the performance of democracies. Finally, it explains how semi-parliamentarism may complement other institutional designs, such as compulsory voting and weaker forms of judicial review.

Chapter 7 discusses the conditions under which semi-parliamentary government can be stable. It responds to two conjectures about "strong" bicameralism: (a) that it requires a presidential system; and (b) that if strong bicameralism is combined with "parliamentarism" in the first chamber, the cabinets formed after the election need to control majorities in the second chamber. The chapter argues that both conjectures are unfounded because they neglect the more detailed design of bicameral systems. Second chambers can be designed to be permissive with respect to cabinet formation. The lack of a no-confidence vote is one important aspect of such a design. The chapter corroborates this argument with conditional logit analyses of cabinet formation in 28 democratic systems in the period 1975–2018.[6] It also uses brief case discussions to show that the more detailed design of second chambers helps us to explain the reform or stability of bicameral systems.

Chapter 8 discusses new and improved ways to design semi-parliamentary government. This constitutional format provides a flexible framework that can be adapted to different contexts and fine-tuned as an alternative to presidentialism. While the tension between simple and complex majoritarianism inevitably resurfaces in the design of inter-branch relations, I argue that semi-parliamentarism allows for ways of resolving legislative deadlock that would be more problematic under presidentialism or other forms of bicameralism. Because the executive is not personalized, it becomes less risky to allow this branch to dissolve the assembly or to initiate a popular referendum on a deadlocked bill. And because the second chamber has at least equal democratic legitimacy to the first chamber, deadlock can be avoided by weakening the veto power of the *first chamber*.

Finally, Chapter 9 uses the book's insights about semi-parliamentarism to articulate a systematic instrumentalist case against presidentialism. Even if one accepts the potential benefits of the separation of powers, presidential government is not a justifiable way to achieve them. These benefits can be achieved by semi-parliamentary government just as well or better, while executive personalism undermines or weighs against them. Justifications of executive personalism are neither well developed nor supported by systematic empirical evidence. Democrats have no principled reason to choose or maintain presidential government.

[6] Switzerland is excluded in this analysis because neither chamber of parliament can dismiss the cabinet in a no-confidence vote.

2

Separation of powers ≠ presidentialism

The separation of powers between executive and assembly is often explicitly conflated with the presidential form of government, as if one could not be had without the other (Calabresi 2001: 54). This is to some extent the legacy of the so-called old institutionalists, who tended to focus on the cases of Great Britain and the United States and paid little attention to systems that were neither parliamentary nor presidential (Bagehot 1867; Laski 1940; Wilson 1844). Their hunch was "that the basic forms of democratic government follow an essentially dichotomous pattern" (Lijphart 1997b: 128). In parts of the literature, this dichotomous thinking has persisted until today. As a result, presidential government is defended in terms of the separation of powers (Calabresi 2001) and the direct election of the chief executive is proposed as the most appropriate way to democratize separation-of-powers systems like that of the European Union (Sonnicksen 2017).

We ought to stop conflating powers separation with presidentialism and instead evaluate forms of government along two separable analytical dimensions. One is the *separation of powers*: roughly, the degree to which the origin and survival of the executive is separated from the assembly. The other is *executive personalism*: roughly, the degree to which the power of the executive is constitutionally focused on a single human being. The main goal in this chapter is to show how the separation of powers can be decoupled from executive personalism—and that semi-parliamentary government is a way to do so.

Table 2.1 summarizes the argument in a simplified manner. In presidential and parliamentary government, the separation of powers and executive personalism are perfectly correlated; semi-parliamentarism decouples them. Executive personalism without the separation of powers could hardly be considered democratic; it would be some form of elective dictatorship.

Table 2.1 is too simple a typology, of course, as there are other hybrid forms of government. Most studies and textbooks in political science work with a trichotomy that distinguishes the two pure types from the most prevalent hybrid: semi-*presidentialism* (e.g. Cheibub et al. 2014; Samuels 2007). Yet, since

Beyond Presidentialism and Parliamentarism. Steffen Ganghof, Oxford University Press.
 DOI: 10.1093/oso/9780192897145.003.0002

Table 2.1 The separation of powers and executive personalism

	Separation of powers	
Executive personalism	**Yes**	**No**
Yes	Presidentialism	(Elective dictatorship)
No	Semi-parliamentarism	Parliamentarism

the latter ties the separation of powers very closely to executive personalism, too, the common trichotomy also reinforces the conflation of the separation of powers and executive personalism. I argue that we ought to distinguish six basic forms of government and highlight how three of them can be understood as efforts to reap some or all of the benefits of the separation of powers, while limiting or avoiding executive personalism. This chapter pays special attention to these oft-neglected hybrids: elected prime-ministerial government in Israel (from 1992 to 2001), assembly-independent government in Switzerland, and semi-parliamentary government in Australia (and Japan).

I begin by elaborating on the concept of executive personalism. Then I discuss the six basic types of government, which come in three logical pairs: presidentialism and parliamentarism, the Israeli and Swiss hybrids, and semi-presidentialism and semi-parliamentarism. The discussion of the two pure types remains short, as a fuller exploration is reserved for Chapters 5 and 9. The chapter ends by synthesizing the argument in a simple typological framework.

Executive personalism

As noted in Chapter 1, executive personalism refers to the extent to which constitutional rules (a) vest executive power in a single human being; (b) who is democratically authorized (more or less) directly by the voters; and (c) who cannot be dismissed for political reasons by any collective and representative entity such as an assembly or a political party.[1] The concept says nothing about how much power the chief executive has, but executive personalism seems to have a causal tendency, under a broad range of background conditions, to

[1] My understanding of this concept thus differs from that of others. Altman (2020: 319) focuses solely on the distinction between "unipersonal" and "collective" executives and thus treats those in parliamentary systems as unipersonal.

strengthen presidential power and undermine and erode formal and informal constraints on executive. While this causal hypothesis is one reason for focusing on executive personalism, it must be distinguished from the concept as such.[2]

As to formal constraints on the executive, presidentialism in the United States is a good example. The history of the US presidency has been one of the gradual expansion of its power and importance, and this expansion has been fueled by executive personalism (Ginsberg 2016: 38–52; Prakash 2020). Madison's idea of checks and balances underestimated the unifying power of presidential leadership, as well as the pressure to work around the deadlock created by numerous institutional veto players (Howell and Moe 2016, 2020). As a result, presidents "dismantled the Madisonian system piece by piece, paving the way for our current president-centered system of national administration" (Posner 2016: 42). Much of the power of the US president is thus not kept in check anymore by constitutional constraints, but "by public scrutiny, the media, and the challenge of leading different institutions and groups in an enormous and diverse country" (Posner 2016: 43). Or so one might hope.

As to informal checks and balances, the picture is similar. It is certainly plausible that more strongly organized parties with an independent leadership and an institutionalized bureaucracy are able to "try to curb the excesses of the president in order to protect their own political prospects" (Rhodes-Purdy and Madrid 2020: 321; see also Martínez 2021). Yet, the problem is that weak organizational and programmatic capacities of political parties are, to a large extent, *endogenous* to executive personalism.

Samuels and Shugart (2010) have shown that parties in presidential and semi-presidential systems often become "presidentialized." This means that they "delegate considerable discretion to their leaders-as-executives to shape their electoral and governing strategies, and that parties lose their ability to hold their agents to account" (Samuels and Shugart 2010: 37). As a result, "political parties in pure and semi-presidential systems are unlikely, under most conditions, to act as voters' representational agents as they do in parliamentary systems" (Samuels and Shugart 2010: 247). Chief executives may even be able to reverse the principal–agent relationship and dominate their parties, rather than being responsible to them. This also means that they can often rely on

[2] The concept of executive personalism as used here must also be distinguished from different causal hypotheses about the so-called "presidentialization" in democratic politics (Elgie and Passarelli 2019). Below I discuss Samuels and Shugart's (2010) important theory of the presidentialization of parties. This presidentialization, to the extent that it exists in a particular case, is a *behavioral effect*, whereas what I call executive personalism is the *institutional cause*.

"their" parties to undermine the separation of powers (Levinson and Pildes 2006). Parties may not be strong enough principals to control the president, but they can be cohesive and polarized agents enough to shield him or her from effective checks and balances.

While my arguments draw heavily on the important theory by Samuels and Shugart (2010), I also argue that it needs clarification and extension. Its main claim is that "to the extent that the constitutional structure separates executive and legislative origin and/or survival, parties will tend to be presidentialized" (2010: 37). Yet, the authors only analyze versions of the separation of powers that imply the direct election of either a president or a prime minister. Assembly-independent government in Switzerland and semi-parliamentary government in Australia (and Japan) are excluded from their analysis (Samuels and Shugart 2010: 28), but these are precisely the versions of the separation of powers that limit or prevent executive personalism by avoiding any direct executive elections. *It is not the separation of powers that presidentializes parties, but executive personalism.* Or so I argue in this chapter.

Presidential and parliamentary government

The two pure forms of government have been distinguished in myriad ways (Lijphart 1992b), but virtually all leading scholars today agree on two definitional criteria (Cheibub et al. 2014; Elgie 2018; Lijphart 1984; Samuels and Shugart 2010; Shugart and Carey 1992). One concerns the *origin* of the executive: Is the (chief) executive selected by the legislature or elected independently from the legislative assembly, in popular elections? The other dimension concerns the executive's *survival* in office: Can the chief executive and cabinet be removed by the assembly in a political no-confidence vote with a simple or absolute majority—or is there only an impeachment procedure of a more judicial and typically supermajoritarian nature (Pérez-Liñán 2020)? These two institutional dimensions affect the degree of branch-based powers separation as well as the degree of executive personalism.

In the two pure types of parliamentary and presidential government, the separation of powers and executive personalism are perfectly aligned (Figure 2.1). *Pure presidentialism* separates the origin and survival of the chief executive in a way that maximizes executive personalism. Presidents, as the chief executives, are popularly (usually directly) elected by the voters for a fixed term; they cannot be removed by the assembly in a political no-confidence vote. Hence, the president's authority does not depend on the assembly or

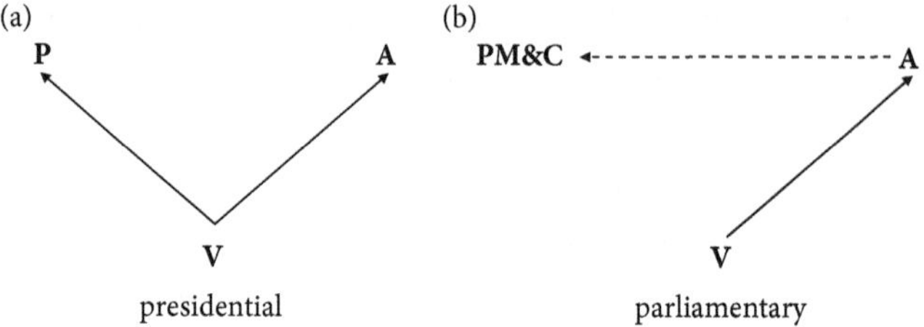

Fig. 2.1 Presidential and parliamentary government: Fig. 2.1(a) presidential; Fig. 2.1(b) parliamentary

Notes: V = voters, A = assembly, P = President, PM = Prime Minister, C = Cabinet, → = election, ⇢ = dismissal.

any other collective entity at the representative level. Presidentialism achieves the separation of powers by vesting massive executive authority in a single human being. As a result, parties in presidential systems tend to become presidentialized (Samuels and Shugart 2010).

While presidentialism's executive personalism is, to some extent, a historical overhang from monarchy (Colomer 2013; Nelson 2014; Prakash 2020: Chapter 1; Scheuerman 2005), the power concentration in a single human being has also been justified in democratic terms. One idea is that it increases clarity of responsibility (DiClerico 1987: 304); another is that the direct election of chief executives is inherently "more democratic" than their indirect selection by the assembly (Arato 2000: 321; Calabresi 2001: 67; Lijphart 1992a: 13). However, if these normative ideas of democratic responsibility and popular control are taken seriously, one might expect proponents of presidentialism to be equally strong champions of the possibility of *direct recall*; that is, the dismissal of presidents in a recall referendum.[3] Presidents would then be responsible to their voters on an ongoing basis. The democratic principal would have more control over its directly elected agent between elections. Executive personalism would become more fully democratized. In fact, though, direct recall is often ignored in comparisons of presidentialism and parliamentarism, it is only possible in a few presidential systems, and, at the time of writing, no recall election has ever succeeded in removing a national executive from office (Pérez-Liñán 2020).

Presidential constitutions also try to limit the perils of executive personalism through various means. Standard examples include impeachment procedures and the prohibition of presidential re-election (Baturo and Elgie 2019).

[3] Recall referenda are about the deselection of representatives and must therefore, in my view, be seen as an element of *representative* democracy. Nevertheless, they are mostly discussed by experts on direct democracy.

As I discuss in Chapter 9, however, these mechanisms are problematic counterweights or tend to weaken the potential benefits of the separation of powers. A much rarer approach—used in Uruguay from 1952 to 1967—is to directly elect a multi-person, collegial executive whose members share power equally and make decisions collectively (Altman 2008, 2020; see also Orentlicher 2013). Its downsides include a potential lack of efficiency and resoluteness (Altman 2020: 322–323).

Pure parliamentarism avoids executive personalism by avoiding any separation of powers between the executive and the legislature. Chief executives are selected by an assembly majority and remain accountable to it on an ongoing basis.[4] They, together with the entire cabinet, can—for purely political reasons—be dismissed by a simple or absolute assembly majority in a no-confidence vote.[5] This also implies that chief executives remain agents of their party. If a party wants to remove its prime minister, it is generally able to do so through a formal no-confidence vote in parliament or as a matter of intra-party politics.[6] Hence, even if politics becomes "personalized" in the sense that candidates' personal characteristics matter greatly, parties remain in control of their prime-ministerial candidates and, if successful, their prime minister (Samuels and Shugart 2010). Under pure parliamentarism, however, this control comes at the costs of losing the potential benefits of the separation of powers (Chapter 5).

Delicate hybrids

If pure parliamentarism and presidentialism exhausted the available design options, the separation of powers and executive personalism would be two sides of the same coin. In fact, though, a number of hybrids blend elements of the two pure types. I begin with two rare hybrids that combine separated power along one dimension—executive origin *or* survival—with fused power along the other. I argue that these hybrids are rare because they mix presidential

[4] "Assembly majority" is ambiguous when an assembly has two chambers. I elaborate on this point below and in Chapter 3.

[5] Parts of the literature associate an ideal-typical parliamentary system with single-seat districts (Strøm 2000). By contrast, I think that forms of government and visions of democratic majority formation should be kept conceptually distinct (see Chapter 5).

[6] The chief executives in a parliamentary system can have different names, such as prime minister or chancellor. They may also be called president, as in South Africa (Kotze 2019).

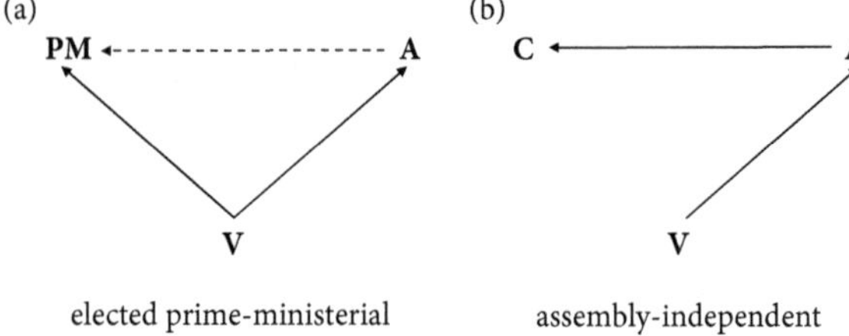

Fig. 2.2 Elected prime-ministerial and assembly-independent government: Fig. 2.2(a) elected prime-ministerial; Fig. 2.2(b) assembly-independent

Notes: V =voters, A = assembly, PM = Prime Minister, C = Cabinet, → = election, --→ = dismissal.

and parliamentary features in ways that create severe tensions. Understanding these tensions will help us to appreciate the more robust hybrids discussed afterwards.

Elected prime-ministerial government in Israel

Under this hybrid form of government, chief executives are directly elected, but their survival in office depends on the parliamentary majority—separate origin but fused survival. This system was used in Israel between 1992 and 2001 for two general elections in 1996 and 1999 and a prime-ministerial election in 2001. It was also discussed at various points in Italy, Japan, and the Netherlands. Samuels and Shugart (2010: 28) refer to it as *elected prime-ministerial*.[7]

From the perspective of democratic legitimacy, this hybrid may be viewed as combining the best of presidentialism and parliamentarism: Voters can choose chief executives directly and get rid of them at least indirectly, via a no-confidence vote in the assembly. In practice, however, this system proved

[7] A system of this kind also exists in other (small) polities, although with important differences. For instance, it was introduced at the local level in Italy, but in a way that connected the direct election of the mayor to the election of the local council so as to make a coherent council majority likely (Fabbrini 2001: 53). At the level of nation-states, Kiribati uses a version in which the candidates for the direct election of the chief executive are *elected by the assembly* after the assembly elections (Van Trease 1993). Part of the reason why this system works (to the extent that it does) is a more general context of personalized politics in a very small state. There are only few parties, which are only very loose groupings and between which assembly members switch to secure influence, promotion, and patronage (Bishop et al. 2020: 11). A directly elected chief executive with an assembly minority can thus hope to turn it into a majority after the election. Nevertheless, there were successful no-confidence votes, on one occasion shortly after the chief executive had taken office (Edge et al. 2019).

unsuccessful and was quickly abandoned. The lessons of this failed experiment are important for the argument in this book. They show how (a) the separation of powers (here of the executive's origin) was sought as a solution to the problems that a highly fragmented parliament created for pure parliamentarism; and how (b) the efforts to limit the perils of executive personalism along the survival-dimension ultimately led to a self-defeating constitutional design.

Prior to 1992, the fragmentation of the party system in Israel had led to severe problems of building and maintaining cabinets. Since attempts to make the electoral system less proportional had failed, reformers hoped that the direct election of the prime minister would reduce the leverage and blackmail potential of smaller parties. It "would replace the uncertainties of narrow, fluid, and fickle parliamentary majorities with a decisive and unambiguous choice of the head of the executive power" (Medding 1999: 205). The underlying normative idea—typically associated with presidentialism and the Westminster model of parliamentarism—was that "a government must be always as much as possible a direct expression of popular will" (Ottolenghi 2001: 115).

These hopes were shattered, however, because it proved impossible to get the benefits of separate origin without also accepting the risks of executive personalism. One desired effect of electing the prime minister directly was to give the winner a clear mandate from the people and a far greater zone of independence in the day-to-day running of the government. Yet to realize these benefits, it would have been necessary to also weaken the power that the parliamentary majority would have over the prime minister. With this power intact, the small parties would retain much of their bargaining leverage, and the popular mandate of the prime minister would partly be cancelled. To work as intended, the system would have needed some degree of powers separation along the *survival*-dimension, too—as in a presidential system.

The protagonists of the reform understood this point. In their original plan, prime ministers would not have needed a parliamentary confidence or investiture vote to install their government, and they could only have been dismissed in a no-confidence vote of a *supermajority* in parliament: at least 70 of the 120 members of the Knesset. This supermajority requirement would have rendered prime ministers somewhat more independent of the parliamentary majority. They would have been somewhat freer to act "like a president, making decisions without needing to keep a weather eye on the shifting moods and alliances in parliament" (Ottolenghi 2001: 112).

But this is where the risks of executive personalism came into play. While the intention was to make the government more powerful vis-à-vis the fragmented parliament, direct election of the prime minister would have implied a simultaneous power shift to the single person occupying the office of the prime minister. And this led to fears that prime ministers "might turn populist or even authoritarian" (Ottolenghi 2001: 112). As a result, the reform could only gain approval without any strengthening of the separation of powers along the survival-dimension: Elected prime ministers could be dismissed with an absolute majority of 61 votes and they would also need a parliamentary vote to install the government. In the case of a lost no-confidence vote, new prime-ministerial and assembly elections were required.[8] These changes meant that the independent electoral legitimacy of the executive made no difference to its survival in office.

The reform, thus, could not achieve its goals. It ended up being counterproductive because the separation of the executive's origin increased the partisan fragmentation of parliament even further. Reformers had hoped for a "coat-tail effect," so that the candidacies for prime minister of the two largest parties, Labor and Likud, would also increase these parties' vote share in the Knesset. Yet the opposite was true: More voters engaged in "ticket splitting" and gave their party vote to one of the smaller parties. This pushed party system fragmentation to new highs and exacerbated all the problems of coalition-building and maintenance that had motivated the reform (Medding 1999; Ottolenghi 2001).

What is more, while the direct election of the prime minister did not achieve its goals, the increased executive personalism nevertheless caused a "presidentialization" of the major political parties (Samuels and Shugart 2010: 181–188). In the electoral arena, Labor and Likud diverted resources away from the Knesset election because they needed other parties' support to win the prime-ministerial race. Without this win, gaining a large share of Knesset seats would have been of little use. The major parties began to choose candidates on the basis of their appeal to a broad constituency, rather than long intra-party service. These candidates sought to appear to be "above" parties, as they focused their campaigns on undecided centrist voters. They also toned down their campaign rhetoric to appease smaller parties and their supporters. The major parties became more vote-seeking and less focused on seeking ideologically rooted policies.

An analogous transformation happened in the governing arena, as direct elections weakened the influence of the prime minister's party over the office holder and, thus, deprived the principle of collective responsibility "of its

[8] If more than 80 Knesset members voted in favor of a no-confidence motion, the Knesset would not be dissolved and there would be elections only for the prime minister (Article 19B of the Basic Law, reformed in 1992).

party core" (Medding 1999: 205). Since the legitimacy conferred by direct elections was personal, prime ministers felt they should govern independently of partisan constraints, and their parties could do nothing about this. In a pure parliamentary system, the prime minister's party can fire the person occupying the office of the prime minister without losing its hold on the office itself. Not so in Israel's hybrid system, as the party had no guarantee that it would retain the premiership in a new election (Samuels and Shugart 2010: 187).

In sum, elected prime-ministerial government in Israel failed to strike a balance between the potential benefits of the separation of powers and the perils of executive personalism. Fused survival cancelled some of the potential benefits of separated origin, while many of the downsides of executive personalism still materialized.

Assembly-independent government in Switzerland

The federal Swiss form of government can be seen as the opposite of the Israeli hybrid. The cabinet is elected by the assembly, but its survival in office does not depend on this assembly: fused origin but separate survival (Figure 2.2). It is often called directorial government or, following Shugart and Carey (1992), "assembly-independent" government.

From the perspective of democratic legitimacy, this hybrid seems to combine the worst of presidentialism and parliamentarism: Voters can neither elect the executive directly, nor can they remove it from office indirectly, via the assembly. In practice, however, it has proved to be highly resilient, which is partly explained by the strength of direct democracy and the conventions of "concordance" (*Konkordanz*). Here, I focus on how the Swiss version of assembly-independent government manages to capitalize on the benefits of powers separation while successfully containing the dangers of executive personalism.

Let us start with the latter. The members of the Swiss cabinet—called Federal Council—serve a fixed term and, thus, cannot be sanctioned by their parties or the assembly majority during their time in office. They can only be denied re-election when their term is completed. This implies a greater degree of executive personalism than in a parliamentary system. Yet this personalism is simultaneously contained in various ways, which was an explicit goal of the framers. While they acknowledged certain advantages offered by an office such as that of the President of the United States, the Constitutional Reform Committee (1992[1848]: 173) "could not think of proposing the creation of an office so contrary to the ideas and habits of the Swiss people who might see therein evidence of a monarchical or dictatorial tendency ... Our democratic feeling revolts against personal pre-eminence."

The perils of executive personalism are reduced in three main ways. The first is the fused origin of the executive. No person can become a member of the Federal Council against the wishes of the assembly majority, by directly appealing to voters. The second is the collegial nature of the executive. The assembly does not elect a single president, who then selects, and can fire, the other members of the cabinet. Instead, a joint sitting of the assembly's two chambers elects each of the seven members of the Federal Council, who serve in the cabinet as equals.[9] Third, the electoral system for the Federal Council, which provides for the individual and sequential election of the seven members, has a systematic tendency to elect more centrist candidates from all parties, as it allows all members of parliament to influence the relative chances of the candidates of their rival parties (Stojanović 2016). For example, in 1999 the centrist Joseph Deiss, one of several Christian Democratic candidates, was elected with 50.2% of the votes in the sixth voting round, after receiving only 8.2% in the first round (Stojanović 2016: 52–53).[10]

While Swiss institutions thus limit the power of any individual cabinet member and counteract monarchical or dictatorial tendencies, the separation of survival is crucial for stabilizing Swiss concordance. It liberates the assembly majority from the task of keeping the cabinet in office, so that different legislative coalitions can be formed on different issues. It is important to understand how this stabilizes Swiss conventions.

The term "concordance" is often understood as a synonym for the so-called *Magic Formula* in Switzerland: the convention that the four largest parties ought to be represented in the Federal Council, with three parties having two members and one party one member.[11] This convention is typically seen as an

[9] This collective control also limits personalism under pure presidentialism, as was the case in Uruguay from 1952 to 1967 (Altman 2020).

[10] Stojanović (2016) argues that the electoral system for the Federal Council resembles the alternative vote (or ranked choice) system favored by the "centripetalist" approach to power-sharing. On this approach, see, e.g. Reilly (2018).

[11] This is the "arithmetic" understanding of concordance. There is also a "political" understanding focused on consensus-seeking and collegiality. Moreover, formal and informal rules require the appropriate representation of language groups and regions in the Federal Council (Linder and Mueller 2021: 36, 46; Giudici and Stojanović 2016).

integral component of so-called "consensus" or "consociational" democracy in Switzerland (Lijphart 1984: 24; Freiburghaus and Vatter 2019). However, its emergence was "not the outcome of *consensus* but of political *struggle* between Christian Democrats and Radicals" (Stojanović 2016: 55, emphasis in the original), and this struggle reflected the underlying majoritarian institutions (see, e.g. Marti 2019: 38–41).[12] The Christian Democrats (CVP, then KVP) sought to reduce the power of the Liberals (also called Radicals) in the Federal Council, who had achieved a majority of four seats in 1953. They wanted to become the pivotal (median) force in the Council, being able to form majorities either with the Liberals on their right or the Social Democrats on their left. They therefore made a political deal with the Social Democrats, who demanded two Council seats. This deal needed some fortunate circumstances and was thus fully executed only in 1959. The Magic Formula was resisted by the Liberals, so that the Social Democrats had to win their two seats in head-to-head contests against Liberal candidates (and they also had to drop their preferred candidate for the second seat in the third voting round to get a more moderate candidate elected). As a result of this struggle, Christian Democrats, Liberals, and Social Democrats ended up with two seats and the People's Party (SVP, then BGB) with one. Only later did this seat allocation rule become known as the Magic Formula.[13]

While the broad Magic Formula coalition further reduces the dangers of executive personalism, it also presents a serious challenge for policymaking. The Swiss government has become highly polarized, as the two largest parties—Social Democrats and the People's Party—occupy rather extreme positions (Bochsler et al. 2015; Vatter 2016). Such a government coalition would be extremely difficult to form and stabilize under parliamentarism because coalition parties' support for the cabinet typically requires their status as legislative veto players on all or most issues, usually codified in a coalition contract. Ideological heterogeneity thus tends to lead to deadlock and cabinet instability under parliamentarism (Tsebelis 2002). But in Switzerland there is no coalition contract and parties are not veto players; they can be outvoted on individual pieces of legislation. In particular, the parties on the left and right wing may be excluded from the minimal-winning coalition (Schwarz et al.

[12] While "concordance" is commonly used in the Swiss political discourse, consociational and consensus democracy are academic concepts associated with specific theories. These theories are controversial, as is the classification of Switzerland as "consociational" (Stojanović 2020).

[13] The formula was changed in 2003, when the Christian Democrats lost one seat to the People's Party, briefly terminated in 2007/2008, and re-established in 2015 (Stojanović 2016: 42).

2011; Traber 2015). Linder and Mueller (2021: 192) note that "the political centre—Christian-Democrats and the Radicals—is the most important policy shaping actor in the parliamentary arena." Of course, this is what we would expect under majoritarian decision rules. The separation of survival creates a form of legislative flexibility that contributes to the resilience of Swiss concordance.

The Swiss combination of fused origin and separate survival has created a behavioral–institutional equilibrium that is not only rather unique but also has important downsides. Due to the Magic Formula, elections do not have much of an (immediate) impact on the composition of the cabinet and voters have no clear choice between alternative political directions. This was obvious, for example, after the parliamentary elections in October 2019. In the wake of increased public concerns about climate change, the Greens and Green Liberals were the biggest gainers of the election. Both parties more than doubled their previous vote shares, to 13.2% and 7.8%, respectively. The Greens surpassed the Christian Democrats (11.4%) and were only slightly behind the Liberals (15.1%). In the subsequent re-election of the Federal Council in December, they attacked one of the seats of the Liberals and tried to get their head of the party, Regula Rytz, elected instead. Yet the assembly's center-right majority rejected the attack and re-elected Liberal foreign minister, Ignazio Cassis. The "Green wave" was thus stopped rather abruptly at the gates of the government. The reduced importance of elections for cabinet composition is also considered one of the main reasons why turnout in Switzerland is very low (Blais 2014; Franklin 2004). In 2019, it was only 45.1%.[14]

In sum, while assembly-independent government in Switzerland has been resilient and fairly successful, it is part of a very complex and demanding behavioral–institutional equilibrium. It is not surprising, therefore, that the Swiss hybrid has not been an export success.

Robust hybrids

How can a mixture of presidential and parliamentary features become more robust and less contradictory? The answer, I submit, is that one branch must be constitutionally separated along *both* institutional dimensions: *origin and*

[14] Of course, direct democratic procedures also matter in this context. On the one hand, they may partly compensate for voters' lack of influence on cabinet composition. On the other hand, the high frequency with which Swiss voters are asked to the ballot box is cited as a reason for Switzerland's low turnout (Blais 2014).

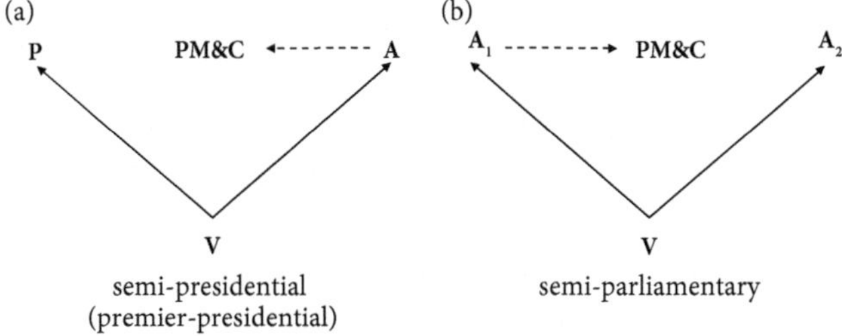

Fig. 2.3 Semi-presidential and semi-parliamentary government: Fig. 2.3(a) semi-presidential (premier-presidential); Fig. 2.3(b) semi-parliamentary

Notes: V = voters, A = assembly, P = President, PM = Prime Minister, C =Cabinet, → = election, ⇢ = dismissal.

survival. The way to achieve this without going back to the pure types is to divide either the executive or the assembly into two democratically authorized parts. In this way, one part of the executive (the president) can be separated along both dimensions or the prime minister and cabinet can be separated along both dimensions from one part of the assembly (the second chamber).[15] The final two hybrids have this structure (Figure 2.3).[16]

Semi-presidentialism

Under semi-presidentialism voters directly elect a president, who survives in office independently from the legislature, but there is also a prime minister, who—together with the cabinet—is dependent on the political confidence of parliament (Duverger 1980; Elgie 1999, 2011).[17] The executive is thus divided into two parts. One part of this "dual executive," the president, has both origin and survival separated from the assembly, while the other part, the prime minister, has its survival fused with the assembly.

In sharp contrast to the Israeli and Swiss hybrids, semi-presidentialism "has become the most emulated democratic regime type in the world" (Samuels and Shugart 2010: 40). Currently, the constitutions of more than 50 countries—not

[15] Both of these divisions can also be present at the same time (see Chapter 3).

[16] Strictly speaking, this figure depicts only one subtype of semi-presidentialism: premier-presidentialism. In the other subtype, the prime minister is also formally accountable to the president. I elaborate on this distinction below.

[17] As Samuels and Shugart (2010: 30) emphasize, for a system to qualify as semi-presidential, the cabinet must be *collectively* responsible to the assembly majority.

all of which are democracies—qualify as semi-presidential (Åberg and Sedelius 2020).

Semi-presidentialism's prevalence is not rooted in its appreciation by scholars. While many constitutional experts warn against this form of government, it suits the self-interest of politicians involved in constitution-making. It provides "a neat compromise between political forces that want presidentialism, usually because they calculate that their party will win the presidency, and those that want parliamentarism, usually because they believe that they are not strong enough to win the presidency, but stand a chance of entering a coalition government, thereby sharing in executive power" (Elgie 2016: 60).[18]

Like presidentialism, semi-presidentialism embraces executive personalism as integral to the separation of powers (Lacerda 2020). The difference to pure presidentialism is that the framers of the US Constitution did not anticipate the rise of mass parties. By contrast, semi-presidentialism was designed as a response to these parties. In Weimar Germany, and later in France, leading proponents of semi-presidentialism mistrusted political parties' capacity to govern and wanted "plebiscitary" presidential elections that would place the president "above" the parties (Samuels and Shugart 2010: 39–40; Weber 1986).[19]

When we analytically distinguish the separation of powers from executive personalism, a specific rationale of the former is difficult to formulate for semi-presidentialism. Robert Elgie's (2011: 14–15) authoritative literature review mentions only two, although he grants the first merely some "intuitive logic." The idea is that semi-presidentialism allows for some degree of power-sharing within the executive, especially in the context of a polarized society (Elgie 2011: 14). This logic is hardly convincing, though. If power-sharing is the goal, *collegial* government under parliamentarism or Swiss-style assembly-independent government appears as the much better option (Lijphart 2012). Semi-presidentialism's executive personalism is likely to undermine the adequate representation of a societal group by a president. A presidential candidate might have to distance himself from the interests of the group to get elected, and the group has little control over an elected president (Samuels and Shugart 2010).

[18] Many studies have explored the way in which the choice of a form of government and the level of executive power concentration are influenced by pre-existing political and institutional conditions. See, e.g. Fortin-Rittberger (2017) and the literature cited therein.

[19] A version of semi-presidentialism was also introduced in Finland in 1919, but the president was indirectly elected.

Elgie's second rationale for semi-presidentialism compares it to presidentialism. Sartori (1997: 124) argues that "[w]hile pure presidentialism is a stalemate-prone structure, semi-presidentialism proposes a gridlock-avoiding machinery." What he means is that the latter allows for the oscillation of power between the president and the prime minister, "reinforcing the authority of whoever obtains a majority" (Sartori 1997: 125). This argument is based on the French experience with "cohabitation" in the 1980s and 1990s. This term describes a situation where the president and prime minister are from opposing parties and where the president's party is not represented in the cabinet. In France, the president—due to his *informal* partisan influence—held executive power when he enjoyed majority support in the assembly but had to accept the *formal* authority of the prime minister under cohabitation.

The problem with this argument is that cohabitation might also lead to conflict between president and prime minister. Åberg and Sedelius's (2020: 1125) review of the literature finds that "intra-executive conflict is more common during instances of cohabitation" and that "[a]s expected, cohabitation can lead to severe tension and undermine general performance, especially when a democracy is young, or when there is no clear-cut constitutional provision setting out the distribution of power among the key actors." In France, the constitution was changed to reduce the likelihood of cohabition. In 2000, voters approved a referendum reducing the president's term from seven to five years, and the National Assembly then passed a bill to the effect that presidential elections would precede parliamentary elections. Since this reform, cohabitation has been avoided.

While the rationale of powers separation thus remains rather unclear, semi-presidentialism is designed to increase executive personalism. The extent of this increase depends on the strength of the president. Here, the distinction between the premier-presidential and president-parliamentary subtypes of semi-presidentialism becomes important (Samuels and Shugart 2010: 30; Shugart and Carey 1992). In the former subtype, the prime minister and cabinet are formally accountable exclusively to the assembly majority (as in Figure 2.3). In the latter, the prime minister and cabinet are dually accountable to the president and the assembly majority. In terms of Figure 2.3, these systems also imply a dashed line from the president to the prime minister and cabinet.

Executive personalism is greatest in the president-parliamentary subtype of semi-presidentialism. Presidents are typically so dominant that these systems are often treated as "effectively 'presidential'" (Chaisty et al. 2018: 26) for many purposes. Presidents' power can even be greater than that of their counterparts in a pure presidential system because they may have the right to dissolve the assembly under certain conditions. President-parliamentarism is also the subtype that is more clearly associated with authoritarian government and/or poses the greatest dangers for the consolidation of democracy (Åberg and Sedelius 2020; Elgie 2011; Stykow 2019).

In the premier-presidential subtype, too, much depends on the specific constitutional powers of the president (Shugart 2005: 338–340). If the president lacks most—or all—of the relevant powers, premier-presidentialism can be barely distinct from parliamentarism with a directly elected figurehead. Ireland is a case in point. Political practice might not always reflect the letter of the constitution, though. On the one hand, we have already seen in the French example that presidents can be dominant, even within a premier-presidential system (especially if they are the head of their parties and enjoy majority support in the assembly). On the other hand, Austria is a well-known example of a president-parliamentary system that, due to constitutional conventions and a particular party-system environment, has effectively functioned like a pure parliamentary system (Müller 1999).

In sum, semi-presidentialism lacks a convincing powers-separation rationale and is essentially about executive personalism. This personalism may not matter much when semi-presidentialism functions like parliamentarism in a particular country or when cohabitation shifts power from the president to the prime minister for a limited period of time. But then a directly elected president does not give the political system much of an advantage either, at least not in terms of the separation of powers.

Semi-parliamentarism

As Figure 2.3 suggests, semi-parliamentarism is, in some sense, the mirror image of semi-presidentialism (Ganghof 2018a). While semi-presidentialism divides the executive into two democratically authorized parts, only one of which—the prime minister—depends on assembly confidence for its survival in office, semi-parliamentarism divides the *assembly* into two equally legitimate parts, in the simplest case two chambers, only one of which possesses the power to dismiss the prime minister in a no-confidence vote.[20] While

[20] More precisely, semi-parliamentarism is the mirror image of premier-presidentialism. Under premier-presidentialism, voters use direct elections to authorize two agents, the president and the assembly, *only one of which* becomes the principal of the prime minister and cabinet. Similarly, under semi-parliamentarism, voters use direct elections to authorize two agents, two parts of the assembly,

semi-presidentialism shifts the locus of powers separation into the executive, semi-parliamentarism shifts it *into the assembly*. It separates the fused powers of the executive and the first-chamber majority from the second chamber. Only the latter is a legislature in a narrow sense of the term, while the first chamber majority becomes fused with the executive. The cabinet-supporting first chamber majority relates to the second chamber as the president relates to the entire assembly in a presidential system (compare Figures 2.1 and 2.3). As a result, the branch-based separation of powers is decoupled from executive personalism.

Chapter 3 will elaborate on the definition and origins of semi-parliamentarism; here, it is best to consider an example: the Australian state of Victoria (Stone 2008; Taylor 2006). The Parliament of Victoria has two chambers: the first chamber (Legislative Assembly) and the second chamber (Legislative Council). Crucially, both chambers are directly elected for concurrent terms and do not differ in their democratic legitimacy. The logic of representation also does not differ between the two chambers: both represent voters' ideological preferences. The idea of territorial representation plays no special role in the second chamber. Yet, while both chambers also have a veto over ordinary legislation, only the first chamber can dismiss the cabinet in a no-confidence vote.[21] Even though individual cabinet members are drawn from both chambers, the *cabinet originates and survives separately from the second chamber*. This is why Victoria can be described as a semi-parliamentary system.[22]

The rationale of semi-parliamentarism is entirely based on the separation of powers. It can combine central advantages of the Swiss and Israeli hybrids, while completely avoiding executive personalism. As in Israel, it is possible for voters to more or less directly select a candidate for the office of the prime minister. The first chamber is elected in single-member districts under majoritarian ("ranked choice") rules, which have so far succeeded in creating an almost pure two-party system. The winning side usually gains an absolute

only one of which becomes the principal of the prime minister and cabinet. If both parts of the assembly become the principal of the prime minister and cabinet, we have the bicameral version of a pure parliamentary system, Italy being one example.

[21] A more detailed analysis must take into account the rules for conflict resolution between the two chambers. These rules favor the first chamber in Victoria, but only because of its much larger size (88 versus 40 members), which is not an inherent feature of semi-parliamentarism. I elaborate on the importance of the second chambers' robust veto power in Chapters 3 and 8.

[22] To be sure, most political scientists and legal scholars would describe Victoria and the other bicameral systems in Australia as "parliamentary" (e.g. Ward 2012). I discuss the need for the concept of semi-parliamentarism further in Chapter 3.

majority of seats and can form a government on its own. First-chamber elections can thus become highly "personalized," in the sense that much attention focuses on the prime-ministerial candidates, but they cannot become "presidentialized" in the sense of Samuels and Shugart (2010). In contrast to Israel, though, the prime minister is not confronted with the need to cobble together a fixed-majority coalition in a fragmented parliament. While the Victorian second chamber is elected under proportional rules and represents various minor parties, it need not vote the cabinet into office and cannot dismiss it in a no-confidence vote. The cabinet is thus free to build second-chamber majorities on an issue-by-issue basis—just as in Switzerland. For example, after the concurrent elections of both chambers in 2018, the Labor Party controlled a large majority in the first chamber (62.5% of all seats) and formed a one-party government but had to govern as a "minority cabinet" in the second chamber (45%). The balance of power in this chamber was held by eight minor parties, only one of which (the Greens) also gained seats in the first chamber. Victorian governments made ample use of the resulting flexibility in coalition-building (Ganghof et al. 2018).

In sum, while semi-presidentialism and semi-parliamentarism are, in some ways, mirror images of one another, their rationales could hardly be more different. Semi-presidentialism is essentially about executive personalism, while semi-parliamentarism is essentially about the separation of powers.

A typological conclusion

Let us summarize the argument by integrating all six basic forms of government into a simple typological framework (Table 2.2). This framework modifies and extends the typological approach of Lijphart (1984: 70) and was first presented in Ganghof (2014).[23] It remains focused on the two crucial questions of how the executive comes into office (origin) and whether it can be removed from office in a political no-confidence vote (survival), but differs from other approaches in two main ways. First, the typology includes democratic criteria in a symmetrical manner. Many definitions require that, in a presidential or semi-presidential system, the president must be authorized in direct or quasi-direct elections, but they say nothing about the democratic legitimacy of the assembly under any executive format. In Table 2.2, the requirement of direct elections is specified for the executive and the

[23] Ganghof (2014) uses the term chamber-independent instead of semi-parliamentary government.

Table 2.2 Democratic forms of government

Is the executive partly or wholly directly elected?	Does the survival of the political executive depend on a directly elected assembly?		
	Wholly	**Partly**	**No**
Yes	Elected prime-ministerial	Semi-presidential	Presidential
No	Parliamentary	Semi-parliamentary	Assembly-independent

Source: Adapted from Ganghof (2018a).

assembly alike.[24] This also implies that the typology applies only to democratic systems.[25] Second, the typology allows for the possibility that the political executive's survival in office is only partly dependent on the assembly. One way in which this partial dependency can exist is that only one part of a dual political executive is dependent on the assembly—the prime minister, but not the president under semi-presidentialism.[26] The other is that the political executive is dependent on the confidence of only one part of a dual assembly: the first, but not the second chamber under semi-parliamentarism (Table 2.2).[27]

The two institutional dimensions of this typology are directly connected to the two sources of executive personalism. One source is the direct (or quasi-direct) authorization of a single human being: the president in a presidential or semi-presidential system and the prime minister in an elected prime-ministerial system. All three systems in the upper row of Table 2.2 are thus institutionally personalized, to various degrees, along the *origin*-dimension. The other source of executive personalism is that the members of the executive are not politically responsible to some collective and representative entity

[24] Elections are not the only possible basis of democratic legitimacy. I neglect this point here, as my goal is to categorize existing forms of democratic government. Chapter 3 takes a broader perspective, which includes random selection.

[25] It is an important question whether typologies of executive formats are meant to apply to all political systems or only to democracies. See, e.g. Stykow (2019).

[26] The focus on the *political* executive is important (see Tokatlı 2020: 111). Under parliamentary, semi-parliamentary, and elected prime-ministerial government, we usually also have parts of the executive that are not dependent on assembly confidence: the heads of state. But these are not political in a narrow sense (Andeweg et al. 2020: 14). As to semi-presidentialism, I would argue that the direct election of the president itself renders this office political, regardless of how much formal power the president is given.

[27] The logics of the four hybrids can be combined, so that the six types are not all mutually exclusive. Rendering them mutually exclusive would require a much more complex classification.

on an ongoing basis. Hence both executive formats in the right column are personalized along the *survival*-dimension. Presidentialism is personalized along both dimensions. This fact is crucial to much of the critical debate around it (see Chapter 9).[28]

Two systems avoid executive personalism: parliamentary and semi-parliamentary government. The crucial difference between them is that parliamentary government has to give up on the potential benefits of the branch-based separation of powers, while semi-parliamentarism is still able to reap some or all of them. This is why semi-parliamentary government deserves our attention. One of the main conclusions of Samuels and Shugart (2010: 261) is that if reformers "truly want parliamentarized parties, they should keep or adopt parliamentarism." My conclusion is that if reformers want parliamentarized parties and a branch-based separation of powers, they should keep or adopt semi-parliamentarism.

[28] The president-parliamentary subtype of semi-presidentialism is also personalized along both dimensions because the prime minister and cabinet are accountable to the president. Their simultaneous accountability to the assembly might be a counterweight to executive personalism, but this depends on the president's power over the assembly, especially with respect to assembly dissolution.

3

Why we need the concept of semi-parliamentary government

In Chapter 1, I suggested that existing democratic systems can be classified as semi-parliamentary when they have bicameral parliaments in which both chambers (a) are directly elected and (b) possess robust veto power over ordinary legislation but (c) only one of them selects and dismisses the prime minister and cabinet. Here, I ask whether we really need a new concept to describe such cases. This question requires an answer because new concepts are introduced too easily in political science; they should be "the last resort and backed by a demonstration of a clear deficiency of the existing vocabulary" (Toshkov 2016: 102). This demonstration is the main goal of this chapter. While I do not deny that the existing vocabulary suffices for some purposes, it does not help us to think clearly about constitutional design. Semi-parliamentary government describes a unique constitutional structure that can achieve the benefits of the branch-based separation of powers without accepting the perils of executive personalism.

The concept has so far been well received in the literature. Albert Weale (2018: 240) considers it "a genuine conceptual breakthrough in political science," and Robert Elgie (2018: 241) predicts that it will become "part of the standard political science lexicon." With respect to Australia, Marija Taflaga (2018: 252) welcomes it as a "simpler," "better," and "more coherent" description of the political process, and Rodney Smith (2018b) observes that bicameral politics "operates according to semi-parliamentary rules and norms." Khaitan (2021) defends a particular version of semi-parliamentarism as an attractive way to optimize four constitutional principles (see also Khaitan 2020). Weale (2019: 74–75) discusses it as the basis for a potential reform of bicameralism in the United Kingdom—one that would turn the House of Lords into "a house of laws" and thus meet "some of the objections to the practice of so called 'accountable' government in the Westminster system."

Beyond Presidentialism and Parliamentarism. Steffen Ganghof, Oxford University Press.
 DOI: 10.1093/oso/9780192897145.003.0003

Meinel (2021: 135-136) considers it as a potential response to the challenges faced by Germany's parliamentary system of government.

As welcome as this reception is, it raises the question of why the time-honored debate about different forms of government has not recognized semi-parliamentarism as a distinct type before. Part of the answer, I suggest, lies in complementary blind spots that characterize prevalent typologies of bicameralism and forms of government in political science. These typologies neglect how directly elected second chambers relate to the executive (Elgie 2018; Lijphart 1984). I highlight this neglect not to enter a more general typological debate but to offer an explanation.

The chapter proceeds from the concrete to the more abstract. It begins with an operational definition of semi-parliamentary government, identifies the cases that fall under it, and sketches their historical evolution. It then explains the blind spots of political science typologies. After responding to a number of worries about the concept of semi-parliamentarism, I compare how well the cases that fall under the operational definition express the underlying, more abstract logic of constitutional design. Finally, I generalize the analysis—and hence the definition of semi-parliamentarism—in two ways. First, I show that semi-parliamentary government can balance competing visions of majority formation at more fundamental levels: partisan and individual visions, electoral and sortitionist visions, democratic and epistocratic visions. Second, I explain why semi-parliamentary government does not require fully fledged bicameralism.

Semi-parliamentarism as a descriptive category

Let us start with semi-parliamentary government as a descriptive category for forms of democratic government that exist today. I propose to use this category for a specific type of bicameral system, based on the following operational definition:

1. There is no direct (or popular) election of the chief executive or head of state.
2. The assembly has two directly elected chambers.
3. Only the first chamber can dismiss the cabinet in a no-confidence vote.
4. The second chamber has veto power over ordinary legislation that is not merely suspensory and/or cannot be overridden by a simple or absolute majority in the first chamber.

The crucial features of semi-parliamentary bicameralism are conditions (2) and (3): even though the second chamber is directly elected, it does not participate in the no-confidence procedure.[1] For the purpose of this book, condition (2) is applied strictly, so that only second chambers in which *all* members are directly elected qualify (see also Elgie 2018). For pragmatic reasons, condition (1) rules out systems that are semi-parliamentary and semi-presidential at the same time (compare Figure 2.2 in Chapter 2).

Condition (4) defines a minimum level of legislative veto power for the second chamber. In Ganghof (2018a), I used the veto power of this chamber only in an ideal-typical definition of semi-parliamentarism. I now believe that some minimal level of veto power should also be part of the operational definition. If the second chamber is denied robust veto power, the constitution itself makes it clear that its role as an agent of the voters is subordinate to that of the first chamber, its democratic legitimacy notwithstanding. To cast the empirical net more widely, though, I do not require absolute veto power but only disregard second chambers whose veto is suspensory and/or can be overruled by a simple or absolute majority in the first chamber. One consequence is that I include Japan, where the veto of the House of Councillors can be overridden by the House of Representatives with a two-thirds majority of the members present.

Based on this operational definition, the empirical cases of semi-parliamentary government are the Australian Commonwealth and Japan, as well as the following five Australian states: New South Wales, South Australia, Tasmania, Victoria, and Western Australia.[2] My focus will be on the Australian cases, but the case of Japan highlights the importance of the electoral systems used in the two chambers of the assembly.

Other countries with wholly directly elected second chambers do not fulfill all four conditions. The Czech Republic, Poland, and Romania have wholly directly elected second chambers but also directly elected presidents. The more important reason for their exclusion, however, is that they all fail to fulfill one additional criterion. The Romanian second chamber has the power to dismiss the cabinet in a no-confidence vote. Romania therefore has a semi-presidential system with symmetrical bicameralism. In Poland and the Czech Republic, the legislative vetoes of the second chambers can be overruled by

[1] This does not rule out the possibility that the cabinet is partly drawn from the second chamber.

[2] The confidence requirements in Australia are generally based on conventions, rather than constitutional law. For instance, the Commonwealth constitution vests executive power in the Queen, exercisable by the Governor General. However, this is "to be understood in a purely formal sense, actual power being wielded by responsible ministers in Cabinet …" (Aroney et al. 2015: 412). The withdrawal of confidence will require the fall of the government. On the Australian states, see Carney (2006).

absolute majorities in the first chambers. Finally, the Senate in Italy's parliamentary system has the power to dismiss the cabinet and it is not entirely directly elected.

The historical evolution of semi-parliamentarism

When was semi-parliamentary government established in our seven cases? If we focus on "full" democracies with universal suffrage, the answer is straightforward. Semi-parliamentarism began when the franchise in *both* chambers was free from property or educational restrictions. Based on this criterion, the first semi-parliamentary systems emerged in the two nation-states in our sample. When the Australian Commonwealth was established in 1901, it was the first democracy to combine a second chamber that was directly elected under universal suffrage with the constitutional convention that cabinets require only the confidence of the first chamber (Smith 2018a; Taflaga 2018). In Japan, semi-parliamentarism was established in 1947 and reflected a compromise between the constitutional ideas of the Japanese government and the Allied powers, especially the United States (Rosenzweig 2010: 294). These two cases were then followed by the Australian states of Victoria (1950), Western Australia (1963), Tasmania (1968), South Australia (1973), and finally New South Wales (1978) (Stone 2002).

This summary paints a somewhat truncated picture, however, because *directly elected* second chambers with robust (absolute) veto power had already been established in the period 1855–1856 in the Australian colonial parliaments of Victoria, Tasmania, South Australia, and Western Australia (Griffith and Srinivasan 2001; Sharman 2015). Moreover, by convention the executives in these polities needed only the confidence of the directly elected first chambers. The resulting bicameral systems departed from the logic of semi-parliamentarism because a restricted franchise in all four systems implied that "the electorates for these second chambers were considerably smaller than the electorates for their respective lower houses" (Smith 2018a: 257). Nevertheless, the move to directly elected second chambers reflected democratic pressures (e.g. Roberts 2016: 44), as well as the desire for a second chamber that would have sufficient "democratic" legitimacy and independence to provide a real and durable check on the first chamber. Even though the framers designed conservative second chambers to defend the interests of the wealthy, they understood that in a conflict between the two chambers, elected members were likely to have greater weight with the public (e.g. Waugh 1997: 343). Moreover, some of them were able to anticipate that a nominee second chamber could be swamped by the government of the day (Serle 1955: 187; Waugh 1997: 344–345). A directly elected—and indissoluble—second chamber was seen as a stronger and more durable counterweight to the first chamber.[3] Crucial elements of semi-parliamentary government—of an assembly-based separation of powers—were thus already established in the Australian colonies in the 1850s.

Members of the New South Wales second chamber remained appointed by the Governor, and Queensland stuck with this model when it separated from New South Wales in 1859. However, Queensland's second chamber was abolished in 1922, after a Labor government had chosen Labor Councillors for this very purpose (Massicotte 2001: 163). By contrast, New South Wales eventually converged on the semi-parliamentary model of bicameralism. Its second chamber was indirectly elected from 1934 and directly elected from 1978 (Clune and Griffith 2006: 494–515; Turner 1969). The first directly elected members took their seats in 1978 and the chamber was wholly elected from 1984 (Smith 2018a).

The blind spots of existing typologies

The seven bicameral systems I classify as semi-parliamentary are typically described as parliamentary systems with "symmetrical" bicameralism (e.g. Lijphart 1984; Stone 2002).[4] I contend that this categorization fails to recognize their distinctiveness. To see why, we have to understand the blind spots in the prevalent typologies of bicameralism and forms of government.

Typologies of bicameralism

The most influential typology of bicameralism was proposed by Lijphart (1984). Importantly, it was never intended to cover all major aspects of bicameral systems. He developed it as part of his particular theory of consensus

[3] It is also worth noting that franchise restrictions based on property or education initially also remained in place in three of the first chambers; only South Australia introduced adult male suffrage in the House of Assembly in 1855 (Carney 2006: 53).

[4] The notion of "symmetrical" bicameralism is closely related to that of "strong" bicameralism, but the latter also takes electoral rules into account (Lijphart 1984). Since the concept of semi-parliamentarism focuses on the constitutional structure, the appropriate comparison is with symmetrical bicameralism. I will say more about strong bicameralism in Chapter 7.

democracy (see Chapter 5) and therefore focused exclusively on how bicameralism contributes to *legislative power-sharing* (Lijphart 1984: 90). Other aspects of bicameralism were deliberately excluded; most notably, how second chambers relate to the executive.

While we are focused on the typological literature and, hence, Lijphart's (1984) seminal contribution, it is worth noting that the neglect of executive–legislative relations characterizes much of the positive and normative theory of bicameralism. For example, Tsebelis and Money (1997: 1–2) note at the outset that bicameralism "appears to have little effect on the relationship between the legislature and the executive" because in parliamentary systems the required parliamentary support of the government "is measured almost exclusively in the popularly elected lower chamber." They do not consider how executive–legislative relations change when the second chamber is directly elected but *nevertheless* lacks a no-confidence vote. Similarly, Waldron (2012: 45) emphasizes from a normative perspective that a second house "should be separated from the authority of the executive in a way that ... the first house is not." But while he discusses, for example, rules that would disallow members of the cabinet to sit in the second chamber, the word "confidence" does not appear in his article.

For Lijphart's (1984) typology, the neglect of executive–legislative relations has two important implications. First, it disregards all potential features of second chambers that are specific to forms of government; for example, whether the second chamber participates in the no-confidence procedure (under parliamentarism) or what kind of role it plays in executive appointments or impeachment procedures (under presidentialism).[5] The Australian and Italian Senates are both deemed "symmetrical," even though only the latter has the power to bring down the government in a no-confidence vote.

Second, since the typology neglects second chambers' potential confidence authority over cabinets, Lijphart does not consider what kind of legitimacy would be needed to actually wield this power in a democracy; he focuses merely on what kind of legitimacy second chambers need to use their legislative veto power. As a result, his notion of symmetrical bicameralism does not require the direct election of second chambers. The German Bundesrat and

[5] Some of the subsequent literature has tried to build on Lijphart, while paying closer attention to the specifics of different forms of government. See, e.g. Swenden (2004), as well as Llanos and Nolte (2003). Other sophisticated measurement attempts remain focused on the legislative veto power of second chambers (Heller and Branduse 2014).

Dutch Senate are considered just as symmetrical as the Australian Senate, even though only the latter is directly elected.[6]

In sum, the deliberate design of Lijphart's typology is such that it cannot capture the distinctiveness of semi-parliamentary bicameralism. This distinctiveness results from the combination of (a) a directly elected second chamber that (b) has robust legislative veto power on ordinary legislation but (c) lacks a no-confidence vote. Only the second of these three conditions plays any role in his typology. Semi-parliamentarism describes a distinct and systematically important subset in the much broader category of symmetrical bicameralism.

Typologies of forms of government

But not only Lijphart's typology of bicameralism has a blind spot when it comes to executive–legislative relations; the prevalent typologies of forms of government have a complementary blind spot when it comes to second chambers. These typologies assume from the outset that it does not matter whether or not the second chamber can dismiss the cabinet in a no-confidence vote—*even when this chamber is as democratically legitimate as the first chamber*. As Elgie (2018: 242) observes, they "are not concerned with where executive accountability lies in the legislature, only with whether there is collective responsibility to some part of it." Second chambers are simply taken out of the equation. And since first chambers can be implicitly assumed to be directly elected in a democracy, the resulting typologies do not need to formulate any democratic criterion for the assembly.

I find this asymmetrical use of the direct election criterion incoherent (Ganghof 2018b). We have seen, in Chapter 2, that the dominant typologies of forms of government take into account whether presidents are directly elected and, if so, whether they have the power to dismiss the prime minister and cabinet. The same treatment should be accorded to second chambers. When they are directly elected, it matters whether or not they also become the principal of the prime minister and cabinet. The concept of semi-parliamentarism is not only necessary to describe a distinct hybrid between parliamentary and presidential democracy, but this hybrid is also logically implied by a coherent application of accepted typological criteria (Chapter 2).

[6] This is also partly due to the fact that Lijphart allows absolute veto power and direct election to be mutually compensatory. Hence, Japan's second chamber is considered symmetrical because it is directly elected (even though the House of Councillors lacks absolute veto power), the Dutch second chamber because it has absolute veto power (even though it is not directly elected) (Lijphart 1984: 193).

Let me reiterate, however, that my aim is not to criticize existing typologies. Different typologies can have different strengths and weaknesses and, thus, must partly be chosen on pragmatic grounds. There are only two nation-states—Australia and Japan—that meet the minimal conditions of semi-parliamentarism, and we will see later in the chapter that these two cases also have features that dilute their semi-parliamentary nature. Depending on the purpose of a particular study, therefore, it may well be a reasonable simplification to treat them as pure parliamentary systems. From the perspective of *constitutional design*, however, the uniqueness of semi-parliamentary government should not be ignored.

Concerns about the concept

Before we take a closer look at our seven cases, let me address some concerns about the concept and its name. One is that the actors that invented semi-parliamentarism did not perceive the resulting system as a hybrid: they "wanted to preserve parliamentarism" (Smith 2018a: 260). This might be a reason for resisting the concept. If it were, though, we would also have to reject the well-established concept of semi-presidentialism. Just as semi-parliamentarism was initially perceived as a parliamentary system counteracted by a strong second chamber, semi-presidentialism in Weimar Germany "was perceived as a parliamentary system counteracted by a strong presidency" (Sartori 1997: 127). It took a long time before the concept of semi-presidentialism was developed and even longer before it was widely accepted.

Another worry about the label "semi-parliamentary" might be that it has already been used to describe other forms of government. Yet these other uses are not only mutually inconsistent (Duverger 1997: 137; Fabbrini 2001; Linz 1994: 48–49; Sartori 1994: 110), but they also lack a clear rationale. Here, too, the comparison with semi-presidentialism is instructive. Elgie (2011: 19–20) notes that the term "semi-presidential" had been used in widely different ways from the mid-1850s. The current understanding of the term developed much later. The use of "semi-parliamentary" suggested here has the advantage of expressing how this form of government mirrors semi-presidentialism (Chapter 2).

Finally, the prefix "semi" may invite a misunderstanding of the concept. Leading experts of Australian bicameralism, such as Campbell Sharman and Bruce Stone, have worried (in personal communication) that it might suggest the system to be defective and its parliamentary aspect to be watered down. They emphasize that Australian bicameralism leads to a greater degree of parliamentary control (less executive dominance), especially compared to the Westminster model of parliamentarism (Stone 2008). The system is, in this sense, more "parliamentary," not less. This worry is important and parallels a common one about semi-presidentialism, which can also be misunderstood as implying some intermediate level of presidential power between parliamentary and presidential systems (Chapter 2).

My first response is that I agree with Stone and Sharman substantively. The potential for greater and more robust parliamentary accountability and control is one of the reasons why we ought to be interested in semi-parliamentary government. So the disagreement is entirely about the use of words. Sharman and Stone understand parliamentary government, at least in part, as a desirable *behavioral equilibrium*: some high level of actual legislative review and parliamentary control of government. By contrast, I follow common definitions that focus strictly on *formal institutions* and, in particular, the no-confidence vote (Strøm 2000). The two views are thus compatible: The institutions of pure parliamentary government tend to cause executive dominance (under some range of background conditions), whereas the institutions of semi-parliamentary government can reduce it.

My second response is that if we could come up with entirely new terms for all hybrid forms of government, the prefix "semi" should better be avoided altogether. Yet the concept of semi-presidentialism is here to stay, and the term "semi-parliamentary" therefore has the advantage of expressing the analogy between these two hybrids (Chapter 2).

Comparing the cases

So far, I have only given a minimal, operational definition of semi-parliamentarism. Now I want to compare how well the seven cases express the underlying "logic" of semi-parliamentary democracy (Ganghof 2018a). I do so along the three analytical dimensions summarized in Table 3.1.

Second-chamber legitimacy

The logic of semi-parliamentary government requires that the second chamber is at least as democratically legitimate as the first. If its legitimacy is

Table 3.1 Semi-parliamentary systems, 2021

	AUS	JPN	NSW	SA	TAS	VIC	WA
Is the second chamber's legitimacy compromised?							
(a) More malapportioned?	Yes	Yes	No	No	No	No	Yes
(b) Unequal term length?	Yes	Yes	Yes	Yes	Yes	No	No
Is second chamber's confidence authority strengthened (budget veto)?	Yes	No	No	Yes	Yes	No	Yes
Is second chamber's veto power compromised?	Yes	Yes	Yes	No	No	Yes	No

Source: Adapted from Ganghof (2018a).

inferior, its lacking power over the cabinet's survival might reflect this inferiority, rather than establishing a different form of government. Even when the second chamber is directly elected under universal suffrage, though, two features may reduce its legitimacy. One is that electoral districts may be more malapportioned (i.e. create more procedural inequality between citizens) than those of the first chamber (Samuels and Snyder 2001). This is the case in the Australian Commonwealth, Japan, and Western Australia (Ganghof 2018a: 265).

The other legitimacy-reducing feature is that the terms of second chambers may be longer than those of first chambers. If the veto power of the second chamber is to be grounded in its equal democratic claim to represent citizens, the two chambers should be elected at the same time and for terms of equal lengths. When second-chamber members serve longer and staggered terms, the legislative program of the first-chamber majority could be blocked by second-chamber members elected several years earlier (Bastoni 2012: 231). This is the case in the Australian Commonwealth (six vs three years) and Japan and Tasmania (six vs four years), as well as New South Wales and South Australia (eight vs four years). Equal term lengths (of four years) have existed in Victoria since 2003 and Western Australia since 1987. In Victoria, the term of the second chamber is constitutionally tied to that of the first chamber (Economou 2019). In Western Australia, the two chambers have been elected concurrently since 1963, but because the second chamber cannot be dissolved under any circumstances, concurrent elections are not guaranteed.

Viewed in conjunction, these two aspects of second-chamber legitimacy imply that the logic of semi-parliamentary government is most clearly expressed in Victoria and is most diluted in the Australian Commonwealth and Japan.

No-confidence authority

The operational definition of semi-parliamentarism requires that the second chamber lacks the right to a no-confidence vote against the prime minister and cabinet. A robust veto over the budget might be used as a functional equivalent (see also Chapter 7), but there is substantial disagreement on this matter.

In the Australian constitutional crisis of 1974–1975, the Senate's right to deny supply led the Governor General and the Chief Justice of the High Court to argue that the survival of the cabinet depended on both chambers (Aroney et al. 2015: 412–417; Bach 2003: 111–119; Barry and Miragliotta 2015; Taflaga 2018). Today, though, many authors doubt that the budget veto makes much of a difference, in part because of how informal constitutional norms changed after the 1974–1975 crisis (Smith 2018a: 258–259; Stone 2008: 181).

By contrast, experts on Japan suggest that the second chamber has "*de facto* power of no confidence" (Thies and Yanai 2014: 70), even though the constitution does not give it the right to veto the budget. They argue that constitutional practice deviates substantially from the text and approaches a bicameral form of pure parliamentarism. One reason is that the second chamber can veto budget-enabling bills. Another is that it has tried to turn formally non-binding censure resolutions against a minister into a no-confidence vote by combining it with a boycott of assembly deliberation (Takayasu 2015: 161). Takayasu suggests that this strategy also applies to the prime minister.

If we treat a robust budget veto as a sort of confidence authority in reserve, then its lack in the cases of New South Wales, Victoria, and Japan expresses the semi-parliamentary logic more clearly.

Absolute veto power on ordinary legislation

Finally, the second chamber can hardly be an equal legislative agent of the voters if it lacks robust veto power on ordinary legislation.[7] As noted above, this is the reason why Japan stands apart from the other semi-parliamentary cases.

[7] The same is not true for the first chamber, whose lack of veto power may be balanced by its power to dismiss the prime minister and the cabinet. Chapter 8 considers such a design.

Even in some of the Australian cases, however, second-chamber veto power is not absolute. A veto of the second chamber in New South Wales can be overturned in a popular referendum, in which the first chamber is the agenda-setter. A veto of its counterparts in the Commonwealth and Victoria can be overturned by a joint session of both chambers, which favors the first chamber due to its size. Only the vetoes of the second chambers in South Australia, Tasmania, and Western Australia cannot be overturned in any way. These cases express the logic of semi-parliamentary democracy most clearly.

The discussion leads to two main conclusions. First, none of the cases express the logic of semi-parliamentary democracy consistently. Second, the two nation-states depart most strongly from it. This fact highlights how important it is to include the Australian states in the empirical analyses of this book, and it helps us to better understand why the comparative literature typically treats the Australian Commonwealth and Japan as parliamentary systems. Even in these cases, though, the combination of direct second-chamber elections with the lack of second-chamber confidence authority over the cabinet is at odds with the logic of a parliamentary system—a fact that has been recognized by country experts (e.g., Bach 2003: 330; Taflaga 2018; Takayasu 2015: 160; Takeshi 2005: 39).

Visions of majority formation and normative balancing

Presuming an underlying logic of a semi-parliamentary democracy helps to highlight important design differences between our cases. But this logic is always relative to certain background assumptions. In this section and the next, I want to explicate and relax two of these assumptions in order to generalize the potential uses of semi-parliamentary government.

The first assumption concerns how the two parts of the assembly are selected. One main attraction of semi-parliamentarism is that they can be selected in different ways, so as to balance different visions of democratic majority formation. In Chapter 1, I discussed the standard political science debate about these visions, which is focused on the choice between majoritarian and proportional electoral systems. How semi-parliamentary government can balance the pros and cons of these systems is what I focus on in Chapter 6. But semi-parliamentarism could also be used to balance competing visions of majority formation at more basic levels, three of which I want to discuss here: (a) partisan and individualist visions, (b) electoral and sortitionist visions, and (c) democratic and epistocratic visions.

Partisan versus individualist visions

When we center our conceptualization of the competing visions of democracy around electoral systems, we usually assume the democratic process to be dominated by parties. However, whether this is desirable is itself controversial. While many authors highlight the importance of programmatically principled and responsible parties, others worry about their negative effects (Muirhead 2006; Muirhead and Rosenblum 2020). Semi-parliamentarism can balance these different perspectives by electing the chamber of confidence in a party-based manner and the chamber of legislation in ways that strengthen the role of independents. We will see in Chapters 6 and 7 that the Australian state of Tasmania uses semi-parliamentary government in this way (Sharman 2013).

Electoral versus sortitionist visions

Both kinds of normative balancing discussed so far implicitly assume that elections are the adequate way to legitimize assemblies, but this view has been challenged by political theorists, who think that selecting policymakers by lot instead of election would be an improvement (for a critical overview, see Landa and Pevnick 2020a). While some propose to replace electoral institutions altogether, thus creating a "lottocracy" (Guerrero 2014), others suggest merely supplementing them. And this is where semi-parliamentary bicameralism comes in. Abizadeh (2020) contends that elections are indispensable for facilitating political agency and the peaceful processing of political conflict but that—for reasons explained further in Chapter 4—sortition is more respectful of the values of political equality and impartiality. Hence, he suggests balancing the competing values by combining an elected first chamber with a randomly selected second chamber. While Abizadeh (2020) does not emphasize this point, only the former would become the principal of the cabinet, whereas the latter would have absolute veto power. In effect, therefore, he proposes a semi-parliamentary system of government in order to balance elections and sortition as competing visions of democracy.

Democratic versus epistocratic visions

Another critique of democratic elections is that they put too much power in the hand of ignorant, irrational, and misinformed voters (Brennan 2016: 23).

According to these "epistocratic" (Estlund 2008) critiques of democracy, it might be better to restrict the franchise through competence-testing. Brennan acknowledges the injustice of historical restrictions grounded on morally irrelevant factors such as race, gender, or possession of property. Given the epistemic flaws of democracy, however, he suggests making suffrage conditional upon morally relevant epistemic qualifications. Just as prospective drivers must pass a driving test, prospective voters ought to pass a voting test.

Of course, this is a highly controversial position for many reasons. One is that even though one might concede that unobjectionable competence tests are conceptually possible, giving political elites the power to design them seems very risky in practice (Bagg 2018: 898). These elites could use these tests to entrench their rule. Many authors therefore conclude that Brennan's epistocracy ought to remain off the table.

This might indeed be the right conclusion. While I do not intend to take a position in this debate, it is worth noting that a semi-parliamentary constitution could balance universal and restricted suffrage in the same way that it could balance elections and sortition. We have seen in the section on "Comparing the cases" that semi-parliamentarism was already used in this way when it emerged in the Australian colonies. Yet, not only were the franchise restrictions based on morally irrelevant factors, but they were also more severe in the chamber of legislation, rather than the chamber of confidence. If morally more acceptable franchise restrictions were to be introduced, they would arguably better be placed in the chamber of confidence—the chamber that authorizes the government to directly exercise power over citizens. The chamber of deliberation, legislation, and control could still be elected under universal suffrage, so that all voices could be heard, new views and interests could form and grow, and the entrenchment of elite rule could be resisted. One way in which it could be resisted is to put the design of the competence test in the hands of the more fully democratic chamber.

All of these more fundamental forms of normative balancing raise many further questions. The goal here has not been to endorse them, but to highlight their commonalities. They are all based on the assumption that the moral and/or practical requirements for selecting a chamber of confidence may differ from those for selecting a chamber of deliberation, legislation, and control. In the rest of this book, I will focus on the kind of normative balancing that we already find in the real world and that is associated with different electoral systems.

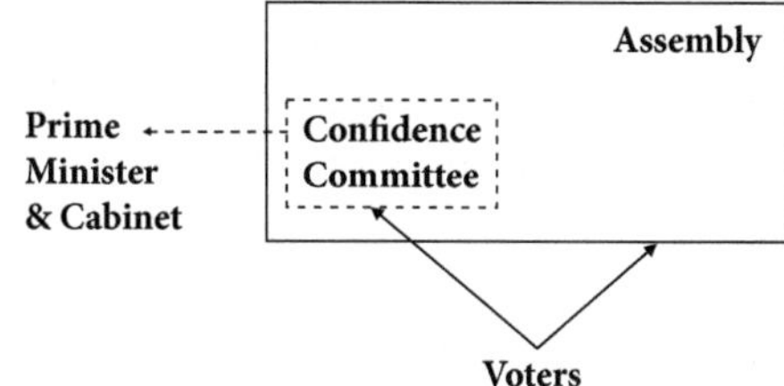

Fig. 3.1 A semi-parliamentary system with a unicameral assembly
Notes: → = election, ⇢ = dismissal.
Source: adapted from Ganghof (2016a).

Semi-parliamentarism within a single chamber

The second background assumption we can relax is that semi-parliamentary government always requires a fully fledged bicameral system with two completely separate chambers. When the goal is to balance the pros and cons of different electoral systems, it is not clear why we need two separate chambers in the first place. If the deliberation and scrutiny of legislative proposals happens predominantly in the (at least) equally legitimate second chamber, while the purpose of the chamber of confidence is mainly to "manufacture" government majorities, the bicameral structure may be inefficient. We might potentially improve upon it by systematically differentiating the right to a no-confidence vote within the assembly. Figure 3.1 illustrates this basic idea by modifying the depiction of semi-parliamentarism in Chapter 2. Rather than having two separate chambers, one part of the assembly, the confidence *committee*, is now embedded within the assembly at large.

Chapter 8 discusses various ways in which the members of the confidence committee can be determined. Here, it suffices to mention one particularly simple option for illustration: a legal threshold of confidence authority. Many electoral systems have legal thresholds of *representation* such that parties whose vote share remains below the threshold are denied seats in the assembly. Analogously, a threshold of *confidence authority* would deny parties below a certain vote share participation in the vote of no confidence procedure. The larger parties with confidence authority would thus form a large confidence committee within parliament. The rules of interaction between the confidence committee and the assembly at large would resemble those between two separate chambers.

This potential design shows once more that we have to distinguish between the operational definition of semi-parliamentary government used to identify empirical cases and a more abstract, ideal-typical definition of the underlying constitutional design. The latter helps us to see new design opportunities. A more general and abstract definition of semi-parliamentarism might go as follows:

> Under semi-parliamentary government, no part of the executive is elected directly. The prime minister and cabinet are selected by an assembly with two parts, only one of which can dismiss the cabinet in a no-confidence vote even though the other has equal or greater democratic legitimacy and robust veto power over ordinary legislation.

This definition does not assume a bicameral system or that both parts of the assembly are elected; and it allows for the possibility that the part of the assembly without confidence authority possesses greater democratic legitimacy than the chamber or committee of confidence. It insists on the robust veto of the former but does not require it for the latter. Chapter 8 also discusses semi-parliamentary designs, in which the chamber or committee of confidence lacks an absolute veto.

Conclusion

We need the concept of semi-parliamentary government because it describes a unique and under-appreciated constitutional structure. This structure is attractive because it establishes an assembly-based separation of powers that can balance different visions of democratic majority formation. We can describe this structure at an abstract level in order to see the full range of design possibilities or based on a minimal definition to identify empirical cases. The cases I have identified as minimally semi-parliamentary are the Australian Commonwealth and Japan, as well as the Australian states of New South Wales, South Australia, Tasmania, Victoria, and Western Australia. The existing literature treats these cases as parliamentary systems because prevalent typologies in political science neglect how directly elected second chambers relate to the executive. While the first fully democratic semi-parliamentary system was the Australian Commonwealth, the basic logic of semi-parliamentary powers separation was already established in the Australian colonies in the 1850s.

4

Are some forms of government more democratic than others?

How do we evaluate forms of government or any other set of formal political institutions? One prominent idea is to evaluate them in terms of their causal consequences. Good institutions are those that lead to good results or outcomes. Another prominent idea is that some institutions are inherently more valuable or democratic than others. This idea is more controversial in political theory, and it is not obvious how the two types of evaluation relate to one another. One goal of this chapter is to clarify the approach to the normative evaluation of democratic institutions taken in this book.

A second, more specific goal is to reject the widespread idea that the direct election of the chief executive—most notably under presidentialism—makes a form of government inherently more democratic (Arato 2000: 321; Calabresi 2001: 67; Lijphart 1992a: 13). This rejection is an important part of my overall argument against presidentialism and in favor of semi-parliamentarism. I also reject the suggestion that semi-parliamentary government is inferior to pure parliamentarism on purely procedural grounds (Meinel 2019, 2021).

The third goal is to clarify three more general desiderata in the egalitarian evaluation of democratic institutions: (a) to distinguish the democratic equality embodied in formal procedures (*procedural equality*) from that realized in the overall political processes (*process equality*); (b) to specify what a particular institutional scheme is compared to; and (c) to consider the two dimensions of political equality in a representative democracy, horizontal and vertical, in conjunction.

The first three sections develop the conceptual framework: they distinguish three ways to value formal democratic procedures, explain how one institutional scheme can be more democratic than another, and highlight the distinction between vertical and horizontal inequality. I then use this framework to show that presidentialism is not democratically superior and semi-parliamentarism not democratically inferior.

Beyond Presidentialism and Parliamentarism. Steffen Ganghof, Oxford University Press.
 DOI: 10.1093/oso/9780192897145.003.0004

Three ways to value formal democratic procedures

Authors that postulate the inherent democratic superiority of presidentialism have never clarified what it means to say that one institutional scheme is inherently more democratic than another. To do so, it is helpful to distinguish three ways to value formal procedures. Figure 4.1 illustrates this distinction with a concrete example, which we will come back to later. The figure depicts a stylized (incomplete) model of some of the causal effects of the mechanical proportionality of electoral systems—a purely procedural feature that has been considered as inherently more democratic in the literature (Christiano 1996; McGann 2006).

Mechanical proportionality requires that *x*% of the votes of any party—real and hypothetical—is translated into *x*% of seats. The degree to which it is realized depends, among other things, on how many seats are to be won in a given district (district magnitude). This procedural feature influences important aspects of the political process, three of which are singled out for illustrative purposes. First, high proportionality is likely to increase citizens' subjective feeling of being represented by a party (Blais et al. 2014; Rodden 2020). It facilitates the emergence of multiple parties with distinct multidimensional platforms, so that voters are more likely to find a party that they feel close to ideologically. Second, multiple parties in parliament and government tend to reduce the so-called "clarity of responsibility" in a political system. This clarity is generally considered to be maximized when a single party dominates the entire political process (Powell 2000; Schwindt-Bayer and Tavits 2016). Third, mechanical proportionality is likely to influence turnout, partly through the two aforementioned variables. The feeling of being represented is likely to increase turnout (Blais et al. 2014), while lacking clarity of responsibility might

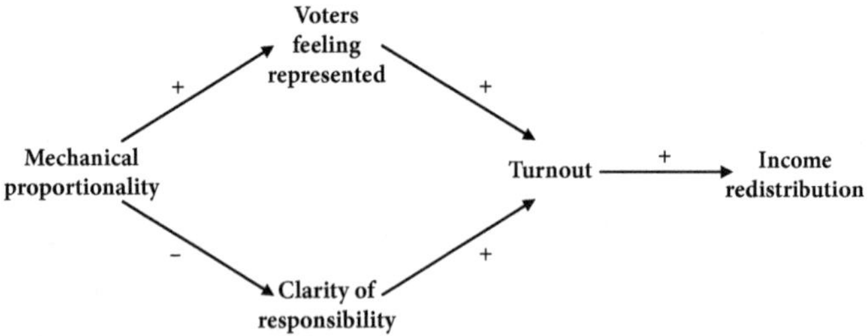

Fig. 4.1 Formal procedures, processes, and outcomes (an illustration)

Source: author's own composition.

reduce it (Park et al. 2019). Mechanical proportionality is also likely to influence certain outcomes of the political process, such as the degree of income redistribution. This influence may partly run through turnout (Kenworthy and Pontusson 2005).

While we will return to some of these causal hypotheses in Chapters 5 and 6, here the model is merely used for illustration. It helps us to distinguish three ways of evaluating a purely procedural feature, such as mechanical proportionality: in terms of

1. its causal effects on the *outcomes* of politics, such as income redistribution;
2. its causal effects on features of the *democratic process*, such as voter feelings, clarity of responsibility, and turnout;
3. its potential *non-instrumental value*, that is, the value that is independent of any causal consequences it might have.

I assume that when authors claim presidentialism to be inherently more democratic than parliamentarism, they have the third, non-instrumental value of political institutions in mind. While they may also have separate concerns about the causal consequences of presidentialism (e.g. Lijphart 1992a), these are discussed in Chapter 9. Here, our goal is to specify a purely proceduralist interpretation of "more democratic." To check whether such an interpretation is meaningful, we first have to consider objections to the idea that formal procedures can have non-instrumental value at all.

Two main groups deny it. One argues that we should only care about outcomes. Its members are often called "instrumentalists" because they see democratic procedures and processes merely as instruments for achieving desirable outcomes, such as a fair income distribution or, more abstractly, justice and truth. They deny that the kind of political equality we associate with representative democracy has any non-instrumental value (Wall 2007; but see Viehoff 2017). Instrumentalists of this type fall into two broad camps: those who believe that representative democracy as we know it is the best instrument (e.g. Bagg 2018; Landemore 2017) and those who doubt this (e.g. Brennan 2016).

The second group that denies the non-instrumental value of formal procedures has a more complex position. It rejects the kind of instrumentalism we have just discussed and embraces political equality as having non-instrumental value. Members of this group have a more robust commitment to democracy because they believe that the substantive outcomes that we ought to pursue in a political system must, in some adequately egalitarian way, be determined by the citizens themselves. For example, James L. Wilson (2019: 111, n. 26) argues that political equality requires the "appropriate consideration" of citizens' political judgment. This concern about equality in the process of political decision-making allows this group to potentially justify adopting democratic arrangements over non-democratic ones, even when the latter lead to better substantive outcomes. It is the achievement or approximation of some equality standard, which I call *process equality*, that is seen as having some kind of non-instrumental value.

When it comes to the evaluation of formal institutions or procedures, any process equality standard is also a kind of outcome standard (see also Estlund 2009: 248–251). So, the second group, too, values formal procedures instrumentally: in terms of their causal consequences for process equality (as well as substantive outcomes). For example, they do not accept procedural features such as mechanical proportionality as a "requirement" for political equality (Wilson 2019: 194). They insist that disproportional electoral systems, such as the so-called first-past-the-post system, are not, in themselves, "undemocratic" (Kolodny 2014: 288; Beitz 1989). Instead, formal institutions such as those of the electoral system must be evaluated in terms of their consequences for an egalitarian political process, all things considered. This group needs a theory of how—through features such as clarity of responsibility or turnout—formal procedures affect overall process equality.

What about those that do ascribe some non-instrumental value to formal institutions, or certain aspects of these institutions, such as mechanical proportionality? They do not deny the importance of overall process equality but suggest that the kind of equality embodied in formal procedures, what I call *procedural equality*, has some kind of priority and establishes some kind of baseline. This baseline deserves special attention and departures from it deserve a special justification. A proportional representation (PR) system with maximal mechanical proportionality is seen as one example of such a baseline institution (Christiano 1996, 2008; McGann 2006).

Before we move on, let me emphasize that I use important terms differently than much of the literature on the justification of democracy. This literature contrasts "instrumental" and "procedural" reasons for democracy but does not typically distinguish between procedural and process equality. It therefore often fails to acknowledge that concerns about process equality are also concerns about the *causal effects* of formal institutions. I highlight this distinction between procedural and process equality and use the term "procedural" with a narrow focus on the evaluation of formal institutions. It is this evaluation that we are concerned with when we try to understand whether one institutional scheme is inherently "more democratic" than another.

How one institutional scheme can be inherently more democratic than another

What kind of priority does the value of procedural equality have, and what kind of baseline does it establish? I believe that process equality and substantive outcomes must have *moral* priority over procedural equality. For example, if it were true that high mechanical proportionality consistently undermined process equality (e.g. by leading to less and more unequal turnout, etc.), we would have reason to avoid it. However, it does not follow that procedural equality has no distinct value at all or that an analytical focus on it is misplaced. It merely means that the non-instrumental value of procedural equality is conditional and that an analytical focus on it cannot be justified on purely moral grounds. I elaborate on both points in turn.

To say that procedural equality has conditional value means that its value can be undercut by considerations about causal effects (Christiano 2008). It can be valued for its own sake but only under certain background conditions. More specifically, procedural equality may be valued non-instrumentally as a particularly visible component of a fair democratic process but only if its causal consequences do not run counter to overall process equality. If they do, procedural equality may lose its non-instrumental value (see also Viehoff 2019).

But if procedural equality is subordinate in this way, why focus on it in the first place? Why not pick some conception of process equality (and desirable substantive outcomes) as our target variable and reason backwards from the available causal knowledge to the desirable set of institutions (Beitz 1989; Kolodny 2014; Wilson 2019)? My answer to these questions highlights the importance and difficulty of publicly justifying procedural inequalities in the real world. We know as a matter of social-scientific fact that instrumentalist justifications of procedural inequalities—including those about process equality—are often insincere or reflect well-known cognitive biases (confirmation bias, status quo bias, etc.). They are often made in a self-interested manner, especially by powerful actors who benefit from some institutional scheme or can predict to do so in the future (e.g. Colomer 2005; Klarman 2016). Against this background, the point of focusing on procedural equality is to shift the onus of justification onto those that argue for procedural inequality.

I suggest that this shift is grounded in an explanatory presumption, not a moral one, the underlying logic being that of Ockham's Razor (Sober 2015). Since the simplest and thus prima facie most likely explanation for any procedural inequality is that it benefits powerful groups or actors, a crucial task in real-world deliberation about justifiable political institutions is to distinguish genuine instrumentalist justifications from pseudo-justifications driven by self-interest and cognitive bias. An important task for political theory is to inform this real-world deliberation. Only if a genuine justification for highly visible procedural inequalities exists can it be publicly available in a way that reassures free and equal citizens that they are not treated unjustly and/or as social inferiors (Christiano 2008; Gaus 1996; Kolodny 2014; Viehoff 2019).

Finally, let us note a problem with the notion of a baseline. It might be thought to imply that there is some ideal set of procedures, which uniquely embodies the value of political equality and thus ought to be approximated (Christiano 1996; McGann 2006). One problem with this thought is that the requirements for procedural equality cannot be uniquely specified without any (implicit) instrumentalist assumptions. For example, a concern about procedural equality in making decisions might lead us to use majority rule, but it may also lead us to flip a coin (Estlund 2008, 2009). Moreover, we will see below that when we consider a *representative* democracy, the desiderata of formal procedural equality along the horizontal and vertical dimensions of the political process may conflict. Hence, it is impossible to determine some ideal design of representative democracy on purely procedural grounds.

A solution to this problem is to conceive of the justification of procedural inequalities in a strictly comparative manner (Wiens 2012). A comparative approach avoids evaluating certain institutional schemes *tout court*. When we compare institutional schemes only along one specific dimension, while keeping others constant, we are often able to say that one institutional scheme is (conditionally) preferable to another in virtue of its greater procedural equality. I will call such a scheme *procedurally preferable*, regardless of whether it is the scheme we ought to adopt, all things considered.

Take, for instance, the comparison between two parliamentary systems that use proportional representation with closed lists in a single district, but different legal thresholds of representation. These thresholds imply that parties have to surpass a certain vote share to win parliamentary seats at all. Suppose that the thresholds are at 5% and 10%, respectively. It is meaningful to say that the former institutional scheme is procedurally preferable and, in this sense, more democratic because it nullifies the votes of fewer (sincerely voting) citizens. Hence, if the scheme with the 5% threshold achieved process equality and good substantive outcomes equally well, it is the one we ought to choose.[1] This is different from saying that this scheme approximates some ideal set of democratic institutions, but it directs our attention where it belongs. Whenever someone proposes to establish or maintain procedural inequality, *we must ask whether some alternative scheme could not achieve the relevant goals equally well but with less procedural inequality.*

Taking vertical inequality seriously

In a representative democracy, procedural equality has two analytical dimensions, horizontal and vertical (Dworkin 2000), but many normative discussions focus only on the former (Ganghof 2015b). As Abizadeh observes:

> Having equal opportunity to wield power in selecting representatives and to influence representatives once selected may be a way of instantiating *horizontal* equality between non-representatives. But horizontal equality fails to address the formal *vertical inequality* intrinsic to representative democracy: between representatives empowered to decide legislation and policy and non-representatives who are not. The tendency to parachute a notion of political equality forged with direct democracy tacitly in mind—as equal say in majoritarian *decision-making*—into a theory of *representative* democracy (Waldron 1999) fails to take seriously this vertical inequality and the fact that elections select office-holders rather than decide laws. Being treated as an equal *qua* selector (and having equal opportunity to influence representatives) is therefore insufficient for political equality [emphasis in the original].
>
> Abizadeh (2020: 6)

Vertical inequality in the formal procedures of democracy may be justified in terms of process equality and/or substantive outcomes. Normative theorists have focused on two types of comparisons. One is between direct and representative democracy. Proponents of representation justify procedural vertical inequality in terms of greater overall process equality and/or better outcomes. For example, Christiano (2008) focuses on process equality and argues that the intellectual division of labor achieved through representation increases

[1] I am not concerned here with the relative importance of process equality and substantive outcomes because my goal is not to present a justification of democracy. Whether the approach outlined here implies a justification of representative of democracy as we know it depends on our causal knowledge.

everyone's control over society so much that it overcompensates for procedural vertical inequality. That is, "even the power of the least powerful is likely to be greater than under direct democracy" (Christiano 2015: 102). Landa and Pevnick (2020b) focus more on good outcomes and justify representation as a sort of compromise between full democracy and "epistocracy," the rule of the knowers (see also Brennan 2016).

The second comparison is between electoral and lottery-based representation. Abizadeh (2020) argues that the only way to make the unavoidable vertical inequality of representation compatible with the value of political equality is to treat citizens equally not qua selectors but qua candidates for office (see also Guerrero 2014; Landemore 2020). Office-holding is seen as a good that consists in extra opportunities to wield power over political decisions and that cannot be distributed equally. Hence the superior institutional scheme is to give everyone "an equal chance or opportunity to hold office" (Abizadeh 2020: 7). However, while this solution establishes a certain form of procedural equality, whether it is better overall can be questioned. Landa and Pevnick (2020a) defend electoral representation in terms of both process equality and better substantive outcomes.

There has been less interest in a third type of comparison, that between different *degrees of procedural vertical inequality* under different forms of representative government. The normative literature is virtually silent on this matter, even at an abstract level. For example, an influential article by Niko Kolodny (2014: 317–318) makes rather detailed claims about horizontal equality and institutional design, but it ignores differences between forms of government and specifies only the most rudimentary procedural requirements for acceptable vertical inequality. Most notably, he requires that the principal controls the selection of the agent and that the agent can be replaced after a short and limited term.

It is here that the claims in political science and constitutional theory about the alleged democratic superiority of presidentialism enter the picture. As I understand them, these are claims about reduced procedural inequality along the vertical dimension. They are misleading, however, because they fail to adequately distinguish and specify the relevant comparisons and disregard conflicts between vertical and horizontal equality.

Is presidentialism inherently more democratic?

It has often been suggested that presidentialism is inherently more democratic than parliamentarism. Arend Lijphart (1992a: 13) states that a "major advantage of presidential government is that its popular election of the chief executive can be regarded as more democratic than the indirect 'election'—formal or informal—of the executive in parliamentary systems." Similarly, Andrew Arato (2000: 321) suggests that the critique of presidentialism "was rarely based on normative considerations for the simple reason that, under a democracy, direct elections are always preferable to indirect elections that can always deny office to the candidate the voters actually prefer." Calabresi (2001: 67) concurs and suspects that "[f]or many readers this advantage of presidentialism over parliamentarianism may be dispositive just by itself." Similar claims can be found in other works (Moe and Caldwell 1994: 172; von Mettenheim 1997).

The underlying argument is not spelled out, though. One intuition is that direct election conserves some of the putative normative appeal of direct democracy (von Mettenheim 1997). Another idea is that the need for direct authorization varies with the power of the office: "Democracy does not require the popular election of all public officials, of course, but the argument that heads of government, who are the most important and powerful office-holders in democracies, should be directly elected has great validity" (Lijphart 1992a: 13; see also Calabresi 2001: 67).

As I interpret these ideas, they suggest that because presidential government gives citizens as the principal more direct control over the selection of the chief executive as a particularly powerful agent, it is procedurally preferable to parliamentary government. This suggestion is mistaken for two reasons: (a) it conflates two distinct comparisons; and (b) it disregards the possibility of conflict between procedural considerations along the vertical and horizontal dimensions.

Consider first the comparison between a presidential system with the direct election of the chief executive and an otherwise identical presidential system, in which presidential selection is processed through intermediate agents such as the members of the Electoral College of the United States. In this comparison, all the other elements of the compared systems remain fixed, so that direct election is indeed procedurally preferable. Concerns about horizontal and vertical equality do not conflict, but point in the same direction.[2] An institution like the Electoral College violates horizontal procedural equality because the votes of some citizens, those in more populous states, do not have the same weight as those of others. The Electoral College echoes the unequal representation of citizens in the United States Senate because states are accorded College votes according to the number of representatives in Congress. It also threatens to undermine vertical equality because its members might choose to violate

[2] For a more detailed discussion of the Electoral College from the perspective of political equality, see Wilson (2019).

their mandate and not elect the candidate that won in the respective state. The intermediate agents may thus have more control over the selection of the president than other citizens. This possibility has been subject to legal controversy. In this particular comparison, it is meaningful to say that the direct election of the president is procedurally preferable and, in this sense, more democratic.[3]

The comparison between a presidential and a parliamentary system of government is different. We have already seen that the arguments about this comparison are not well developed, but a charitable interpretation might go as follows. It is procedurally preferable, along the vertical dimension of procedural equality, that each and every agent in a representative democracy be directly elected by the entire electorate: each member of parliament, each member of the cabinet, each member of the Supreme or Constitutional Court, and so on. That representative democracy is not ultimately set up in this way is because of weighty instrumental reasons: Members of parliament ought to be accountable to their parties or local constituencies; there must be some hierarchy in the cabinet to create clarity of responsibility; judges ought to be shielded from electoral competition; and so on. Hence, the idea might be that the general procedural preference for direct election does not survive instrumentalist scrutiny for most individual agents, but it does for the heads of government, as the most important and powerful office-holders.

The problem is that this kind of argument about vertical procedural equality may conflict with reasonable concerns about horizontal equality. After all, it is not enough to directly elect a set of individual agents. These agents must also interact with each other under specific rules in order to produce collectively binding decisions. Our concerns about procedural equality must also include these horizontal rules of interaction, which might well point towards making the chief executive an agent of the assembly.

Consider, for instance, McGann's (2006) justification for a parliamentary system of government. He argues that political equality requires that decision-making power be concentrated in a legislative assembly that makes internal decisions by simple majority rule and whose members are elected under rules that are mechanically proportional. In this way, citizens have formally equal opportunity to influence binding decisions via groups of representatives with similar views (see also Christiano 1996). Moreover, McGann (2006: 85) notes

[3] Of course, defenders of the Electoral College might accept this but insist that its instrumental benefits undercut the procedural value of direct election. This question need not concern us here, although it is worth noting that there are also weighty instrumental reasons against the Electoral College, including those associated with process equality. One reason is that presidential campaigns tend to focus on a few swing states, thus potentially not giving adequate consideration to the interests and judgments of citizens in other states.

that one way to extend this equality in legislative voting to the process of agenda-setting is to let the assembly majority select and deselect the chief executive and cabinet. In this account, it is procedurally preferable along the horizontal dimension of equality to select the chief executive indirectly.

A proponent of presidentialism might respond to McGann by insisting that a presidential system could be designed to match the horizontal procedural equality achieved by proportional-representation (PR) parliamentarism (Colomer and Negretto 2005). The mechanical proportionality in assembly elections could match that of a parliamentary system, presidents could be denied absolute veto power over legislation, and whatever specific powers (e.g. in legislative agenda-setting) presidents might have could be fairly authorized by an absolute majority of voters in a separate presidential election.[4] When we compare this kind of system to the one favored by McGann, purely procedural considerations are insufficient to rank them. While the proponent of presidentialism can point to the procedural value of electing chief executives directly, McGann can point to the value of having them selected by a proportionally elected majority coalition.

We can certainly try to weigh the conflicting considerations against one another but not without bringing in instrumentalist assumptions about process equality and the requirements of adequate representation. For example, the proponent of parliamentarism might deny that a single human being can adequately represent a heterogeneous citizenry and emphasize that a prime minister must continuously accommodate the preferences of the majority in a proportionally elected assembly to stay in office. One might also argue from a social choice perspective that a PR parliamentary system is more reliable in empowering the median voter (if it exists) as the Condorcet winner or, at least, in preventing the victory of the Condorcet loser (see Colomer and Negretto 2005; McGann et al. 2002).[5] By contrast, the proponent of presidentialism might point to the fact that the endogenous selection of the chief executive in a pure parliamentary system can lead to a bias against whichever side on the general left–right dimension is fragmented into a greater number of parties (Döring and Manow 2015). This is because the party that leads the cabinet-formation process is often the largest party but not necessarily the one preferred by a majority of voters. Both sides have to make assumptions

[4] Perhaps the most egalitarian way to directly elect a president is an alternative vote (or "ranked choice") system. All voters can rank as many candidates as they like, and the candidates with the lowest vote shares are sequentially eliminated and their votes reallocated to determine the candidate with an absolute majority (more than 50% of all votes). For further discussion, see Chapter 8.

[5] The Condorcet winner (loser) is the alternative that would win (lose) every pairwise majority contest.

about human psychology and the causal effects of institutions; they cannot make purely procedural arguments. Hence, the claim that presidentialism is inherently more democratic than parliamentarism is false.

The neglect of direct recall

It is also worth noting that the proponents of this claim do not apply their concerns about vertical procedural equality consistently. After all, the vertical equality between principals and agents not only depends on how the agents are selected but also—and more fundamentally—on how their authority can be *revoked*.[6] The possibility of recalling all directly elected agents is arguably procedurally preferable to its absence. Under presidentialism, the possibility of directly recalling a directly elected president would reduce procedural inequality along the vertical dimension without affecting the horizontal dimension.[7] This possibility is preferable in the same way in which it is preferable, on egalitarian grounds, that we as individuals can fire our doctors or lawyers. It is striking that proceduralist arguments for presidentialism neglect this procedural superiority of direct recall.

To be sure, one can claim that the recall of directly elected representatives would have undesirable *causal* effects on process equality and substantive outcomes. But such a claim has to be part of a more general instrumentalist evaluation. In Chapter 9, I argue that presidentialism cannot be defended on instrumental grounds. The argument essentially reverses the logic of Lijphart (1992a) and Calabresi (2001). The direct power that the holders of the office of the chief executive exert over their citizens does not give us procedural reasons for their direct election (as we have seen), but it does give us instrumental reasons to make their authority politically revocable by some collective and representative entity.

[6] Abstract discussions about the equality between principal and agent also ignore this crucial aspect of their relationship (e.g. Kolodny 2014). This is surprising, given that all of the archetypical agents Kolodny and others use to motivate the argument for delegation (doctors, lawyers, accountants, and financial planners) can usually have their authority revoked at any time and for whatever reason. The call for the possibility of recalling public officers also has a long pedigree in political thought (Qvortrup 2020; Whitehead 2018).

[7] Of course, the democratic superiority of direct recall applies more generally. In particular, it is procedurally preferable under any form of government that citizens can recall individual members of parliament (when these are directly elected in geographically defined districts) and/or the parliament as a whole.

Is semi-parliamentarism less democratic?

Let us finally consider the comparison of parliamentarism and semi-parliamentarism from the perspective of procedural equality. Some authors worry that there is something democratically defective about semi-parliamentary government (Meinel 2019, 2021; Weale 2018). Here I want to respond to Meinel; Weale's concerns are discussed in Chapter 6.

Meinel (2019, 2021) sees semi-parliamentarism as an interesting response to the challenges faced by pure parliamentary government, such as the increased partisan fragmentation of parliaments. However, he considers semi-parliamentary government to violate a "principle of egalitarian representation" (Meinel 2019: 212; see also Meinel 2021: 135-136). The idea seems to be that under parliamentarism, the equality of the members of parliament symbolizes the equality of citizens. Since semi-parliamentarism creates a privileged group of assembly members (those that can participate in the no-confidence procedure), it gives up on this symbolic representation of citizens.

I want to make two main points in response. First, I do not view Meinel's concern as one about the procedural equality of citizens. I have argued that this equality conditionally requires that citizens have equal institutional entitlements, not that their status is symbolized in a particular manner. When we think about semi-parliamentary government in terms of these entitlements and specify the relevant comparisons systematically, we can see that it can be procedurally preferable to parliamentarism.

Meinel's comparison of parliamentarism and semi-parliamentarism lacks precision because he does not specify the relevant levels of mechanical (dis)proportionality in the electoral system. Elsewhere in his book he considers the 5% legal threshold of representation in the German electoral system to be instrumentally justified because it makes an "indispensable contribution" (2019: 121) to the formation of stable governing majorities in a parliamentary system. Yet, such a threshold means that the actual or potential voters of below-threshold parties are procedurally discriminated against. By denying these voters representation in parliament, they are denied all the opportunities associated with it, including the opportunity to participate, via their chosen parties, in the vote of no confidence procedure. As a result, whether or not parliamentarism treats citizens more or less equally than semi-parliamentarism in purely procedural terms depends on the level of the respective thresholds of exclusion.

To see this, let us consider the simple version of semi-parliamentary government introduced in Chapter 3: a *legal threshold of confidence authority* (see Ganghof 2018a and Chapter 8). Parties whose vote share is above the threshold of representation but below the threshold of confidence authority gain representation in parliament and the rights associated with it, but not the right to participate in the no-confidence procedure. The bicameral versions of semi-parliamentarism that we find in Australia create essentially the same result. The implicit electoral threshold created by the majoritarian electoral systems of the first chamber becomes the threshold of confidence authority, while the lower implicit threshold of the proportional systems of the second chamber becomes the threshold of representation.

Semi-parliamentary government can be procedurally preferable to parliamentary government because a threshold of confidence authority denies certain citizens fewer rights than a threshold of representation. Whether this is the case depends on the respective thresholds. When we compare a parliamentary system with a 5% threshold of representation to a semi-parliamentary system without such a threshold but a 5% threshold of confidence authority, the latter is procedurally preferable, everything else being equal. It denies the actual or potential voters of below-threshold parties fewer opportunities. They are merely denied the opportunity to influence the formation and dismissal of the government, not the opportunity to participate fairly in legislative deliberation and voting. It is precisely in this sense that semi-parliamentarism can be considered more democratic than parliamentarism, everything else being equal.[8]

When we vary the thresholds in the comparison, the evaluation becomes more complicated. Consider, for instance, a parliamentary system with a 5% threshold of representation and a semi-parliamentary system with no such threshold but a 10% threshold of confidence authority. The reduced procedural inequality in legislation and deliberation under semi-parliamentarism must now be weighed against the increased procedural inequality in choosing the government. Here instrumental concerns, for example about the importance of the government's control of the legislative agenda, must enter the picture and a purely procedural comparison becomes inconclusive.

My second response to Meinel is to grant that the symbolism of semi-parliamentarism might raise valid *instrumentalist* concerns, as it makes the

[8] A fuller evaluation must also take into account the procedures regulating inter-branch relations; see Chapter 8.

procedural discrimination of certain voters more visible. When parliamentary systems deny some voters fair representation in parliament, this discrimination becomes hidden to some extent once parliament is formed. It is almost as if these voters did not exist. By contrast, if these voters are represented in a semi-parliamentary system but denied participation—via their representatives—in the formation and dismissal of the government, the procedural discrimination becomes highly visible. This visibility might have negative causal effects, for example, on the overall support for the democratic system. This is an empirical hypothesis worth considering, although it does not seem to find a lot of initial support in the bicameral cases of semi-parliamentarism in Australia (Stone 2008).

Conclusion

Presidentialism is not inherently more democratic than parliamentarism—a purely procedural comparison of these two systems is inconclusive. Parliamentarism is also not preferable to semi-parliamentarism on purely procedural grounds, but semi-parliamentarism is preferable if the relevant thresholds of exclusion are held constant in the comparison. Denying the voters of below-threshold parties power over the cabinet creates less procedural inequality than denying them any representation in the assembly. There are no conclusive procedural reasons for presidential government or against semi-parliamentary government.

5

Visions of democracy and the limits of parliamentarism

Is a separation of powers between the executive and the assembly desirable? Proponents of parliamentary government do not believe so. They highlight the advantages of the fusion of power between the government and the assembly majority, not least the avoidance of executive personalism (Ackerman 2000; Linz 1994; Samuels and Shugart 2010).[1] Yet the parliamentary fusion of powers also creates important trade-offs in the design of democracy (Lijphart 1992a; Shugart and Carey 1992). Voters directly authorize a single collective agent, the assembly, who is charged with the two different, and partly conflicting, tasks: selecting a government and keeping it in office, on the one hand; making laws and controlling the government, on the other. As a result, the design of the assembly's electoral system and of the confidence relationship between executive and legislature must respond to conflicting goals. Designs that allow voters to make a clear choice between competing cabinet alternatives conflict with those that represent voters fairly and allow legislative proposals to be deliberated and decided upon issue by issue.

Since trade-offs exist under any form of government, our task is (a) to understand how competing goals can be balanced under parliamentarism; and (b) to compare this balancing to what is possible under the separation of powers. This chapter tackles the first part of this task. I distinguish two polar visions of democracy—simple and complex majoritarianism—and argue that trying to approximate them under pure parliamentary government is difficult and risky. Many parliamentary democracies position themselves between the two conceptual extremes. They thereby achieve a form of normative balance but have to give up on the most demanding goals of each vision.

I first explain why I consider it necessary to replace well-known distinctions such as that between majoritarian and consensus democracy (Lijphart

[1] Of course, they may believe in other aspects of a broader notion of the separation of powers, which includes, e.g., the judiciary or federalism.

Beyond Presidentialism and Parliamentarism. Steffen Ganghof, Oxford University Press.
 DOI: 10.1093/oso/9780192897145.003.0005

1984, 2012). Then I elaborate on the proposed conceptual contrast between simple and complex majoritarianism. Next, I discuss the risks and difficulties of trying to approximate these two polar visions, especially within the confines of a parliamentary system of government, and I explore the strategies for achieving some normative balance between the extremes. Finally, I operationalize each vision in terms of three goals and map the resulting patterns of democratic majority formation for 22 non-presidential democracies in the period 1993–2018 (see appendix). The sample includes pure parliamentary systems, semi-presidential systems, and the assembly-independent system in Switzerland.

Visions of democracy and the separation of powers

Political science has long suggested that there exist competing visions of democracy, and it has produced a number of proposals about what these visions are (Gerring and Thacker 2008; Lijphart 1984, 2012; Powell 2000). I add another one here, for two main reasons. First, I do not accept the widespread idea that one of these two visions is "majoritarian," while the other is not (Lijphart 1984, 2012; Powell 2000). Democracy is fundamentally built on the idea of majority rule, and our conceptualization of competing visions of democracy should reflect this. These visions should be understood as *different visions of majority rule.*[2]

Second, I am interested in exploring how visions of majority formation interact with forms of government. The existing conceptual approaches are not well suited for this purpose. One reason is that they often make the fusion or separation of powers between executive and assembly part of the definition of the two visions. For example, Gerring and Thacker (2008: 18) distinguish two comprehensive models of democratic governance, which they call decentralism and centripetalism. Each model lumps together many distinct institutions and features, including the form of government and the structure of the assembly. This approach fixes the relationship between forms of government and visions of democracy conceptually from the outset. It does not help us to explore this relationship empirically or to think creatively about constitutional design. The question whether bicameralism can be an alternative to

[2] Of course, some democracies may depart from majority rule and require supermajorities to pass ordinary legislation (e.g. McGann 2006: 183). Such departures are not my focus here and the extent to which they exist in democracies is frequently exaggerated. Institutions such as strong second chambers may render legislative decision-making supermajoritarian, but I argue in Chapters 6 and 8 that this is not necessarily the case.

presidentialism—central to my argument in this book—does not arise at all, as both institutional schemes are presumed to be part of the same "decentralist" model.

Another downside of existing approaches is that important causal consequences of the separation of powers are neglected (Ganghof 2010). This point is best illustrated with the influential case of Switzerland. The seminal works of Lijphart (1984, 2012) and Powell (2000) ground one of the polar visions of democracy in the so-called Westminster model. Crucial components of this model are (a) a parliamentary system of government; (b) plurality elections in single-seat districts; (c) a two-party system; and (d) one-party majority cabinets.[3] Both authors associate this model with the very idea of democratic majority rule and thus call it majoritarian democracy. The alternative model, which they respectively call "consensus" and "proportional" democracy, embraces proportional representation (PR) and multiparty competition. The tricky task is to specify the *conceptual* alternative to the Westminster model. As Lijphart (1984: 14) asks: What is its logical opposite? Both authors take their cues from the Swiss case. They interpret the country's convention of representing the four largest parliamentary parties in the cabinet (the "Magic Formula") as a rejection of majority rule. Lijphart (1984: 23, emphasis added) sees it as an effort to "maximize the size of the ruling majority instead of being satisfied with a bare majority." For Powell (2000: 92), it embodies the idea that "all the representative groups in the assembly should have influence on policy making in proportion to their size."

Yet both of these interpretations neglect a key fact: Switzerland does not have a parliamentary system. As discussed in Chapter 2, the Magic Formula cabinets imply neither consensus nor proportional influence because the cabinet parties are not veto players. Since the assembly does not have to keep the cabinet in office, there is no need for coalition discipline. Swiss parties do, in fact, form minimal-winning coalitions on controversial issues and, hence, are indeed often satisfied with a bare majority.[4] As discussed in Chapter 2, the majoritarian features of the Swiss constitutional system also help to explain why the Magic Formula emerged in the first place. By neglecting the separation of powers, we risk painting a biased picture of how democracy works in Switzerland.

[3] I focus on these four features, but the alleged model has many potential attributes. Russell and Serban (2021) argue that the concept has become too stretched to be useful.

[4] None of this is to deny other "proportional" or "consensual" features of Swiss politics (Linder and Mueller 2021). But it matters whether consensual behavior and conventions are grounded in constitutionalized minority vetoes or, rather, in fundamentally majoritarian institutions (McGann 2006).

The empirical studies of Lijphart (1984, 2012) and Powell (2000) have been groundbreaking in many ways, but neither of them was designed to corroborate the conceptual ideas on which they are built. These ideas are presumed and become the theoretical lens through which reality is perceived. To understand how the fusion or separation of powers shapes democratic majority formation in different countries, we might need a different lens.

Simple versus complex majoritarianism

I propose to contrast two polar visions of democracy: complex and simple majoritarianism (Ganghof 2015a).[5] Both of these ideal-typical visions embrace majority rule but differ in their views on how majorities ought to form in a democracy. What distinguishes the two ideals is not how large majorities ought to be or how much relative influence parties ought to have, but how they approach the inherent cognitive and coordinative complexity of politics in modern societies.[6]

The ideal of simple majoritarianism is to reduce this complexity as much as possible in order to reduce the cognitive demands on voters and the coordinative demands on separate political parties. Too many partisan options are seen as presenting voters with a "conceptual obstacle" (Carey and Hix 2011: 385). In its most extreme version, therefore, simple majoritarianism envisions a process in which only two disciplined political parties compete in a unidimensional conflict space; one party becomes the clear winner and dominates the legislative process. In this ideal, voters can directly select a government and clearly see who is responsible for past decisions (Rosenbluth and Shapiro 2018).

Complex majoritarianism, by contrast, embraces the cognitive and coordinative complexity that results when multiple parties stake out distinct positions in a multidimensional conflict space. Institutional constraints on the emergence of new parties and the dimensionality of party competition are seen as unfair and unnecessary simplifications of public deliberation and legislative

[5] The term "complex majoritarianism" is also used, in a different sense and context, by Melissa Schwartzberg (2013). She is concerned with the stability of constitutions and uses the term in opposition to supermajority requirements for constitutional changes. In her conception, complex majoritarianism in constitutional change involves public deliberation and time delays.

[6] "Majoritarianism" does not here describe a particular normative conception and justification of democracy. For this use of the term, see, e.g. Abizadeh (2021).

voting (e.g. Christiano 1996: 261; McGann 2006, 2013). In its most extreme version, complex majoritarianism also envisions that different legislative majorities can be built on different issues—just as in Switzerland. This is seen as a way to include all voters fairly in legislative deliberation and decision-making (e.g. Nagel 2012; Powell 2000: 256, n. 9; Ward and Weale 2010). In the words of Powell (2000: 256, n. 9), different sets of parties and citizens will form the majority on different issues, so that "it is important that the policy-making coalition not be locked into place by the immediate election outcome."[7]

Importantly, both of these visions of majority formation embrace the values of electoral accountability and fair representation, but they engage different *theories* about what the realization of these values requires (Ganghof 2016b).[8] Proponents of simple majoritarianism equate accountability with simplicity: two-party competition is "easy for voters to comprehend; and comprehension aids accountability" (Rosenbluth and Shapiro 2018: 236). Accountability is essentially equated with "clarity of responsibility" (Powell 2000; Schwindt-Bayer and Tavits 2016). By contrast, proponents of proportional representation highlight how low entry barriers for new parties help to keep *all* parliamentary parties accountable (McGann 2013: 111). Issue-specific decision-making even allows voters to keep parties accountable for their participation or non-participation in specific legislation coalitions, thereby making the idea of accountability even more cognitively demanding (Ganghof 2016b: 226).

The respective theories of representation are different, too. For example, a large literature in political science follows Powell (2000) in measuring the "congruence" between the policymakers and the median voter in some conflict space (for a critical review, see Sabl 2015). Within this approach, the difference between the two visions boils down to their conceptions of the relevant median. Simple majoritarianism tries to reduce the conflict space to a single dimension and to approximate the position of some "global" median voter (Huber and Powell 1994; Powell 2000, 2019).[9] Complex majoritarianism, by contrast, assumes a multidimensional conflict space and is concerned with the position of the median voter on each separable issue (Ganghof 2015a; Nagel 2012; Ward and Weale 2010).

[7] As I discuss elsewhere, Powell's study embraces conceptual ideas that are in tension with one another (Ganghof 2015a).

[8] In contrast to this view, it is often suggested that one democratic vision prioritizes accountability, the other representation (e.g. Carey and Hix 2011: 385).

[9] E.g., Rosenbluth and Shapiro (2018: 236) claim that with "only two parties in the game, political competition tends to be based on economic interests … ."

The two visions under pure parliamentarism

Having sketched the two polar visions in general terms, we can now apply them to the stages of democratic majority formation in a pure parliamentary system. While Powell (2000) focuses on the distinction between the pre-electoral and post-electoral stages, I distinguish four possible stages at which the process of coalition-formation and majority-formation can be completed (Figure 5.1). These stages are related to the two polar visions for a simple reason. When the process of democratic majority formation is completed at an early stage, complexity is reduced; when it is postponed to a later stage, complexity increases. The first and last of these stages thus correspond roughly to the two polar visions, while the two intermediate stages can be understood as attempts to achieve some normative balance (Ganghof 2015a). We will see that these two intermediate stages also dominate the actual political processes of advanced parliamentary democracies. The following considers each of the four models of majority formation in turn.

Party-centered majority formation

This corresponds roughly to the Westminster model or what I have called simple majoritarianism. It aims at completing majority-formation at the first stage: only two parties form, both of which need to be broad, long-term coalitions of different societal groups. If the winning party forms a majority cabinet and dominates the legislative process as a single veto player, the process of majority formation is essentially completed at the first stage. Cases like the United Kingdom or the Australian state of Queensland approximate this model.

Alliance-centered majority formation

There are multiple parties, but they group into two competing alliances before the election. One alliance gains a majority and dominates the legislative

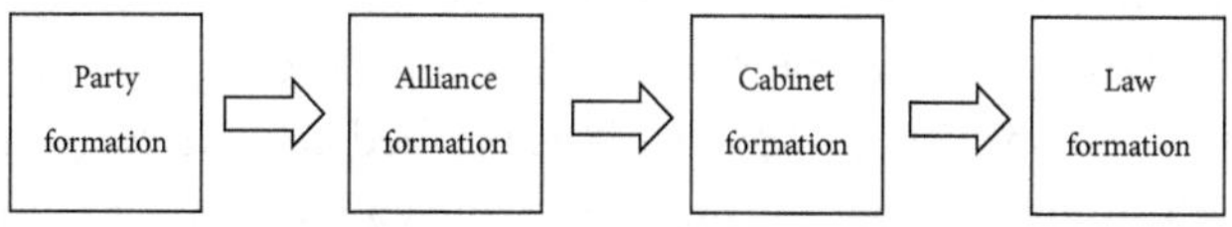

Fig. 5.1 Four stages of democratic majority formation
Source: adapted from Ganghof et al. (2015: 62).

process as a veto-player coalition. Majority formation is essentially completed at the second stage. Germany in the 1980s and 1990s approximates this model.

Cabinet-centered majority formation

Multiple parties compete separately in elections but form a fixed majority coalition afterwards. They establish each other as veto players and execute a joint coalition program, for which they take joint responsibility. Majority formation is essentially completed at the third stage. Finland approximates this model (Ganghof et al. 2015).

Legislature-centered majority formation

Multiple parties compete separately in elections and one of them forms a minority cabinet that builds issue-specific legislative coalitions in the legislature. These coalitions on specific laws or issues complete the process of democratic majority formation. Denmark approximates this model to some extent (see "How parliamentary government constrains issue-specific decision-making").

While the polar models of completing majority formation at the first or the last stage may seem attractive under idealized conditions, they are associated with significant risks and difficult to stabilize in practice—especially under pure parliamentary government. I discuss these risks and difficulties for both visions in turn.

The limits and perils of simple majoritarianism

In a complex world with multiple dimensions of political conflict, a two-party system is difficult to create and maintain. The attempt to do so creates a number of risks. I will focus on biased representation, power concentration, and affective polarization. It is important to keep in mind that the following discussion is about the *ideal* of simple majoritarianism—as espoused, for example, by Rosenbluth and Shapiro (2018)—and the implied normative justification of electoral institutions. I make no empirical claims about why certain electoral institutions were chosen or have been maintained in particular countries (see, e.g. Colomer 2018).

Note first that a two-party system *in the assembly* would be easy to engineer. For example, we could allow voters to choose between party lists in a single, jurisdiction-wide electoral district. If no party achieved an absolute majority in the first voting round, a second round (or "run-off") between the two top parties could determine the winner. These two parties would gain assembly seats in proportion to their final vote shares. The problem with this kind of system is that it would not only concentrate a lot of political power in the elite of the two winning parties, but it would probably also fail to reduce the number of parties that participate and gain votes in the first round. Voters' cognitive burden would still be high.

Partly for this reason, proponents of simple majoritarianism defend the practice of electing representatives in single-seat districts (SSD), preferably under plurality rule (Rosenbluth and Shapiro 2018). They hope that this type of majoritarian electoral system will reduce the number of candidates and lead to the same two-party system in each district. Yet this hope rarely turns into reality (Dunleavy and Diwakar 2013; Kollman 2018; Moser et al. 2018). In parliamentary systems such as Canada, India, or the United Kingdom, SSD-plurality elections do not generate two-party systems, certainly not in terms of voters' choices. The ideal of simple majoritarianism can therefore have important negative consequences in the real world.

Biased representation

One is that SSDs tend to severely bias democratic representation. This happens even when district boundaries are drawn in a fair way—which they often are not (McGann et al. 2016). Many votes for a party can be wasted when they are located in districts where a party normally wins with large majorities. This has been a particular problem for left parties, whose voters are concentrated in urban areas (Rodden 2019). Partly as a result of this fact, two-thirds of post-war (1945–2003) governments in SSD systems were right or center-right, whereas the distribution of governments under PR was rather balanced (Döring and Manow 2015). A related problem is that SSD systems can lead to a large number of districts that are uncompetitive and thus "safe" for a particular party.

Within the logic of simple majoritarianism, some of these problems could in principle be tackled by creating larger electoral districts designed to be "microcosms of the country itself" and thus allowing parties "to stand for the nation's average voter" (Rosenbluth and Shapiro 2018: 238–239). However, the geography of modern societies makes this extremely difficult, if not impossible. Taken to its logical extreme, simple majoritarianism might require the random assignment of voters to nonterritorial districts (Rehfeld 2005).

Power concentration

Another potential consequence of SSD-plurality elections is the concentration of power. In contrast with other studies (e.g. Bernauer and Vatter 2019), I do not see power concentration as a part of any democratic *ideal*. After all, if the ideal of simple majoritarianism could be approximated in the real world, power concentration would be limited by the fact that (a) electoral districts are microcosms of the country; (b) the winning party has an absolute majority in the electorate and in parliament; and (c) this party is itself a long-term coalition of different groups (Bawn and Rosenbluth 2006; Rosenbluth and Shapiro 2018). In reality, though, SSD often allow an electoral plurality—and sometimes even an electoral minority—to win a majority of seats in parliament and dominate the legislative process. The ideal of simple majoritarianism then degenerates into "pluralitarian" democracy (Nagel 1998; Santucci 2020).

Further power concentration can result from the attempt to process multidimensional political conflicts within, rather than between, separate parties. To see this, consider how Rosenbluth and Shapiro (2018) describe the underlying ideal. They emphasize that, while two-party competition necessarily involves coalition-building between different groups and interests within the catchall parties, these coalitions are built and maintained for the long term—as opposed to the short-term interparty coalitions in multiparty systems. Their hope is that the leadership of this long-term coalition "implements the policy that maximizes the joint utility of the groups from which it draws its electoral support" (Bawn and Rosenbluth 2006: 253). Rosenbluth and Shapiro (2018: 35) compare these intra-party coalitions to marriages, while likening inter-party coalitions to hookups.

Yet the quality of relationships depends not only on their time horizon, but also on the control that participants have over it. Inter-party coalitions tend to give their member groups greater control through the ever-present exit option, while intra-party coalitions tend to delegate a lot of power to the party leadership. Maybe this leadership has good incentives in a unidimensional conflict space—for example, the incentive to represent a society's median voter. In a multidimensional space, though, a skilled party elite can maneuver in ways that different voter groups can hardly track and are incapable of controlling.

It can engineer logrolls across dimensions, and strategically reconfigure these logrolls over time. As a result, it may be able to implement far-reaching changes *against the preferences of a voter majority*. And since the entry of new parties is heavily restricted by the electoral system, voters may not have any plausible way to sanction this behavior at the ballot box (McGann 2013). Jack Nagel (1998) brilliantly analyzed this form of hidden, elite-driven minority rule in New Zealand before the move to PR. He concludes that the "facade of majority government too often conceals a logrolled reality of minorities rule over specific policies" (Nagel 2012: 9–10). If one-party majority government is like a marriage, it may involve quite a bit of marital domination and neglect.

Polarization

Another potential consequence of trying to represent multidimensional voter preferences with only two parties is social and affective polarization. The parties tend to be pushed towards bundling separable issues into heterogeneous and incoherent platforms, shaped more by the underlying political geography of modern societies than any logical relationship between the different issues (Rodden 2019, 2020; see also Drutman 2020). The resulting programmatic heterogeneity and incoherence within the parties also imply that voters' cognitive burden might not, in effect, be lower than in a multiparty system—and more susceptible to systematic misinformation. Both parties have incentives to focus their campaign resources on providing voters with targeted information about the *most extreme* positions within the *other* party, rather than accurate information about their own platform (Cox and Rodden 2019). As a result of such "demonization," voters feel distant to the out-party and increasingly hostile towards its supporters, while not feeling close to their preferred party either.[10] Some long-term marriages make everyone miserable.

Intensified polarization can also become a danger to democracy, as polarized voters become more willing to turn a blind eye on democratic backsliding as long as it helps their own side (Graham and Svolik 2020; Przeworski 2020). By contrast, when multiple parties stake out distinct positions in a multidimensional space, they make it easier for voters to find parties they feel close to, and they allow for the formation of parties and coalitions that bridge

[10] The demonization of the other party may be more likely when a two-party system exists in the context of a presidential system of government (Cox and Rodden 2019).

the geographical divide of modern political societies, at least to some extent (Rodden 2019, 2020).

The limits and perils of complex majoritarianism

Complex majoritarianism rejects any constraints on the number of parties and envisions issue-specific inter-party coalitions in a multidimensional conflict space. This polar vision of democratic majority formation, too, is difficult to approximate in the real world and is associated with specific risks. I will first discuss these difficulties and risks in general terms and then with a specific focus on the constraints of a parliamentary system of government.

Dealing with complexity

Complexity may overwhelm voters (Carey and Hix 2011: 385). A greater number of options and a greater dimensionality of political positions may lead them to learn less about these options, to use problematic heuristics, to commit voting errors, or to abstain from voting altogether (see Cunow et al. 2021 and the literature cited therein). Complexity also reduces clarity of responsibility, which may have a number of negative consequences, for example, reduced turnout or increased corruption (Park et al. 2019; Schwindt-Bayer and Tavits 2016). Responsibility becomes particularly hard to assign when coalitions are formed in an issue-specific manner (Ganghof 2016b).

The complexity of multiparty politics in a multidimensional conflict space may also overwhelm parties' capacities for coordination and compromise. Much-discussed risks include lengthy and failed attempts at forming governments, unstable governments, legislative deadlock, and particularistic or clientelistic legislative deals that externalize the costs of decision making to excluded groups (Rosenbluth and Shapiro 2018). Complexity might also become a danger for democracy itself, for example, by making it too difficult for the opposition of would-be authoritarians to coordinate effectively (Rosenbluth and Shapiro 2018: Chapter 11).

Parties can choose strategies of coalition-building and majority formation that may reduce complexity and facilitate effective coordination, but these strategies will often lead them away from the ideal of issue-specific decision-making. This ideal is sometimes formulated in terms of highly simplified analytical models, in which uncertainty and transaction costs play no role

(Ward and Weale 2010; see also Lupia and McCubbins 2005). In the real world, political actors' interest in reducing transaction costs and making legislative processes more routine and predictable may lead them to build a fixed majority coalition that legislates on all issues.[11] One way in which such a coalition may facilitate compromise and decision-making is logrolling (de Marchi and Laver 2020). This means that parties trade issue positions: Party A accepts party B's position on an issue B cares strongly about, and B returns the favor on an issue A cares strongly about.[12]

How parliamentary government constrains issue-specific decision-making

While actors may try to limit issue-specific majority formation under any form of government (see, e.g. Chaisty et al. 2018: 46), parliamentarism subjects them to specific constraints. Since the assembly has the task of keeping the cabinet in office, parties face strong incentives to stabilize governments by building majority coalitions of veto players (Tsebelis 2002). This can be actual majority coalitions or minority cabinets with formalized majority support in the legislature (Strøm 1990). In both cases, issue-specific majority formation becomes more difficult or is ruled out completely. The majority coalition is typically fixed as long as the cabinet is in office, which tends to lead to better legislative performance (Thürk 2021).

Issue-specific legislative coalitions become more likely when parties build "substantive" minority cabinets—those that lack formalized majority support in the assembly (Strøm 1990; Ward and Weale 2010: 26). Even then, however, the resulting flexibility in legislative coalition-building remains constrained by parliamentarism. Since each cabinet party tends to be a veto player on all issues, flexibility is greatest when substantive minority cabinets are formed by a *single party* (Tsebelis 2002: 97–99).[13] But such cabinets are rare, especially in fragmented and multidimensional party systems. In the data set used in

[11] Much of the political science literature suggests that issue-specific decision-making must be enforced through specific institutional structures; e.g. the delegation of decision-making power to committees or ministries that have exclusive jurisdiction over particular issues (Laver and Shepsle 1996; Shepsle 1979).

[12] A more technical question is whether actors' preferences are separable; that is, whether their ideal policy on one dimension is unaffected by the outcome on another (for a discussion of this "separability" requirement, see Ward and Weale 2010: 33–34).

[13] As Ward and Weale (2010: 26) note, this is not necessarily the case. An important example is Denmark in the 1980s, when a liberal-conservative minority cabinet consisting of four parties lost more than hundred final voting decisions and accepted an "alternative," center-left majority on certain issues (Damgaard and Svensson 1989). But such a constellation is exceptional.

this book, they account for only 7% of all cabinets (20 of 285).[14] Most of them were formed in systems with moderate to high mechanical disproportionality and/or relatively few effective parties. In systems with high mechanical proportionality and many parties, substantive one-party minority cabinets formed only in Norway (but not after 2000) and once, for 17 months, in Denmark (in 2015).[15] Such minority cabinets are rare, in part, because they tend to be more fragile. Comparative research shows that the substantive nature of minority cabinets tends to decrease government stability (Krauss and Thürk 2021). The rarity of substantive one-party minority cabinets reflects the constraints of parliamentary government, and so does the resulting lack of legislative flexibility.[16]

In addition, the logic of parliamentarism makes it difficult to clearly *legitimize* a substantive one-party minority cabinet in a fragmented parliament. When there are several larger parties, none of which holds a majority of seats, which one should have the right to form a one-party minority cabinet? A common answer may be the party with the most votes, but this party may be intensely disliked by the voters of other parties. It might even be the "Condorcet loser," meaning that it would lose pairwise majority contests against every other party. Since the parliamentary system does not separate the selection of the government from the assembly elections, there is no way for voters to legitimize a single-party minority cabinet directly.

[14] These numbers are for the period 1993–2018 and include the semi-parliamentary systems (see appendix). They exclude Switzerland's non-parliamentary system.

[15] Thürk (2020: 7, 222) also notes how the relative frequencies of different types of minority cabinets have changed. While important studies emphasize the prevalence of single-party (Strøm 1990; Tsebelis 2002: 97) and substantive minority cabinets (Crombez 1996), the share of supported and multiparty minority cabinets has increased over time.

[16] To be sure, specific constitutional rules can stabilize substantive minority cabinets, but they can also make the formation of such cabinets more difficult. This is most obvious in the case of a "constructive" no-confidence vote that requires the election of a new cabinet by absolute majority in order to dismiss the existing one. This rule makes the formation of a minority cabinet *between elections* more difficult, as opposition parties cannot facilitate this formation by abstaining. The rules for government formation after an election could be more permissive, but differing requirements for cabinet formation after and between elections may not be easy to justify. Sieberer (2015) shows that restrictive no-confidence procedures tend to go hand in hand with restrictive investiture procedures. Spain's constitution is somewhat exceptional in this regard. It requires an absolute majority for a constructive no-confidence vote but only a simple majority in the second round of an investiture vote (Ajenjo 2015; Cheibub et al. 2021). Even in this case, though, the constructive no-confidence vote may work against (single-party) minority cabinets. Since opposition parties can anticipate the difficulty of removing a minority cabinet, they may be hesitant to support it—by voting for it or abstaining—in an investiture vote. After the Spanish elections in April 2019, the conditions for a single-party minority cabinet were in many ways very favorable (Field 2016, 2019), but the left-wing Unidas Podemos demanded inclusion into the government, which resulted in a failed attempt to invest a Socialist minority cabinet and new elections in November 2019. After these elections, the Socialists finally agreed to a minority coalition, thus establishing Unidas Podemos as a veto player and reducing the potential for issue-specific coalitions.

Normative balancing strategies under parliamentarism

Having sketched the difficulties and risks of the two polar visions, we can now better understand why many parliamentary democracies may try to position themselves between the extremes. To achieve some normative balance, they can essentially choose one of the two intermediate models of majority formation in Figure 5.1.

Alliance-centered majority formation

This strategy defends the goals of simple majoritarianism, while allowing for some substantial degree of proportional representation. The central requirement is that there be multiple proportionally elected parties which group into two competing alliances *before* the election. If this grouping is successful, voters can make a clear choice between two cabinet alternatives (Shugart 2001). Pre-electoral alliances may also improve retrospective clarity of responsibility by creating "tighter bonds" between the parties (Powell 2000: 53), and these tighter policy bonds may stabilize cabinets. Electoral systems of the mixed-member proportional or the bonus-adjusted proportional type have been justified as institutions that fit and support this alliance-centered model (Renwick et al. 2009; Shugart and Wattenberg 2003).

This approach to normative balancing has obvious limits, though, as multiple parties must essentially behave like two parties. Such behavior may be more likely to arise when there is only a single dimension of conflict (Ganghof et al. 2015). Pre-electoral coalitions limit individual parties from staking out a clear policy profile in a multidimensional issue space (e.g. Christiansen and Damgaard 2008: 69). For pre-electoral alliances to be credible, they must also continue after the election and are thus incompatible with the issue-specific or policy-specific formation of legislative coalitions. The normative balance achieved by the alliance-centered model is demanding and remains tilted towards simple majoritarianism.

Cabinet-centered majority formation

The second balancing strategy is rarely discussed as such in political science (but see Ganghof et al. 2015). It allows multiple, proportionally elected parties to compete independently in a multidimensional space, while also encouraging them to build a stable majority coalition of veto players after the election.[17] In this way, elements of complex majoritarianism (PR and multidimensional competition) can be balanced with those of simple majoritarianism (collective responsibility of the coalition, as well as cabinet stability). This sort of balancing may be facilitated by certain constitutional rules of cabinet formation and termination. The requirement of voting the government into office with an absolute majority provides incentives to build majority cabinets (Bergman 1993; Cheibub et al. 2021; Sieberer 2015), and a "constructive" no-confidence vote helps to stabilize cabinets once they are formed (Bergmann et al 2021; Lento and Hazan 2021).

This strategy is limited in that it rules out the most demanding goals of each of the polar visions. Since government formation depends on post-election bargaining, voters cannot choose the government directly; and since majority cabinets tend to establish each cabinet party as veto player on all issues, there is not much flexibility in legislative majority formation. If a constructive no-confidence vote is used to stabilize cabinets, parliaments' power vis-à-vis the cabinet is also substantially weakened (Sieberer 2015). Finally, clarity of responsibility is reduced because voters cannot easily observe cabinet parties' relative influence on government policy (Martin and Vanberg 2020).

The need for mechanical disproportionality

There is a further limitation that the two balancing strategies have in common. They both require a constraint on the (effective) number of parties in parliament and government. In the alliance-centered model, this constraint helps to maintain unidimensional competition and facilitates the formation of two comprehensive alliances. In the cabinet-centered model, fewer parties reduce the cognitive burden for voters and increase clarity of responsibility as well as cabinet stability. Some degree of mechanical disproportionality in the electoral system (e.g. in the form of a moderate legal threshold) seems necessary for normative balancing.

For many authors, the resulting reduction in mechanical proportionality is not much of a problem because they care mainly about how proportionally *actual* votes are translated into seats (e.g., Carey and Hix 2011). If some degree of mechanical disproportionality deters voters from voting for small parties, this is as it should be. Strategic voting helps to limit the number of parties

[17] This can be multiparty majority cabinets or formal minority cabinets (Strøm 1990).

without reducing observed proportionality too much. Carey and Hix (2011) argue for electoral systems with a moderate district magnitude; that is, with a moderate number of members elected in each electoral district. They estimate the sweet spot to be between three and eight members.

But this argument has limits, too. The evidence shows that even in the electoral sweet spot, the most likely outcome is to have either few parties or high observed proportionality, not both (Carey and Hix 2011; Linhart et al. 2018; Raabe and Linhart 2018; St-Vincent et al. 2016: 8). In addition, proponents of complex majoritarianism insist that mechanical proportionality is what matters. It differs from other goals in that it can reasonably be seen as having intrinsic democratic value (see Chapter 4). In any case, reducing mechanical proportionality shifts the overall balance towards simple majoritarianism.

The empirics of normative balancing

To explore the patterns of democratic majority formation empirically, I focus on a sample of 22 advanced democracies in the period 1993–2018 (see appendix). It includes pure parliamentary systems, semi-presidential systems, and the Swiss assembly-independent system. Switzerland is included because there is a single chain of delegation from voters via parliament to government—and because this inclusion allows us to see the consequences of cabinets that cannot be dismissed in a no-confidence vote. For the semi-presidential systems, I focus on their parliamentary aspects, as explained in more detail below. The parliamentary system of Queensland is included as the only subnational system because it serves as a contrast case for the analysis of the semi-parliamentary Australian states in Chapter 6.

Operationalizing the two visions

I operationalize each vision in terms of three central goals, which are derived from the above discussion as well as the previous literature, not least the literature on the advantages of presidentialism (Cheibub 2006, 2007; Ganghof and Eppner 2019; Lijphart 2012; Mainwaring and Shugart 1997; Powell 2000; Shugart and Carey 1992; Shugart 2001; Strøm 2000). I briefly discuss each goal and summarize their operationalization in Table 5.1 (see appendix for details). Second chambers are taken into account in this operationalization whenever

Table 5.1 Operationalizing the two visions of democratic majority formation

Simple majoritarianism	Complex majoritarianism
Identifiability measures how much votes are concentrated on the two biggest competing parties or pre-electoral blocs and whether the cabinet is based on a single party or bloc.	**Proportionality** is the log of the effective district magnitude.
Clarity of responsibility is a duration-weighted measure of cabinet types, where cabinets are ranked according to the clarity of responsibility they create.	**Multidimensionality** measures the "effective" number of dimensions, based on a factor analysis of issue-specific party positions.
Cabinet stability relates the average term length of cabinets to the constitutional maximum.	**Legislative flexibility** is a duration-weighted ranking of cabinet types, based on their potential for issue-specific coalition-building between parties.

Source: See appendix for details of data sources.

they are directly elected and matter for the achievement of the respective goal.[18]

1. The pre-electoral *identifiability* of cabinet alternatives captures the extent to which voters can directly choose between two cabinet alternatives (Strøm 1990; Powell 2000: 71–76). Under parliamentarism, perfect identifiability requires that voters face a choice between only two parties or alliances and that the winning side forms the cabinet. Since we are here focused on the parliamentary system, the potential role of directly elected presidents in creating identifiability under semi-presidentialism is neglected. This role is discussed further in Chapter 9.
2. Retrospective *clarity of responsibility* is generally considered to depend on the number of parties in government, whether the government has majority status in the first or only chamber of the assembly, and whether it faces additional veto players (Powell 2000: 50–67; Schwindt-Bayer and Tavits 2016). It is greatest when a single cabinet party controls all institutional veto points.
3. The relevance of *cabinet stability* is largely derived from the previous two goals (Powell 2000: 61). If an identifiable cabinet alternative is voted

[18] Italy's Senate is not wholly directly elected. It is treated as such here because the institutions of parliamentary democracy are fully extended to the Senate (see Chapters 3 and 7).

into office but soon replaced by some other coalition without new elections, the potential gains of identifiability are likely to be lost. And even if new cabinets are empowered by new elections, frequently changing cabinets make it more difficult for voters to see who is responsible for policy outcomes.

4. *Mechanical proportionality* requires that *x*% of the votes of any party—real and hypothetical—is translated into *x*% of seats. As discussed in Chapter 4, it is the only one of the six goals that can also be valued in purely procedural terms, rather than as a means to an end. It is here approximated with the (logged) effective district magnitude (see appendix).[19]
5. The *multidimensionality* of party positions is measured as the effective number of dimensions based on expert surveys of party positions (Benoit and Laver 2006; Ganghof et al. 2018). It is an imperfect proxy, as we would ideally measure the extent to which formal institutions suppress potential multidimensionality. The actual measure may also capture differences in the societies' conflict structures.
6. *Legislative flexibility* is measured based on a ranking of cabinet types and the differences between forms of government. It is greatest under assembly-independent government in Switzerland, as explained above. In parliamentary systems, it depends on the majority status of the cabinet (substantive minority cabinets being more flexible) and the number of veto players in the cabinet (single-party minority cabinets being more flexible).[20]

Empirical results

Table A.1 in the appendix provides the cases' average values for these six variables in the period 1993–2018. Here, I focus on the broader picture by averaging the three standardized variables for each vision. The resulting summary scores for simple and complex majoritarianism are standardized so that the average value is zero and one unit corresponds to one standard deviation. Figure 5.2 shows these scores together with a linear regression line.

[19] I do not claim that this is the best way to measure mechanical proportionality. The important point is to focus on formal institutions. An alternative measurement might be based on Taagepera's (2007) seat product. See Li and Shugart (2016), as well as Shugart and Taagepera (2017).

[20] As discussed above, single-party majority cabinets may have a lot of flexibility in intra-party majority formation. Here, the focus is on flexibility in inter-party coalition-building.

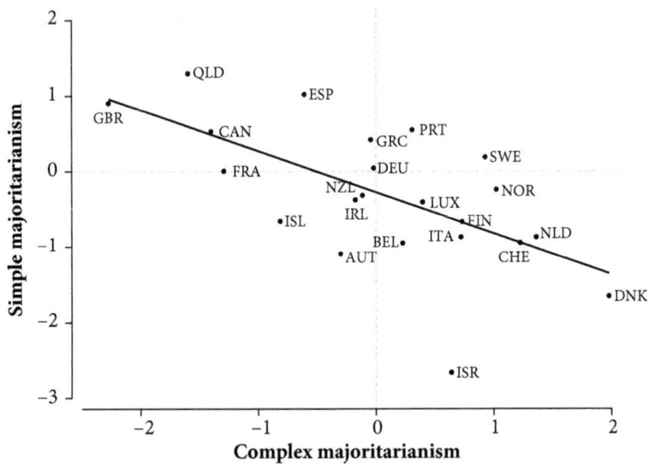

Fig. 5.2 Simple versus complex majoritarianism in 22 democracies, 1993–2018
Notes: see text.

The figure provides two main insights. First, we see the expected trade-off between the goals of simple and complex majoritarianism. No country can simultaneously achieve high values on both dimensions; Portugal and Sweden are the only cases to have above-average values. Second, most countries do have intermediate locations on the trade-off line. The two polar visions are not easy to approximate.

Israel is an obvious outlier, with very low values on simple majoritarianism. This outlier status is partly rooted in the country's electoral system (Shugart 2021) but solely driven by low cabinet stability. Israel's scores on identifiability and clarity of responsibility are low, too, but similar to those of Austria, Belgium, or Finland (see Table A.1 in the appendix). While its outlier status should thus not be over-interpreted, the case of Israel suggests that some countries may pay a higher price for complex majoritarianism than others.

Note also that we only recognize this outlier status if we aggregate the goals of the two visions separately. The comparison with Lijphart's (2012) approach is interesting here. The regression line in Figure 5.2 captures something rather close to his "executives-parties" dimension, but separating the goals of the two visions allow us to distinguish cases like Israel and Finland. While these two cases achieve similar values on the executives–parties dimension (Lijphart 2012: 244) and complex majoritarianism, they differ substantially with respect to simple majoritarianism. Israel is also one of the cases that "can only be described as having highly contentious and conflictual political cultures"

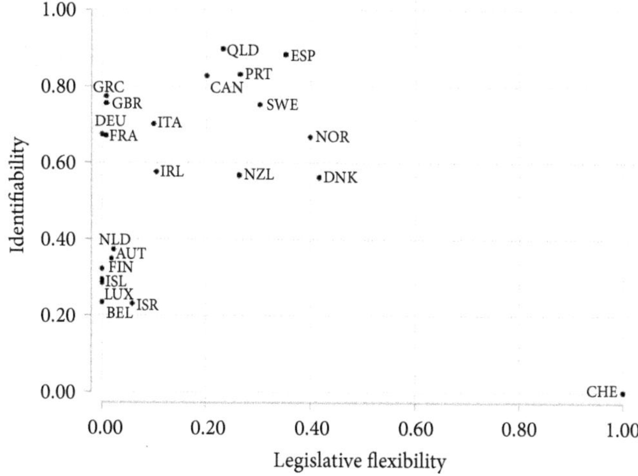

Fig. 5.3 Identifiability versus legislative flexibility in 22 democracies, 1993–2018
Notes: see text.

(Lijphart 2012: 302). This serves as a reminder that complex majoritarianism does not measure any kind of consensus.

To analyze the results further, Figure 5.3 takes a separate look at the trade-off between the two most ambitious goals of each polar vision—identifiability and legislative flexibility—and provides several insights. First, and most importantly, combining high values on both goals is empirically (and logically) impossible under parliamentarism; there are no cases in the upper-right quadrant.

Second, the figure highlights the unique position of Switzerland. Due to its non-parliamentary form of government (i.e. a cabinet whose survival in office does not depend on the assembly), it is the only case to achieve perfect flexibility without any veto players. The price to be paid for this flexibility is the lack of any pre-electoral identifiability of competing cabinet alternatives: cabinet composition is fixed prior to the election by the Magic Formula convention.

Third, Switzerland also puts the degree of legislative flexibility of the parliamentary systems in perspective. Cases like Denmark have substantially lower flexibility because minority cabinets typically consist of multiple parties with veto-player status. As argued above, this is partly due to the inherent logic of parliamentary government.[21]

[21] Given Switzerland's legislative flexibility, one might wonder why its overall score on complex majoritarianism is not higher. The main reason is that the data of Benoit and Laver (2006) suggests a unidimensional conflict space. Other studies paint a similar picture (e.g. Rovny and Polk 2019).

Finally, among the parliamentary and semi-presidential systems in Figure 5.3, we can distinguish three clusters. The first approximates party-centered or alliance-centered forms of majority formation and thus achieves relatively high levels of identifiability at the cost of low legislative flexibility (Greece, Italy, United Kingdom, etc.). The second achieves neither of the two goals because majority formation is predominantly cabinet-centered (Austria, Finland, Israel, etc.).[22] The third cluster reconciles high identifiability with some degree of flexibility. It includes two types of cases: those whose electoral systems imply substantial mechanical disproportionality but whose governments frequently fail to achieve majority status (Canada, Spain, etc.), and those with high proportionality and frequent minority cabinets but also a fair degree of pre-electoral alliance formation (New Zealand and Scandinavia).

Conclusion

How can parliamentary systems of government balance competing design goals? To answer this question, I have distinguished two polar visions of democratic majority formation: simple and complex majoritarianism. Both visions embrace democratic majority rule but have different visions of how majorities ought to form. They reflect different approaches to the cognitive and coordinative complexity of modern politics. Under parliamentarism, the two visions can be spelled out in terms of the stages at which the process of majority formation is completed. Simple majoritarianism aims to complete this process early to keep things simple; complex majoritarianism prefers late completion to fairly represent all voters in actual deliberation and decision-making. In their extreme forms, however, both polar visions create significant risks and do not constitute very robust equilibria. Many parliamentary democracies achieve some degree of normative balancing by taking intermediate positions on the continuum from simple to complex majoritarianism, but they tend to give up on the most ambitious goals of each polar alternative. These democracies do not enable voters to make a clear electoral choice between competing cabinet alternatives, and they do not represent them fairly in the deliberation and legislative decision-making on specific issues or policy areas.

[22] Recall that in semi-presidential systems with (in practice) strong presidents such as France, presidential elections may increase identifiability (although cognitive complexity remains high in the first round of presidential elections). This is not reflected in the data.

6
How semi-parliamentarism can balance visions of democracy

A semi-parliamentary system creates a separation of powers between the executive and one part of a directly elected assembly. In the bicameral case, the prime minister and cabinet can be dismissed in a no-confidence vote by the first chamber but not by the second chamber, even though the latter is directly elected and has robust veto power. What makes this constitutional structure attractive?

To answer this question, I apply the framework established in Chapter 5 to the semi-parliamentary cases (as identified in Chapter 3): Australia and Japan, as well as the Australian states of New South Wales, South Australia, Tasmania, Victoria, and Western Australia. The analysis shows how semi-parliamentarism can balance different visions of democracy in ways that are unavailable under parliamentarism. In particular, it enables voters to make a clear choice between competing cabinet alternatives, while also being fairly represented in an issue-specific or policy-specific process of deliberation and legislative decision-making.

The next section discusses normative balancing under semi-parliamentarism from a theoretical perspective. I then compare the institutional designs of the seven semi-parliamentary cases and the resulting patterns of democratic majority formation. The two-dimensional mapping of these cases is complemented with comparative analyses of legislative coalition-building in Australia and legislative success rates under different forms of government. The remaining sections of the chapter discuss challenges to my argument, sketch its broader implications for the performance of democracies, and explain how semi-parliamentarism may complement other desirable institutional designs, such as compulsory voting and weaker forms of judicial review.

Beyond Presidentialism and Parliamentarism. Steffen Ganghof, Oxford University Press.
 DOI: 10.1093/oso/9780192897145.003.0006

Normative balancing in theory

In Chapter 5, I specified the competing visions of simple and complex majoritarianism in terms of six goals. Here, I explore theoretically how semi-parliamentarism can balance them. The goals are discussed in the order that best reflects the logical connections between the relevant arguments.

Mechanical proportionality

Under semi-parliamentarism, the chamber of legislation and control has no constitutional power over the selection and dismissal of the cabinet. Therefore, the mechanical proportionality of its electoral system is less constrained by the desire to create identifiable cabinet alternatives, stable cabinets, and clarity of responsibility.

Identifiability

At the same time, a majoritarian electoral system for the chamber of confidence can enable voters to make a clear choice between alternative one-party governments. As discussed in Chapter 5, when majority or plurality rule is applied in single-seat districts, identifiability is not guaranteed (Dunleavy and Margetts 2004; Kollman 2018; Moser et al. 2018), but the same is true for the Westminster model of pure parliamentarism. Chapter 8 shows how using majoritarian methods (ranked-choice voting or run-off elections) in a single, jurisdiction-wide district allows voters to choose a single cabinet party directly.

Multidimensionality

For multiparty parliamentary systems to achieve identifiability, a low dimensionality of partisan conflict may be required (Ganghof et al. 2015). It makes the formation of two competing pre-electoral alliances more likely. Under semi-parliamentarism, by contrast, voters can choose the cabinet through the first chamber, so that the dimensionality of partisan competition need not be constrained in the second chamber.

Legislative flexibility

Chapter 5 has shown that legislative flexibility is constrained under parliamentarism because multiparty and multidimensional parliaments make substantive minority cabinets of a *single party* unlikely to form and difficult to legitimize. When minority cabinets consist of multiple parties, this tends to establish each of them as a veto player on all issues. Under semi-parliamentarism, by contrast, voters can directly legitimize a single government party in the first chamber, even when this party's seat share in the proportionally elected second chamber is well below an absolute majority. Legislative flexibility thus tends to increase.

To see this more clearly, we can apply the argument that Tsebelis (2002: 97–98) develops on the basis of the standard spatial model for one-party minority cabinets under pure parliamentarism (see also Laver and Schofield 1990; Strøm 1990). Figure 6.1 illustrates it in a simplified version, showing the ideal points of five parties in a two-dimensional political space. The government party G has a first-chamber majority but minority status in the second chamber. The latter also includes party C, which is the opposition party in the first chamber, as well as three further parties (A, B, D) that are represented only in the second chamber. For the sake of simplicity, we assume that each party has 20% of the seats in the second chamber, so that every possible three-party legislative coalition is a minimal-winning coalition with the power to pass legislation.

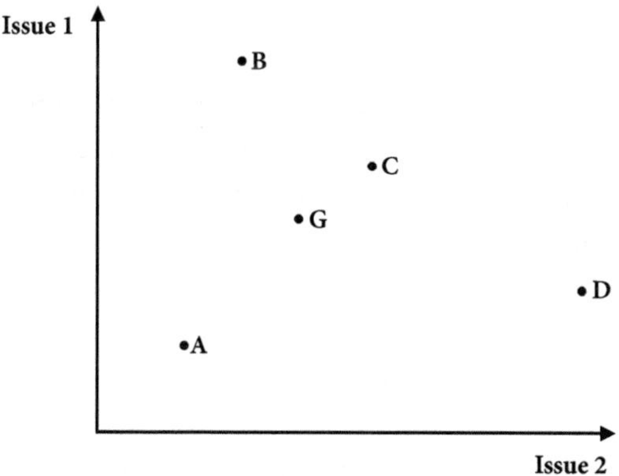

Fig. 6.1 Legislative flexibility of single-party cabinets in two dimensions

Notes: see text.

In the constellation shown in Figure 6.1, and if all parties are predominantly policy-seeking, G is likely to find support for its proposals, regardless of where the status quo is located. If the two issues are decided separately, G benefits from its median status on both dimensions and will get support for its own ideal point. If the decision is made in a genuinely two-dimensional manner, G will typically be able to move the status quo towards its own ideal point. The reason is that it can always exclude two parties from the winning coalition and, hence, at least one of the parties with more extreme preferences (A, B, or D). If G has strong agenda power, it will typically not have to make any concessions at all; it will get majority support for proposing its own ideal point. Some minimal-winning coalitions could also form against the government; for example, ACD or BCD. The government might accept these alternative majorities as long as its basic program remains intact, or seek a compromise with members of the alternative coalition, or use its agenda or veto power to block undesired policy change.

Cabinet stability

Semi-parliamentarism can create stable cabinets by combining two institutional engineering solutions: reducing the number of parties in the chamber of confidence, while making government survival independent from parliamentary confidence in the more proportional chamber of legislation. One advantage of this combination over pure parliamentarism is that the legislature can be simultaneously "strong" vis-à-vis the executive in two distinct ways. The first chamber remains strong in its ability to dismiss the chief executive and the cabinet, while the second chamber remains strong in its ability to control the executive. By contrast, efforts to stabilize cabinets in multiparty parliamentary systems tend to reduce parliament's control capacity (by creating majority cabinets that dominate parliament) and/or its dismissal capacity (by making no-confidence rules "constructive").

Clarity of responsibility

The final goal, clarity of responsibility, is necessarily compromised in any separation-of-powers system—except perhaps when a single (disciplined) party has sole control of both branches (Powell 2000; Schwindt-Bayer and Tavits 2016). However, by facilitating the formation of single-party majority cabinets in the first chamber, semi-parliamentarism can achieve an aspect of clarity of responsibility that is often considered to be especially important (e.g. Cheibub 2006).

Institutional comparison of the cases

Table 6.1 compares the current institutional design of the seven cases identified as (minimally) semi-parliamentary in Chapter 3. These designs fall into three groups, the biggest of which is *mainland Australia*. It includes the cases that use the semi-parliamentary constitution to balance simple and complex majoritarianism. First chambers are elected under majoritarian rules in single-seat districts (alternative vote, AV), second chambers under proportional rules in multi-seat districts (single-transferable vote, STV). As a result, there is a substantial difference in the disproportionality—as measured by Gallagher's (1991) Least Squares index—with which votes are translated into seats in the two chambers. Yet, the disproportionality in the second chambers is not particularly low (perfect proportionality would equal a value of zero) due to small assembly sizes and moderate district magnitudes (Farrell and McAllister 2006).[1] This results in relatively compact party systems with three to four effective parliamentary parties.

The second "group" consists of *Tasmania*, which uses semi-parliamentarism to balance party-based and personalized majority formation. The resulting balance is that "[p]rogrammatic choices can be made through parties at lower-house elections, supplemented with local representation through Independents in the upper house" (Sharman 2013: 344). Sharman (2013) explains in detail how personalized majority formation in the second chamber is achieved. A crucial element is that second-chamber members are elected by the AV and have fixed, staggered, six-year terms, with one-sixth of the membership retiring at annual periodic elections held on a fixed day each year. These annual elections cannot be overridden by dissolving the chamber and forcing a general election for all seats, and they cannot be held on the same date as elections for the first chamber. In Tasmania, second-chamber elections are thus like a series of annual by-elections in two or more electoral districts, whose timing is beyond the control of the government. This institutional structure results in a long-established dominance of independents in the second chamber, which has been reinforced in recent years by rules on election spending that severely limit party influence.

[1] In the two states that elect the second chamber in a single state-wide district, New South Wales and South Australia, the district magnitude is reduced due to staggered elections of only half of the chamber.

Table 6.1 Electoral systems in the semi-parliamentary cases

	NSW	VIC	SA	WA	AUS	TAS	JPN
First chamber							
Assembly size	93	88	47	59	150	25	465
Electoral system	AV	AV	AV	AV	AV	STV	FPTP+PR
District magnitude	1	1	1	1	1	5	1/6–28
Effective magnitude	1	1	1	1	1	5	7.7
Disproportionality	10.6	12.7	16.5	21.8	12.2	6.2	21.6
Effective parties (votes)	3	3	3.6	3.5	3.3	2.7	4.8
Effective parties (seats)	2.1	2.1	2.2	1.9	2.1	2.3	2.5
Second chamber							
Assembly size	42	40	22	36	76	15	242
Electoral system	STV	STV	STV	STV	STV	AV	SNTV+PR
District magnitude	21	5	11	6	2–6	1	1–6/48
Effective magnitude	21	5	11	6	5.6	1	20.0
Staggered?	Yes	No	Yes	No	Yes	Yes	Yes
Disproportionality	4.9	5.5	11.7	5.6	5.3	–	11.2
Effective parties (votes)	3.4	3.9	4.3	4.0	4.5	–	4.7
Effective parties (seats)	3.1	3.3	3.2	4.1	3.4	–	3.3

Note: Data is for the latest election (if this was not a double dissolution election). In the Australian cases, the Liberal and National parties are treated as separate parties unless they competed jointly. AV = alternative vote, FTPT = first past the post, PR = proportional representation, SNTV = single non-transferable vote, STV = single transferable vote.

Source: For data sources, see appendix. Disproportionality is Gallagher's (1991) index.

While Sharman does not emphasize this, the semi-parliamentary constitution is also crucial for the Tasmanian institutional–behavioral equilibrium. For if the second chamber possessed the right to dismiss the prime minister, it would be democratically unacceptable that voters can never hold the second chamber as a whole accountable for its actions and that these actions are not organized in terms of programmatic choices (see also Fewkes 2011: 91).

The Tasmanian use of the semi-parliamentary constitution also implies that the partisan politics in the first chamber is subject to the same tension between simple and complex majoritarianism as a pure parliamentary system (Chapter 5). Tasmania has dealt with this by adopting proportional representation (STV) with a small district magnitude (M = 5 since 1998). As Table 6.1 shows, this strategy has been successful in keeping both the effective number of parties and empirical disproportionality fairly moderate.

Finally, electoral system design in Japan is not geared clearly towards normative balancing. Japan uses mixed-member majoritarian electoral systems in both chambers (Nemoto 2018), and while empirical disproportionality in the first chamber is substantially greater, the effective numbers of parties in the two chambers differ less than in some of the Australian cases.

Normative balancing in practice

To quantify and visualize the balancing potential of semi-parliamentary government, we can build on the empirical framework developed in Chapter 5. Since the variables that capture the goals of simple and complex majoritarianism take directly elected second chambers into account, they can be applied to semi-parliamentary systems. The variables reflect whichever chamber is more relevant for a particular goal in a semi-parliamentary system (see appendix for details). In particular, the three variables capturing complex majoritarianism all reflect the value of whichever chamber achieves higher values. In mainland Australia, this is typically the second chamber.

Figure 6.2 reproduces Figure 5.2 from Chapter 5 and now includes the semi-parliamentary cases. It illustrates three main points. First, it reveals semi-parliamentarism's potential to mitigate the trade-offs between simple and complex majoritarianism. The cases of the Australian Commonwealth, New

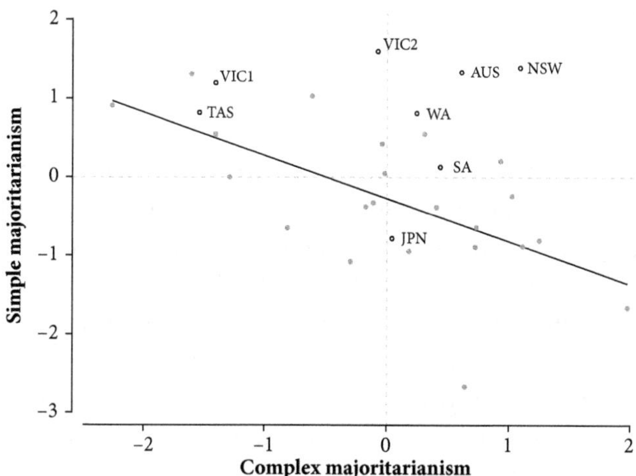

Fig. 6.2 Simple and complex majoritarianism in semi-parliamentary democracies, 1993–2018

Notes: see text.

South Wales, Victoria (after the constitutional reform of 2003), and Western Australia are positive outliers: they combine goals of simple and complex majoritarianism to an extent that is not observed in pure parliamentary systems.

Second, these cases' *absolute* levels of goal achievement differ along the two dimensions. With respect to simple majoritarianism, they are on par with Westminster systems like that of Queensland—the Australian state that abolished bicameralism in 1922. Along the complex majoritarianism dimension, by contrast, even New South Wales does not come close to the values of Denmark's parliamentary system. The reasons are that, while some semi-parliamentary cases outperform Denmark with respect to legislative flexibility, proportionality and dimensionality remain limited even in the second chambers (see appendix). This is a limitation of the specific designs in Australia, however, rather than of the semi-parliamentary constitution as such (see Chapter 8).

Finally, the profiles of the semi-parliamentary cases vary greatly. Since Tasmania uses the semi-parliamentary constitution for a different purpose, its approach to balancing simple and complex majoritarianism is not different from a pure parliamentary system. Japan and pre-reform Victoria do not make full use of semi-parliamentarism's potential for normative balancing, mainly because the electoral systems in the two chambers are similar. South Australia follows the same institutional template as the other cases in mainland Australia (Table 6.1) but does not achieve similar outcomes. Reasons include the small size of the second chamber, the relative frequency of minority situations in the first chamber, and the major parties' resulting need to gain support from minor parties and/or independents in the process of cabinet formation (Brenton and Pickering 2021; Ward 2012: 81–87).

As in Chapter 5, it is useful to take a closer look at the two goals that are most difficult to reconcile under a pure parliamentary system: identifiability and flexibility (Figure 6.3). Three points stand out. First, the semi-parliamentary systems can achieve the same levels of identifiability as Westminster democracies. Second, they can achieve higher levels of flexibility than even the most flexible parliamentary systems because they provide a more secure path towards cabinets with only a single veto player.[2] Third, semi-parliamentary government can reconcile these two goals to a large extent, which is impossible under pure parliamentarism. Voters can more or less directly select a single-party government and be fairly represented in issue-specific legislative decision-making.

[2] The semi-parliamentary cases can never get beyond 0.75 on our measure of flexibility, because a single majority party in the first chamber is a veto player. This contrasts with the situation in Switzerland, where every party can, in principle, be excluded from the legislative coalition.

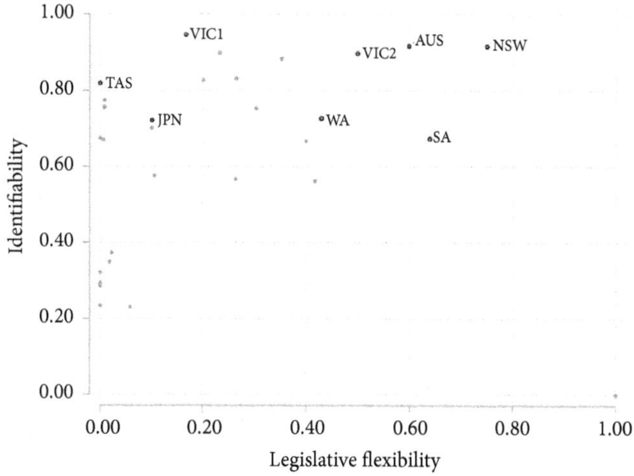

Fig. 6.3 Identifiability versus legislative flexibility in semi-parliamentary democracies, 1993–2018
Notes: see text.

A closer look at legislative flexibility

The indicator of legislative flexibility is rough and captures merely the *potential* for flexibility. One way in which this potential might not be realized is that governments tend to rely on the same legislative coalition throughout a legislative period. Another concern—well known from the literature on presidentialism—is that governments' efforts at issue-specific coalition-building may fail and result in legislative deadlock. I discuss both possibilities in turn.

How much flexibility is there in practice?

We know from the research on minority governments that the potential for legislative flexibility is not always realized. One reason can be the location of parties' policy positions relative to the status quo. If a minority cabinet wants to change the status quo in the same direction (left or right) on all issues, it might consistently seek support from the same party or parties (Ganghof et al. 2019). In practice, therefore, legislative coalitions might not shift much from issue to issue. Another possibility is that some potential support parties care only about a small set of issues, while accepting the government's mandate on

Table 6.2 Legislative flexibility in mainland Australia (divisions), 1996–2019

Legislative coalition (%):	Left	Mixed	Right
Government: Labor			
With median control (N = 300)	17	27	56
Without median control (N = 80)	1	53	46
Government: Coalition			
With median control (N = 185)	19	34	42
Without median control (N = 17)	82	18	0

Note: Entries are successful divisions in the second chamber on third or, alternatively, second readings of assented bills introduced by governments that have majority status in the first chamber, but minority status in the second chamber. The numbers give the percentages of left, mixed, and right coalitions. They do not always add up to 100% because coalitions with independents only are excluded.

Source: The data is taken from Pörschke (2021).

all others. The Christian Democrats in New South Wales have partly played this role.[3]

To explore actual legislative flexibility with available data, we can look at the patterns of coalition-building in second-chamber divisions. Table 6.2 does so for mainland Australia in the 1996–2019 period. It focuses on governments that have majority status in the first chamber but minority status in the second chamber. The main lesson is the importance of whether governments include the median party in the second chamber. When they do not, a "grand coalition" between the two major parties becomes likely, if not inevitable, and legislative flexibility is reduced. When they do control the second chamber median, however, governments tend to take advantage of this position. They become more likely to build coalitions on "their" side of the political spectrum, while excluding the major opposition party—although, in Australia, Labor governments tend to do this less often than Coalition governments (17% versus 42%). Since governments tend to include the second chamber median frequently, the division data suggests a fair degree of actual flexibility in legislative majority formation. This is corroborated by qualitative accounts (e.g., Clune 2021).

[3] On coalition-building in New South Wales, see Clune and Griffith (2006), as well as Smith (2006, 2012).

Table 6.3 Government legislative success by form of government, 1979–2019

	Parliamentary	Semi-presidential	Presidential	Semi-parliamentary
Overall	85.8% (390)	82.4% (110)	66.4% (189)	83.6% (150)
Single-party	87.0% (169)	78.6% (21)	64.1% (101)	84.1% (113)
Coalition	84.9% (221)	83.3% (89)	69.0% (88)	82.3% (37)

Note: Observations are years, with their number given in parentheses. Since most semi-parliamentary systems are found at the subnational level in Australia, the unicameral parliamentary system of Queensland is also included.

Source: The data is taken from Pörschke (2021) and includes data from Saiegh (2011) and McKelvy (2013).

Does the separation of powers lead to deadlock?

But perhaps the attempt to build issue-specific or dimension-specific coalitions often results in legislative deadlock. To explore this possibility, I follow Cheibub (2007) and Saiegh (2009, 2011) in comparing governments' legislative "success" or "effectiveness" in democracies by form of government. These studies define this success as the ratio of the number of proposals introduced by the government to those approved by the legislature. Pörschke (2021) assembled a data set that builds on Saiegh (2009, 2011), as well as McKelvy (2013) and also includes the semi-parliamentary systems in the Australian states.[4] Based on this data, Table 6.3 provides, for the period from 1979 to 2019, a modified version of Cheibub's (2007: 89, Table 4.6) comparison.[5] While Cheibub collapsed parliamentary and semi-presidential systems, I treat the latter as well as semi-parliamentary systems as distinct types.

Since Table 6.3 integrates different data sets and compares across different time periods and levels of government, it must be interpreted cautiously. Nevertheless, the data suggests that success rates are rather similar under parliamentary, semi-presidential, and semi-parliamentary government but substantially lower under presidential government. How can this be explained?

Cheibub (2007: 89–90) suggests a partial explanation for the lower success rates under presidentialism based on selection bias. The idea is that presidents are more likely to initiate bills that they know will be defeated, whereas prime ministers under pure parliamentarism must be more careful to protect

[4] Saiegh's data focuses on first chambers, while McKelvy also takes second chambers into account; so does, of course, Pörschke's data on the semi-parliamentary systems.

[5] While Saiegh's data goes back to 1946 (for some cases), that of McKelvy and Pörschke only starts in the early 1990s.

their survival in office. If this were true, though, prime ministers under semi-parliamentarism might be expected to behave like presidents with respect to the second chamber. Table 6.3 provides no evidence for this.

A different potential explanation is that the negative effect of presidentialism on legislative success—whatever its true size may be—is only partly due to the branch-based separation of powers. It may also result from the way that presidential constitutions connect this separation to executive personalism (Chapter 2). Concentrating executive power in a single individual may reduce legislative success both directly and indirectly. An example of a direct effect is that presidentialism facilitates the election of outsiders or newcomers (Carreras 2017; Samuels and Shugart 2010), which tends to increase the likelihood of executive–legislative conflict (Carreras 2014).[6]

An example of an indirect effect is that executive personalism arguably makes it more risky to include a deadlock-resolution mechanism like assembly dissolution in the constitution (see Chapter 8 for further discussion). When presidents are allowed to dissolve the assembly, the threat of dissolution becomes a weapon not only of governments but of single human beings. Presidents can use it to "quell dissent" (Sanchez-Sibony 2018: 105) within their own parties and thus strengthen party "presidentialization" (Samuels and Shugart 2010). Under semi-parliamentarism, by contrast, the possibility of a double dissolution can be used more safely as a weapon of the government and/or first chamber against a potentially obstructive second chamber. Any strengthening of prime ministers vis-à-vis their party or coalition in the first chamber is balanced by this chambers' confidence power. In the semi-parliamentary systems, it is often possible to dissolve the entire second chamber (e.g. in a double dissolution procedure) or half of it (e.g. after a lost no-confidence vote in, and dissolution of, the first chamber). This possibility may facilitate governments' legislative success—regardless of how often it is actually used.

To take a closer look at the comparison between parliamentary and semi-parliamentary systems, I focus on the data sets of McKelvy (2013) and Pörschke (2021), as their measurement of legislative success consistently takes second chambers into account (Table 6.4). Pörschke's data also allows us to single out those legislative periods under semi-parliamentarism in which the government is identical to or includes the median party in the second chamber.

We see—as we did in Table 6.3—that parliamentary systems tend to have higher success rates overall but that the difference is not large. Moreover, if

[6] "Outsiders" are defined by becoming politically prominent from outside the national party system, "newcomers" by their lack of political experience in a party, a cabinet, or a legislature (Carreras 2017: 365–366).

Table 6.4 Government legislative success by form of government, 1993–2019

	Parliamentary	Semi-parliamentary	Semi-parliamentary with government controlling the median in both chambers
Overall	88.4%	84.8%	90.1%
	(67)	(31)	(15)
Single-party	85.0%	85.0%	90.7%
	(30)	(26)	(13)
Coalition	91.2%	83.7%	86.1%
	(37)	(5)	(2)

Note: Observations are legislative terms, with their number given in parentheses. Since original expert survey data on party positions in Australian states is used to determine the median party in both chambers (see appendix), Japan is excluded from the semi-parliamentary columns due to missing data.

Source: The data is taken from McKelvy (2013) and Pörschke (2021).

governments control the second chamber median in a semi-parliamentary system, legislative success rates are not lower. A particularly interesting comparison is that between coalition governments under parliamentarism (91.2%) and single-party cabinets with second-chamber median control under semi-parliamentarism (90.7%). The high levels of legislative success in the latter constellation may partly be explained by the governments' flexibility in building legislative coalitions. The relevance of median status also highlights the importance of institutional design (see Chapter 8).

In sum, the more detailed analysis shows that the semi-parliamentary separation of powers does not lead to severe and persistent legislative deadlock. It thus reinforces the results of the previous section: semi-parliamentary systems can balance simple and complex majoritarianism in ways that are unavailable under other forms of government. Most importantly, they simultaneously allow voters to clearly legitimize a single-party government and to be fairly represented in issue-specific legislative decision-making. In contrast to presidential government, these two goals are reconciled without concentrating executive power in a single human being.

Is normative balancing desirable?

But is it really desirable to balance simple and complex majoritarianism? One way to challenge this idea is to insist that some goals are inherently more important than others. Weale (2018) makes an argument to this effect.

He contends that the values of simple majoritarianism are "largely instrumental values," whereas those associated with complex majoritarianism are "intrinsic"—they follow from the "very definition of democracy" (2018: 238). For him, the normative standard implied by the ideal of political equality is the "issue-by-issue median," which he describes as a "voting rule" (Weale 2018: 237; see also Ward and Weale 2010). He suggests that a parliamentary system like Denmark can approximate this standard, so that the kind of normative balancing possible under semi-parliamentarism is not desirable.

My response is twofold. Conceptually, I see the issue-by-issue median not as a voting rule, at least not in the real world, but an abstract standard of what I have called process equality (Chapter 4). Its value is not intrinsic.[7] The three goals of simple majoritarianism are just as much standards of process equality, but they emphasize the vertical, rather than horizontal dimension of the democratic process. The only goal of complex majoritarianism that is focused on formal institutions and might thus have some priority in institutional design is mechanical proportionality. But, as I argued in Chapter 4, semi-parliamentarism has an *advantage* over a pure parliamentary system in this regard, everything else being equal. If Denmark replaced its 2% legal threshold of representation with a 2% legal threshold of confidence authority (thus introducing semi-parliamentarism), the voters of new and very small parties would be treated more equally by the formal procedures, not less. The idea of democracy's intrinsic value does not challenge the importance of normative balancing.

My second response is empirical. Weale's argument presumes that substantive minority cabinets under parliamentarism actually achieve legislative flexibility and do empower the issue-by-issue median. As I have shown in Chapter 5, however, parliamentary government limits legislative flexibility. Minority cabinets in countries like Denmark tend to consist of multiple veto players, each of which can block a movement of policy towards the issue-specific median or demand movements away from it as part of a larger logroll. If the goal is to empower the issue-specific median, some version of Swiss-style assembly-independent government might be a better choice because every party can be excluded from the winning legislative coalitions. Yet we have seen in Chapters 2 and 5 that this form of government has severe disadvantages, too. Normative balancing is unavoidable.

[7] As explained in Chapter 4, process equality may be considered "intrinsically" valuable in the sense that we might give it some priority over achieving good substantive outcomes. Here, we are concerned with the evaluation of formal institutions, whose capacity to achieve any process equality standard must be evaluated instrumentally.

What about democratic "performance"?

Another way to challenge the desirability of normative balancing is to question whether it actually improves the "performance" of democracies as measured in terms of variables such as voter turnout, corruption, or various socio-economic indicators (Bernauer and Vatter 2019; Lijphart 2012). One response is that it is impossible to directly estimate some relatively context-independent "average causal effect" of well-designed semi-parliamentarism on democratic performance. The reasons include (a) the small number of semi-parliamentary cases; (b) their currently far-from-optimal designs; (c) their geographical concentration in a single country; and (d) their prevalence at the subnational level. There is simply no valid way to directly estimate how well-designed semi-parliamentarism would perform, say, at the national level in Scandinavia, Israel, Brazil, or the United Kingdom.

Lest this response appear too apologetic, let me also turn the tables a bit and note that existing studies of democratic performance do not deal adequately with the constitutional separation of powers. For example, the kind of normative balancing arguments that I have advanced here for semi-parliamentarism have been made about presidentialism for some time (e.g. Cheibub 2007; Mainwaring and Shugart 1997; Shugart and Carey 1992) and there is also some empirical evidence to support them (e.g. Cheibub 2006). Yet, Lijphart's (2012) empirical approach implies that when presidential systems approximate simple majoritarianism in the executive branch and complex majoritarianism in the legislative branch, they are similar to parliamentary systems with intermediate levels of proportionality, multipartism, and clarity of responsibility (Ganghof and Eppner 2019: 118). The optimization potential of the separation of powers is ruled out from the outset. Another example for the conceptual neglect of the separation of powers is the comparative analysis of Bernauer and Vatter (2019: 80, but see 11), which classifies the Swiss form of government as "semi-presidential" and, like Lijphart (2012), equates Swiss cabinets with oversized cabinets in parliamentary systems (Bernauer and Vatter 2019: 84).

These examples lead me to question that the institutional and behavioral variation of real-world democracies can be reduced to a few composite variables that explain democratic performance. This reductionist approach may lead to invalid causal claims (Ganghof and Eppner 2019). Moreover, it may limit our ability to think creatively about constitutional design by reinforcing a sort of cognitive path-dependency. Rather than to learn from unusual institutional configurations such as those in Switzerland or Australia, the effort to fit them into broad conceptual boxes, such as "consensus" or "majoritarian" democracy, may lead us to distort their characteristics. The thick strokes with which we paint reality may keep us from recognizing deeper explanations and new design possibilities.

Given this danger, I am content with outlining the *theoretical* plausibility that a well-designed semi-parliamentary constitution *may* improve performance, everything else being equal. Turnout is a good example. Quite a few studies suggest that simple and complex majoritarianism have conflicting causal effects on turnout (Ganghof and Eppner 2019). On the one hand, proportional representation, multiple parties, and multidimensional preferences make it easier for voters to find a party they feel represented by, which renders them more likely to vote (Blais et al. 2014; Rodden 2020). On the other hand, all of these features, by reducing identifiability and clarity of responsibility, also seem to reduce turnout (Park et al. 2019; Tillman 2015). Parliamentary systems may try to balance these conflicting causal effects by providing incentives for alliance formation, but this balancing strategy is demanding (Chapter 5). The balance achievable under semi-parliamentarism *may* be superior because it can combine high levels of identifiability with proportional and multidimensional representation. This potential superiority is difficult to test empirically, partly because Australia uses compulsory voting, but this fact does not invalidate the theoretical argument.

Corruption is another example. Here, too, some studies point to a corruption-reducing effect of proportional representation and a high effective number of parties (Lijphart 2012), while others ascribe such an effect to high clarity of responsibility (Schwindt-Bayer and Tavits 2016). Still other studies try to reconcile these conflicting results by suggesting a corruption-reducing sweet spot at some intermediate level of party system fragmentation (Schleiter and Voznaya 2014). Well-designed semi-parliamentary systems may provide a different path towards optimization because single-party cabinets can provide for relatively high clarity of responsibility, while multiparty systems can increase party system competitiveness and achieve horizontal accountability. In fact, Schwindt-Bayer and Tavits (2016: 56–57) single out the Australian Commonwealth as a case that was more effective in fighting corruption when it was governed by single-party majority cabinets. What they neglect is that these cabinets usually lacked a majority in the proportionally elected Senate with a well-developed committee system. This fact may also have contributed to Australia's performance on corruption.

Arguments along these lines could probably be developed for additional performance indicators such as median voter congruence or satisfaction with democracy (see, e.g. Stecker and Tausendpfund 2016). Here, though,

I want to go one step further and explore how a semi-parliamentary constitution may benefit democratic performance indirectly, by complementing other performance-enhancing constitutional features. We might call this the synergistic benefit of semi-parliamentarism.

Synergistic benefits of semi-parliamentarism

To illustrate potential synergies, I will focus on two examples: compulsory voting and weak(er) judicial review of legislation. They relate directly to the two main advantages of well-designed semi-parliamentarism: (a) the kind of normative balancing it enables; and (b) its potential to achieve a genuinely political form of horizontal accountability.

Compulsory voting

Arend Lijphart (1997c) has famously argued that "'democracy's unresolved dilemma'" is that elections do not accurately reflect the preferences of the citizenry. There appears to be a "cycle of disengagement" (Chapman 2019), in which many citizens with lower wealth and education levels vote relatively less, partly because they do not perceive the political system as responsive to them, and this non-voting reinforces the lack of responsiveness. Compulsory voting—when adequately sanctioned—has been discussed as a way to break this cycle, but only between 20 and 30 countries (depending on counting rules) have implemented this practice. Australia stands out in this group as having a well-designed and systematically enforced system (Bonotti and Strangio 2021).

There is also clear evidence that compulsory voting can have massive effects on democratic processes and substantive outcomes. For example, Fowler (2013) estimates that its introduction in the Australian states caused a 24-percentage-point increase in voter turnout and a 7–10-percentage-point increase in the vote and seat shares of the Labor Party, and that its national adoption increased voter turnout by 18.6 percentage points and pension spending by more than 40%. Other studies come to similar conclusions (Bechtel et al. 2016).

Compulsory voting nevertheless continues to be controversial (e.g. Brennan and Hill 2014; Birch 2018; Lever and Volacu 2018; Umbers 2020). What seems clear is that its successful justification depends on some broader configuration of basic institutions, on penalties for nonvoting being mild, on the burdens of voting being minor, and on appropriate exemptions being allowed (Chapman 2019; Elliott 2017; Umbers 2020). I contend that its justifiability also depends on the mechanical proportionality of legislative elections being as high as possible, everything else being equal. For it seems objectionable to coerce citizens to vote whilst *restricting the very options they can vote on*. One might allow voters that feel constrained in their choices an exemption, of course, but if the democratic state coerces voters to turn out, it plausibly assumes a corresponding obligation to increase their freedom of choice as much as possible. And this, in turn, implies an obligation to search for a constitutional structure that is conducive to this goal.[8]

The empirical results by Fowler and others underline this point. It is not objectionable that compulsory voting shifts policies towards the left, if this shift corrects an existing bias, rather than creating a new one. But we know that legal or implicit thresholds of representation can also create bias and invert election results; they may turn electoral minorities into legislative majorities and vice versa. If, say, voters with libertarian beliefs are coerced to vote, they should be able to be represented by a libertarian party, even if this party remains very small and lacks constitutional power over the cabinet. Parliamentary representation can help this party to grow and make a principled case for and against certain policies (including compulsory voting). If coercion is justified as a way to level the playing field, then its combination with a biased electoral system is problematic. To the extent that semi-parliamentarism allows for a greater degree of mechanical proportionality than parliamentarism, everything else being equal, it might be a better structure to complement compulsory voting.

Weak(er) judicial review

Another contentious issue of constitutional design concerns the power of courts. Many authors emphasize the risks and downsides of adopting "strong" forms of the judicial review of legislation to protect individual rights (e.g. Bellamy 2007; Waldron 2006).[9] These authors are often labelled advocates of "political constitutionalism" (Goldoni 2012). One main concern of theirs is

[8] To my knowledge, this point has not been made in the literature. Lisa Hill, in Brennan and Hill (2014: 114, n. 10), considers "some degree of genuine choice" preferable and "some degree of proportionality ... optimal." I worry that these requirements are too weak.

[9] The distinction between strong and weak judicial review is a simplification, of course. The reality is a gradual one along multiple dimensions of strength and weakness (Dixon 2019).

that strong judicial review undermines political equality. Political constitutionalists hold that the legislature is the right place to decide disagreements about rights. These concerns about political equality are also linked to concerns about substantive outcomes; for example, because judicial review may be used to entrench the political preferences of (formerly) powerful actors (Ginsburg 2003; Hirschl 2004). Again, my aim here is not to dive deeper into this debate but to highlight a widely accepted precondition for the absence or weakness of judicial review: an effective form of *political* accountability (e.g. Waldron 2006, 2012; Stephenson 2019).

Stephen Gardbaum (2014: 639) argues that the "[c]onstitutional evolution towards judicial review in established parliamentary democracies has been, in significant part, the result of changing institutional practices that have combined to undermine faith in traditional political modes of review and accountability, and render judicial ones the only seemingly practical alternative." What he means in particular is the dominance of the executive in a parliamentary system with disciplined parties. He identifies as an overlooked contributing cause for the growth of judicial review the lack of an effective political separation of powers and, hence, a lost faith in "political accountability as an effective and sufficient check on government action" (Gardbaum 2014: 618).

Gardbaum (2014: 636) also notes that Australia is "one of the few countries to resist constitutionalization and judicial review of rights" and suggests that its bicameralism may help to explain this fact. The Senate exercises real legislative power and actively scrutinizes government legislation, primarily through its Standing Committee for the Scrutiny of Bills (Stephenson 2013), and this capacity to hold governments accountable is strengthened by the use of proportional representation for Senate elections. Gardbaum contrasts this situation with that in Italy, where similar electoral systems in both chambers diminish the Senate's role as an agent of accountability.

While Gardbaum's explanation for the relative lack of constitutionalization and rights review in Australia is somewhat speculative, semi-parliamentary government with a proportionally elected second chamber is without doubt an attractive constitutional structure for achieving political accountability (Stone 2008). In explicating it, though, Gardbaum focuses on the comparison to Italy and the electoral systems of the two chambers, while neglecting the form of government. Italy has a parliamentary system because the confidence relationship between cabinet and assembly is extended to the Senate, and this is the deeper reason why the electoral systems of the two chambers *cannot* be very different without causing problems (see Chapter 7). Only because the Australian Senate does not have the constitutional power to dismiss the cabinet is there a true separation of powers and the electoral systems of the two chambers can be allowed to differ. The semi-parliamentary constitution is central to political accountability in Australia.[10]

None of this is to say that rights review in the Australian parliaments is satisfactory. There is probably a lot of room for improvement in terms of both institutions and political culture (Debeljak and Grenfell 2020). To the extent that rights review does work, however, second chambers play an important role as counterweights to executive and major party dominance (e.g. Grenfell 2020; see also Saunders 2021). Moreover, once we fully understand the structure and potential of semi-parliamentary government, we may be able to increase its potential to foster political accountability and reduce executive dominance (see Chapter 8).

Conclusion

The semi-parliamentary separation of powers can balance competing visions of democratic majority formation in ways that are unavailable under pure parliamentary government. The resulting normative balance may improve democratic processes and outcomes, and it may complement other potentially desirable constitutional designs, such as compulsory voting and weaker forms of judicial review. These insights remind us that there are no free lunches in choosing a form of government. Pure parliamentary government does have downsides.

This is not the same as claiming that semi-parliamentarism is superior to pure parliamentarism, all things considered. One reason not to exaggerate its advantages is that the tension between different visions of democratic majority formation is bound to resurface in the design of inter-branch relations. Roughly speaking, the more powerful the first chamber becomes relative to the second chamber, the more we strengthen simple vis-à-vis complex majoritarianism—and vice versa. I will discuss this issue further in Chapter 8.

[10] Finland used to be another example of legislative supremacy in the constitutional review of legislation (Lavapuro et al. 2011), and this supremacy was complemented by a one-third minority veto in the unicameral parliament. However, since a minority veto biases the political process, it was abolished as soon as the political right felt as constrained by it as the left. I discuss this abolishment further in Chapter 7 (see also Eppner and Ganghof 2017).

The main conclusion here is not that normative balancing under semi-parliamentarism is necessarily *better* than that under pure parliamentarism, but that it is *importantly different.*

Another reason to remain cautious is that there are certainly more goals in constitutional design than I have covered here. I have deliberately focused on goals that have played a prominent role in the political science literature and especially in defenses of the presidential separation of powers (Cheibub 2006, 2007; Mainwaring and Shugart 1997; Shugart and Carey 1992). This will help me make my case against presidentialism in Chapter 9. If a broader range of goals is taken into account, however, the kind of normative balancing achieved by pure parliamentary systems might well be considered superior. For example, in times of increasing affective polarization between citizens and the overarching importance of the urban–rural divide in shaping this polarization, the formation of multiparty cabinets might be an important unifying force in society (Rodden 2020). While such cabinets tend to create veto players and reduce clarity of responsibility, as well as legislative flexibility, they may also help to create trust between different societal groups, build executive expertise in different parties, and so on. Perhaps a deeper understanding of semi-parliamentarism will also help us to better appreciate the strengths of pure parliamentary government.

7

Design matters: second chambers, cabinet formation, and constitutional reform

(With Sebastian Eppner)

Semi-parliamentary democracies establish a separation of powers between the executive and one part of a directly elected assembly. As Chapter 6 has shown, this powers separation makes it possible to balance different visions of democratic majority formation in ways that are not available under pure parliamentarism. In particular, voters can rely on the first chamber to choose between competing cabinet alternatives and on the second chamber to be fairly represented in issue-specific deliberation and voting. In contrast to the presidential separation of powers, voters can achieve this normative balancing without having to vest executive power in a single human being (Chapter 9). This combination of features makes semi-parliamentary government an attractive constitutional format.

This assessment may seem to be challenged by two prominent conjectures in political science and constitutional theory. The first argues that strong bicameralism—of which Australian semi-parliamentarism is one example—is only viable in presidential systems (Ackerman 2000; Calabresi 2001). The second suggests that a strong second chamber can only be combined with the logic of a parliamentary system in the first chamber if parties form "oversized," and thus often ideologically heterogeneous, cabinets (Lijphart 1984). If these two conjectures were true, the patterns described in Chapter 6 could not be viable in the long run.

We argue in this chapter that both conjectures pay insufficient attention to the design of second chambers. If this design reduces their constraint on cabinet formation, second chambers are compatible with parliamentarism in the first chamber and with cabinets that lack a majority in the second chamber. We corroborate these claims with empirical analyses of cabinet formation and constitutional reforms in 28 advanced democracies in the period 1975–2018.

Beyond Presidentialism and Parliamentarism. Steffen Ganghof and Sebastian Eppner, Oxford University Press.
 DOI: 10.1093/oso/9780192897145.003.0007

The chapter thus also contributes to the literatures on cabinet formation under different forms of government (Cheibub et al. 2004) and on the stability and reform of second chambers (Russell and Sandford 2002; Vercesi 2019).

The next section elaborates on the two conjectures about strong bicameralism. We then consider the more detailed design of symmetrical second chambers and build two indices of how restrictive these chambers are with respect to cabinet formation. Next, we show, in a conditional logit analysis, that the control of a second-chamber majority only affects cabinet formation when the chamber in question is restrictive. Finally, brief case discussions reveal how the restrictiveness of second chambers also helps to explain patterns of second-chamber reform. Most importantly, reducing the restrictiveness of a second chamber—rather than its legitimacy or veto power—can be sufficient to stabilize a bicameral system.

Two conjectures about strong bicameralism

We begin by elaborating on the two conjectures that form our starting point. The first is that truly strong bicameralism requires a presidential system. As Bruce Ackerman (2000: 675) puts it, if constitutional designers "insist on a really powerful and independent senate, they must also be willing to accept something else: a really powerful and independent presidency" (see also Calabresi 2001: 87; Lijphart 1984: 101). The underlying argument is that when a second chamber becomes too symmetrical or strong, it leads to a "legitimacy tie" between rival parties in the two chambers (Ackerman 2000: 672; Lijphart 1984: 101). Presidential systems are assumed to be better at handling this problem because the government is legitimized directly by the voters and does not depend on parliamentary confidence at all.

A different way to state this conjecture is to postulate a fundamental incompatibility between the parliamentary accountability of governments and strong bicameralism (Lijphart 1984: 101). A recent example of this incompatibility thesis can be found in the final report of the State Commission on the State of the Parliamentary System in the Netherlands (2019). It advises against the direct election of the Dutch Senate because the resulting increase of its strength is considered a problem:

> greater legitimacy poses a threat to the bicameral system as we know it. In this system, the political primacy of the First chamber is expressed to a significant degree in its direct election, as opposed to the indirect election of the Upper House. This relationship between the Houses is necessary to prevent

> a stalemate arising between the Houses on the basis of two deviating election results. Such a stalemate is not easy to resolve in a parliamentary system.
> (State Commission 2019: 225)

The second conjecture is related to the first. It suggests that a legitimacy tie can be avoided in one specific way: the "obvious solution" is "to form an oversized cabinet" (Lijphart 1984: 104). The idea is that if parties form coalition cabinets that control majorities in both chambers, strong bicameralism can be rendered compatible with the logic of parliamentary government. This hypothesis has also gained quite a bit of empirical attention in political science.

If the two conjectures were true, they would question the potential of semi-parliamentarism. The first conjecture suggests that strong bicameralism cannot be viably combined with a government that emerges from and is responsible to parliament, the second that this combination can only be achieved at high costs. If an oversized coalition of veto players were needed to make the combination work, many potential advantages of semi-parliamentarism discussed in Chapter 6 would be undermined.

Fortunately, the two conjectures can be refuted, and this refutation is instructive. They both fail to adequately consider the more detailed design of second chambers. Most importantly, they do not clearly distinguish between the *legislative veto power* of a second chamber on the one hand and its constitutional *power over the cabinet* on the other. As we have already seen in Chapter 3, Lijphart's (1984) notions of symmetrical and strong bicameralism deliberately neglect second chambers' constitutional relationship to the government.[1] Yet, when the second chamber lacks constitutional power over the cabinet, the problems of legitimacy ties or legislative stalemate are no greater than in a presidential system. After all, Juan Linz's (1990a, 1994) famous critique of presidentialism focuses on these very problems. Indeed, I will argue in Chapters 8 and 9 that, to the extent that these problems do exist at all, they may be *more* severe under presidentialism—precisely because this form of government connects the separation of powers to executive personalism (Chapter 2).

[1] Ackerman (2000) is more attentive to second chambers' specific powers over the cabinet. Yet, he still mixes them with legislative veto powers at crucial parts of his argument. Parliamentarism and bicameralism are considered compatible if the members of the second chamber "may delay or defeat some measures, but they do not have the power to unseat the prime minister or the cabinet *or unduly sabotage the government's program*" (674, emphasis added). While Ackerman is right to focus on second chambers' power to unseat the prime minister and cabinet, this power should be strictly distinguished from their legislative veto power.

When second chambers are strong in terms of their legitimacy and legislative veto power but weak in their power over the cabinet, they are a viable alternative to presidentialism and do not necessitate the formation of oversized cabinets. Showing this empirically is the main task of this chapter.

The restrictiveness of second chambers

We start by looking at the more detailed design of symmetrical second chambers. In doing so, we exclude Switzerland from our general sample of 29 democracies, as the Swiss government does not require the confidence of any chamber of parliament to stay in office (Chapter 2). To increase the number of observations, we here consider the period from January 1975 to March 2018. Table 7.1 shows the twelve second chambers in the sample that were symmetrical in this period according to the criteria of Lijphart (2012): They had substantial legislative veto power and sufficient democratic legitimacy to use it.[2] Two cases had symmetrical second chambers only during some of the period of investigation: New South Wales from 1984 and Belgium until 1993. Due to constitutional reforms during the period under consideration, the second chambers of Victoria and Western Australia enter our analysis as three and two observations, respectively. We also include Finland, which used a unicameral veto of a one-third minority as an alternative to bicameralism until 1987 (Eppner and Ganghof 2017). Including this veto is preferable to excluding Finland or treating it as a case without any institutional veto point (Volden and Carrubba 2004).

The design of symmetrical second chambers can be more or less restrictive with respect to cabinet formation. To investigate the empirical consequences of the relevant design differences for cabinet formation and institutional stability, we construct two simple additive indices of restrictiveness. The first focuses only on the constitutional design of executive–legislative relations; the second adds institutional features that affect actor and bargaining constellations. We discuss both in turn.

[2] To make our point about second design, we follow the literature here as closely as possible. However, treating the symmetry of second chambers as a dichotomous variable is a strong simplification. Some second chambers have weaker symmetry; for example, because they are not directly elected (e.g. in the Netherlands), because their veto can be overridden (e.g. in Japan), or because their absolute veto only applies to certain types of legislation (e.g. in Germany).

Table 7.1 The restrictiveness of symmetrical second chambers

	Confidence (budget veto)	Investiture	Dissolution	Restrictiveness I	Party discipline	Decision-making flexibility	Compositional instability	Restrictiveness II
Italy	1(1)	1	−1	**1**	0	0	0	**1**
Belgium pre-1993	1(1)	1	−1	**1**	0	0	0	**1**
Victoria pre-1984	0(1)	0	0	**0**	0	0	0	**0**
WA pre-1987	0(1)	0	0	**0**	0	0	0	**0**
Netherlands	0(1)	0	0	**0**	0	0	0	**0**
Japan	0(0)	0	0	**0**	0	0	0	**0**
Finland pre-1987	0(0)	0	−1	**−1**	0	1	0	**0**
WA post-1987	0(1)	0	0	**0**	0	−1	0	**−1**
Tasmania	0(1)	0	0	**0**	0	0	−1	**−1**
Victoria 1984–2003	0(1)	0	−1	**−1**	0	0	0	**−1**
Germany	0(0)	0	0	**0**	−1	0	−1	**−2**
South Australia	0(1)	0	−1	**−1**	0	−1	0	**−2**
Australia	0(1)	0	−1	**−1**	0	−1	0	**−2**
Victoria post-2003	0(0)	0	−1	**−1**	0	−1	0	**−2**
New South Wales	0(0)	0	−1	**−1**	0	−1	0	**−2**

Notes: See text for explanations. Coding is based on the respective constitutions.

Restrictiveness I: Executive–legislative relations

The literature on parliamentary government highlights the design of no-confidence, investiture, and dissolution procedures (e.g. Bergman 1993; Cheibub et al. 2021; Goplerud and Schleiter 2016; Sieberer 2015) but has tended to neglect these procedures in theorizing the effects of second chambers on cabinet formation (but see Diermeier et al. 2007; Eppner and Ganghof 2017). Restrictiveness I captures them.

Confidence

If the second chamber possesses the right to a no-confidence vote against the cabinet, it becomes more restrictive with respect to cabinet formation. The likely "equilibrium response to this institutional constraint is to form larger (perhaps even surplus) coalitions (possibly constituting a majority in both chambers)" (Diermeier et al. 2007: 248). In our sample, a second chamber with confidence authority existed in Belgium until 1993 and still exists in Italy (André et al. 2015; Russo 2015).

As explained in Chapter 3, the second chamber's power to veto supply—that is, legislation appropriating funds for the ordinary annual services of government—might be used as a functional equivalent to a no-confidence vote, although many legal and political experts believe that is not actually the case (anymore) in Australia. We focus on the no-confidence vote but use the budget veto for a robustness test (see Table A3 in the appendix). The "confidence" column in Table 7.1 shows the values for the absolute budget veto in parentheses. Among the Australian cases, New South Wales, and Victoria (after the constitutional reform of 2003) stand apart as lacking it. A case that is more restrictive with respect to the budget is the second chamber in the Netherlands.

Investiture

A second chamber also becomes more restrictive if it must explicitly agree to a new government taking office, typically called an investiture vote. This vote may be needed before the government can assume office or it may take the form of a compulsory confidence vote after the government has assumed office (Rasch et al. 2015: 3–4). The strictest version of an investiture vote requires an absolute majority (Cheibub et al. 2021). Even when only a simple majority is required, however, the need to achieve this majority *in both chambers* plausibly "incentivizes the formation of large coalitions" (Russo 2015: 137). Not surprisingly, we see the involvement of the second chamber in the government's investiture only in the two cases with a second chamber no-confidence vote: Italy and pre-1993 Belgium. In both cases, the vote is a compulsory confidence vote (Rasch et al. 2015: 343, Table 19.1).

Dissolution

While no-confidence and investiture votes render second chambers more restrictive, the possibility of their dissolution works in the opposite direction. The threat of assembly dissolution can render obstructive behavior by opposition parties costly (Becher and Christiansen 2015). While the detailed rules for dissolution vary significantly in democracies (on first chambers, see Goplerud and Schleiter 2016), we focus on whether second chambers can be dissolved (full or in part) under any circumstances (see also Thies and Yanai 2014: 60–61). This is impossible in Germany, Japan, pre-1984 Victoria, Western Australia, and Tasmania. The second chamber in the Netherlands can be dissolved, but since it is elected by provincial councils, a dissolution "could not possibly solve a political problem, should one arise between the government and the Upper House" (Besselink 2014: 1216).[3] Hence, we also treat this case as restrictive with respect to dissolution.

Restrictiveness II: Taking actor and strategic constellations into account

While Restrictiveness I focuses on the core institutions regulating executive–legislative relations, Restrictiveness II adds specific institutional features that may reduce the effects of second chambers on cabinet formation. These design features imply important variation in the nature of the relevant actors and strategic situations. While we will model actors' behavior in the statistical analysis, some important constitutional design differences cannot be adequately captured in the statistical model and thus ought to be part of the index.

Party discipline

Studies of cabinet formation usually assume disciplined parties and thus use variables such as the number of parties or their ideological differences. While this assumption is generally justifiable, state delegations in the German Bundesrat are *constitutionally required* to vote as a block. This requirement renders

[3] It is perhaps more adequate to say that it would be unlikely to solve a political conflict between parties, but it might solve one within parties. If there is a lack of party discipline, for instance, dissolving the second chamber could potentially be used to replace defectors with party loyalists.

strict party discipline impossible and party unity in legislative voting less probable. The Bundesrat is therefore a more permissive veto player (Tsebelis 2002, Chapter 2).[4]

Decision-making flexibility

As argued in detail in Chapter 6, the specific combination of electoral systems in the bicameral systems of mainland Australia renders second chambers less restrictive. First chambers' alternative vote systems tend to lead to one-party majority cabinets in the center of the political space, which can often build flexible, issue-specific legislative coalitions in second chambers that are proportionally elected and lack confidence authority. This design facilitates an actor constellation in which the majority party has incentives to govern with flexible, issue-specific legislative coalitions (Tsebelis 2002: 97–99). As a rough approximation, we therefore consider a bicameral system to be more permissive when single-seat district electoral systems in the first chamber are combined with proportional representation in the second chamber.

Decision-making flexibility is also affected by the difference between bicameralism and supermajority requirements. When a one-third minority in parliament can veto legislation, the flexibility of the government in choosing between different support parties is reduced and the incentives for building larger cabinets increases. The Finnish minority veto is therefore coded as more restrictive.

Compositional instability

The standard approach to modeling cabinet formation looks at distinct bargaining situations; for example, when a new cabinet is formed after an election. The cabinet-builders are assumed to make a decision about what kind of coalition they want to form and whether it will have a majority in the first and second chambers. However, they are likely to seriously consider the majority status in the second chamber only when this status will be stable for some time. If actor and preference constellations in the second chamber change frequently, coalition-builders may disregard the second chamber and prefer to seek issue-specific support for particular pieces of legislation (see Fortunato et al. 2013).

[4] The lack of party discipline also makes it harder for opposition parties to create a credible veto threat based on vote-seeking incentives (Ganghof and Bräuninger 2006). A good example is a major German tax reform in 2000, when a Social Democratic–Green government made no concessions to the oppositional Christian Democrats because it was able to strike minor deals with different state governments (Ganghof 2006: 133–134).

We have therefore compared the average number of changes in second-chamber composition during one first-chamber term. This number is below or around one for all cases except Germany and Tasmania, which have values around four. In Germany, the composition of the Bundesrat can change with every state election. In Tasmania, it can change every year due to the system of yearly staggered elections. As explained in Chapter 6, this system facilitates the dominance of independents in the second chamber (Sharman 2013: 341) and further increases permissiveness (see our reasoning on party unity in 'Party discipline' above). The respective constitutional rules in Germany and Tasmania thus reduce restrictiveness.

Summary

The two indices reveal important design differences between symmetrical second chambers. Restrictiveness I applies standard arguments about executive–legislative relations to second chambers. The more comprehensive Restrictiveness II adds more case-specific design features. While we have isolated the different features for the purpose of index construction, they can, to some extent, be seen as packages. This is one of the reasons why we will focus mainly on the more comprehensive Restrictiveness II. The values on this index reflect the different models of bicameralism. At one end of the spectrum are the highly restrictive second chambers in (pre-reform) Belgium and Italy, which fully extend the logic of a parliamentary system to the second chamber. As we will see, these cases rely on high congruence in the composition of the two chambers of parliament, so that more specific features of permissiveness are unnecessary. At the other end, we have the more permissive second chambers in Australia and Germany. These cases are designed to allow for bicameral incongruence. Hence, they not only tend to be more permissive in the basic design of executive–legislative relations, but also add specific permissive features. These features differ according to the underlying model of representation. In Germany's territorial model, second-chamber composition changes frequently and states are required to vote as a block. In Tasmania's non-partisan model, frequent composition changes go hand in hand with a chamber dominated by independents. In mainland Australia's partisan model, majoritarian elections for the first chamber are combined with proportional representation in the second chamber. Without denying the coherence of these models, we can use the two indices to explore how the restrictiveness of second chambers conditions their effects on cabinet formation, as well as their institutional stability.

How do second chambers affect cabinet formation?

How do second chambers affect cabinet formation? A fairly large literature on this question has remained inconclusive (e.g. Druckman and Thies 2002; Druckman et al. 2005; Eppner and Ganghof 2015, 2017; Ganghof 2010; Mitchell and Nyblade 2008; Sjölin 1993; Thürk et al. 2021; Volden and Carrubba 2004). We argue that this is partly due to the neglect of second chambers' more detailed design; that is, their restrictiveness. More specifically, we want to explore two hypotheses. The main one is that more restrictive second chambers tend to have a greater effect on cabinet formation. The supplementary hypothesis is that constitutional designers are likely to understand this causal consequence and thus have strong incentives to make sure that a highly restrictive second chamber has a similar or identical composition as the first chamber.

To explore these hypotheses, we analyze 369 government formations in 28 democratic systems between January 1975 and March 2018 (see appendix for details and data sources). Of these, 154 government formations happened in the presence of a symmetrical second chamber. Our analysis is unique in that it includes the bicameral Australian states into the comparison of democratic nation-states. To the best of our knowledge, the combination of parliamentarism (in the first chamber) and symmetrical bicameralism at the subnational level exists only in Australia. Given the important institutional variation that the Australian states add to the sample, as well as the similarity of cabinet formation processes at national and state levels, we have strong reasons to combine the information at national and state levels. For consistency, we also include the unicameral Australian state of Queensland.

A simple descriptive look

To take a first look at the data, consider Figure 7.1. It evaluates both hypotheses by displaying the degree of bicameral congruence and veto control at different levels of restrictiveness. We use Restrictiveness I here, since it is simpler and better suited to a bivariate analysis.[5] *Congruence* is the share of potential first-chamber majority cabinets that control the institutional veto point (i.e. have a second-chamber majority or a first-chamber two-thirds majority in Japan

[5] Recall that Restrictiveness II is meant to capture aspects of actor constellations in ways that complement the regression model. Its additional items logically imply a lack of congruence and would thus bias the bivariate analysis.

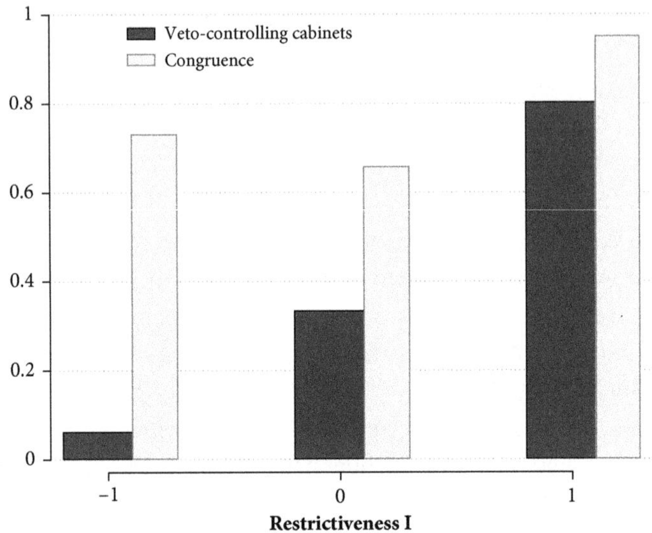

Fig. 7.1 How second-chamber restrictiveness shapes congruence and veto control in 28 democracies, 1975–2018
Notes: see text.

or a two-thirds majority in Finland). *Veto-controlling cabinets* is the share of actually formed cabinets that control the institutional veto point.

The analysis supports our two hypotheses. When restrictiveness is very high, congruence is very high, too: around 95% of potential first-chamber majority cabinets *automatically* control majorities in the second chamber. Cabinet-builders rarely have to make a special effort to achieve a second-chamber majority. By contrast, when restrictiveness is intermediate or low, congruence is lower. Veto control becomes less necessary and more difficult to achieve. The degree to which it is achieved is higher at an intermediate level of restrictiveness, as we would expect.

A multivariate analysis

Of course, a host of other variables influence cabinet formation and thus need to be controlled for. To do so, we follow the standard approach to modeling cabinet formation in political science (Druckman et al. 2005; Martin and Stevenson 2001). We use conditional logit regression models to estimate how the various properties of all governments that could form—all potential governments—affect their relative probabilities of being chosen as the actual

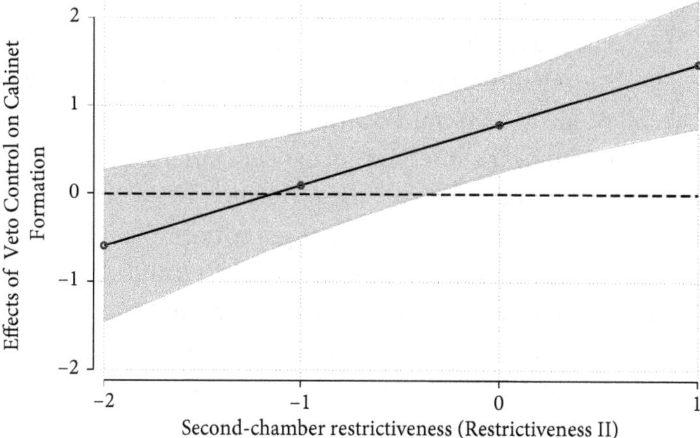

Fig. 7.2 The interplay of second-chamber restrictiveness and veto control in 28 democracies, 1975–2018
Notes: see text.

government. Any combination of parties with parliamentary representation at the time of government formation is one potential government. Our sample contains 577,879 potential governments. The dependent variable in the statistical model indicates the potential governments that actually formed. These 369 governments are coded one, the others zero.

To evaluate our main hypothesis, we focus on the *interaction* of the two explanatory variables analyzed in Figure 7.1. The first indicates whether the potential government controls a second-chamber majority or equivalent veto point (Veto control),[6] the second measures second chamber restrictiveness (Restrictiveness II).[7] As in Figure 7.1, our interest is in how restrictiveness *conditions* the causal effect that veto control has on the likelihood that a potential government is chosen. We discuss the specification of cabinet formation opportunities, the choice of control variables, their empirical measurement, and the detailed regression results in the appendix. Here, we want to get straight to the estimated interplay of restrictiveness and veto control, which is visualized in Figure 7.2.

[6] In Finland, the value is one if the potential cabinet holds 66% or more of the seats (thus making a minority veto against the coalition numerically impossible). In Japan, it is one if the potential cabinet either has a majority in the second chamber or a two-thirds majority in the first chamber (which can override a second-chamber veto).

[7] We use Restrictiveness II because we used Restrictiveness I above and the composition of the two chambers can now be captured by various controls. As before, however, our conclusion for the other index would not be substantially different (see Table A3 in the appendix).

The horizontal axis shows the different levels of second-chamber restrictiveness. The vertical axis shows the statistical model's answer to the question whether governments with a second-chamber majority (i.e. with veto control) are more likely to form: Positive values suggest a positive answer. The diagonal line shows the interplay of the two variables, with the shaded area representing the uncertainty of the estimation (95% confidence interval). The results are as expected. Potential governments are more likely to become the actual government if they control a second-chamber majority (or a minority veto) *and if the design of the second chamber is restrictive.* In systems with the most restrictive second chambers, the chance of a potential government to be chosen as the actual government is about 4.5 times larger if its parties jointly control a second-chamber majority, everything else being equal.[8] The estimated effect of veto control reaches statistical significance only at the two highest levels of restrictiveness. Permissively designed second chambers have no measurable effect on cabinet formation.

Since these results are based on a number of simplifying assumptions, they should be seen as multivariate observations that corroborate the simpler picture in Figure 7.1. However, our causal interpretation of the regression analysis is corroborated by much qualitative evidence. Most importantly, this evidence also shows that the permissively designed second chambers in Australia have not affected cabinet formation (Ward 2012). For Germany, the qualitative evidence for a second chamber effect is also weak, given that more plausible explanations exist for the formation of "grand coalitions" of the two major parties (Proksch and Slapin 2006). For restrictive second chambers, by contrast, qualitative studies have consistently underlined their effects on cabinet formation, especially in Italy (when congruence was not perfect) and Japan (Hyde 2011: 172; McCargo 2010: 472; Rosenbluth and Thies 2010: 106–107; Takenaka 2012). The same is true for the Finish minority veto (Karvonen 2014: 80–82).

Our analysis thus provides a deeper understanding of why strong bicameralism does not generally require the formation of broader, oversized cabinets to be stable. If the design of the second chamber is sufficiently permissive, a behavioral equilibrium can emerge in which ideologically compact cabinets, backed by first-chamber majorities, seek flexible and issue-specific majorities in the second chamber—regardless of whether the legislative support partners

[8] The effect size has to be exponentiated to calculate the change of the odds ratio, in this case $e^{1.5} \approx 4.5$.

in this chamber are parties, independents, or state governments. This interpretation of the evidence is further corroborated when we turn to comparative patterns of second-chamber reform.

Restrictiveness and constitutional reform

If strong bicameralism were fundamentally incompatible with a no-confidence vote in the first chamber, we should expect this institutional combination to be relatively unstable. This section shows that this is not the case. When we take into account how restrictive the design of second chambers is with respect to cabinet formation, we can better understand patterns of constitutional reform or stability. More specifically, we have to look at the interplay of how restrictive second chambers are and how they are composed. High congruence and low restrictiveness are alternative ways of stabilizing symmetrical second chambers. If either of these conditions is present, we do not necessarily expect strong pressures for constitutional reform. By contrast, if a restrictive design of the second chamber combines with incongruent compositions of the two chambers, a strong impetus for reform becomes more likely.

Symmetrical and restrictive second chambers can be stable, when they are congruent

Symmetrical and restrictive second chambers can be stabilized by a congruent composition of both chambers. Figure 7.3 shows the congruence over time in the relatively restrictive second chambers in Belgium, Italy, Japan, and the Netherlands.[9] As before, congruence is defined as the proportion of potential first-chamber majority cabinets that control a second-chamber majority. Let us take a closer look at these cases.

Belgium

Congruence in Belgium was almost perfect, so that restrictiveness did not necessitate reform. However, high congruence raises questions about the purpose of a second chamber. The Senate was reformed in 1993 as part of a broader reform of Belgian federalism. It became not only less restrictive, with the cabinet becoming accountable only to the first chamber, but also asymmetrical.

[9] While the data set for the regression analysis extends only until 2018 (see appendix), we extended the analysis of congruence in these four cases to September 2020.

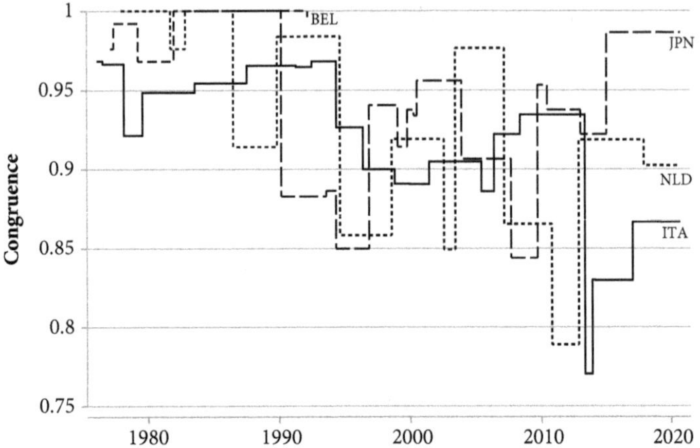

Fig. 7.3 Bicameral congruence in four democracies with symmetrical and restrictive second chambers, 1975–2020
Notes: see text.

In 2014, it was weakened further and lost its participation in the standard legislative procedure (Goossens and Cannoot 2015; Vercesi 2019).

Italy

Congruence was very high in Italy until the early 1990s but declined afterwards, due to electoral reforms. This decline combined with the Senate's restrictiveness to intensify constitutional reform pressures. While initiatives to reform the Senate's powers date back to the 1980s (Vercesi 2017: 606), the last attempt was made in 2016, shortly after bicameral congruence had reached a low point (Figure 7.3). A constitutional reform proposal was accepted by both chambers but ultimately rejected in a referendum (Baldi 2018). The reasons for this rejection are numerous (Bergman 2019; Ceccarini and Bordignon 2017; Di Mauro and Memoli 2018). What is crucial here is that the proposal went far beyond reducing the Senate's restrictiveness. It would have turned the Senate into a much smaller and asymmetrical chamber: indirectly elected and with only suspensive veto power on ordinary legislation (Romeo 2017; Vercesi 2019). Moreover, the reform was connected to a previously passed—and subsequently replaced—electoral reform that would have increased the disproportionality of the electoral system (D'Alimonte 2015). The new electoral system (named "Italicum") granted an absolute majority of seats to the list obtaining at least 40% of the votes or—in case no list reached this threshold—to the winner of a run-off election held between the top two parties. Rather than merely reducing the

Senate's restrictiveness, the reform would have been a rather drastic shift towards simple majoritarianism (Chapter 5). This allowed the opponents of the reform to successfully frame it as undermining checks and balances and threatening democracy (Ceccarini and Bordignon 2017: 294). After the constitutional reform had been rejected, the electoral system was changed once more (Massetti and Farinelli 2019) and congruence increased again—thus helping to stabilize, for the time being, Italy's symmetrical and highly restrictive bicameralism.

Japan

Japan's second chamber is relatively restrictive, despite fulfilling the minimal conditions for a semi-parliamentary system (Chapter 3). It cannot be dissolved and it lacks the kind of specific restrictiveness-reducing features we find in the Australian cases or in Germany (see Figure 7.1). As noted in Chapter 3, moreover, experts on Japan hold that the second chamber has a de facto no-confidence vote because it can veto "budget-enabling bills" and combine censure motions with a boycott of assembly deliberations (Thies and Yanai 2014: 70; Takayasu 2015: 161). The House of Councillors may thus be even more restrictive than the formal constitutional rules captured in Table 7.1 suggest. Hence, we might expect bicameral incongruence to trigger debates about constitutional reform.

This is also what we see (Heeß 2017: 280–287), but the phases of troubling incongruence were very brief. From 1956 to 1989, the Liberal Democratic Party (LDP) held single-party majorities in both chambers. Incongruence increased afterwards, but Thies and Yanai (2014) show that we have to distinguish two types of situations. When the government merely lacks a majority in the second chamber, it is often able to round up party support on an ad hoc basis for each bill. By contrast, when the second chamber is controlled by the main opposition party or coalition, legislative effectiveness drops substantially and the government's ability to govern may be undermined. The latter periods were rare and brief, however. They existed from 2007–2009 and 2011–2012 and, in the first of these, the government actually controlled a veto-proof supermajority in the first chamber. It is not surprising, therefore, that constitutional reform debates did not gain much traction (Heeß 2017: 280–287). As reflected in Figure 7.3, the dominance of the LDP in both chambers has been re-established in recent years (Jain 2020), which weakens incentives for a reform of bicameralism.

The Netherlands

In the Netherlands, congruence had also been very high until the end of the 1980s but decreased and fluctuated afterwards. The second chamber thus became a significant constraint some of the time. Coalition-builders were not always willing or able to control a majority in the second chamber but instead sought issue-specific support. While this pattern bears some similarity to what we see in Australia, it also differs in crucial respects. Due to the permissive proportional representation system in the first chamber, (a) the government consists of two or more veto players; and (b) issue-specific agreements with opposition parties are often already achieved in the first chamber (and merely accepted by the second chamber). Hence, the second chamber plays a very limited role in the process, and its main effect is to increase the de facto majority requirement in the first chamber (State Commission 2019: 217). Due to this increase, however, the reduced congruence contributed to a broader debate about constitutional reform.

Incongruent second chambers can be stable, when their design is permissive

That a similar composition of the two chambers can stabilize a powerful second chamber is no new insight. What has been neglected in the existing literature is how incongruent second chambers can also be stabilized by a permissive design. Five cases entered the period under consideration with relatively permissive designs (based on Restrictiveness II, see Table 7.1): the Australian Commonwealth, Germany, New South Wales, South Australia, and Tasmania. If a no-confidence vote in the first chamber were fundamentally "incompatible" with strong bicameralism, we would expect these cases to be inherently unstable. But this is not what we see.

Australia

In the four Australian cases, second chambers did not see a reduction of their legislative veto power, and they did also not become more congruent. The institutional equilibrium was stabilized by the fact that second chambers did not affect cabinet formation. Second-chamber reform or abolishment is sometimes proposed publicly, of course, especially by proponents of "simple majoritarianism" (Chapter 5), but there were no serious attempts in that direction. As Mainwaring et al. (2019: 267) note for South Australia, for example: "From time to time, there have been calls to abolish the second chamber …

There appears, however, to be limited appetite for a unicameral system, such as in Queensland." Similarly, Clune and Smith (2019: 229) maintain that after the development of the Legislative Council from an appointed to an elected house of review, the "institutional framework of NSW politics currently appears to be relatively settled."

Germany

Germany differs from the Australian cases in that, as part of a broader federalism reform, symmetry was reduced somewhat. However, the goal was not to change but to restore what the designers of the Germany constitution had originally intended. Germany's Basic Law makes a distinction between consent laws (*Zustimmungsgesetze*) and objection laws (*Einspruchsgesetze*); only for the former is the Bundesrat's active approval (by absolute majority rule) indispensable. The German second chamber was thus never intended to be fully symmetrical. The Parliamentary Council that designed the constitution had expected the share of consent laws to amount to no more than 10%, but it ended up fluctuating around an average of 55% (Stecker 2016). The federalism reform enacted in 2006 reduced this share to 39% overall, while failing to achieve any reduction in the area of tax laws (Stecker 2016). Hence, the reduction of symmetry constituted no systematic departure from the original design, which is relatively permissive and reduces the Bundesrat's effect on cabinet formation. Had this design been more restrictive, the German reform debate would have been completely different.

Restrictive and incongruent second chambers tend to trigger reform

We expect stronger pressures for second-chamber reform when this chamber is (a) symmetrical; (b) incongruent; and (c) restrictive. We can also formulate more precise expectations about what kind of reforms to expect. Reducing symmetry or increasing congruence are not the only two options; it might also be sufficient to make the second chamber less restrictive with respect to cabinet formation.

Our evidence corroborates these expectations. The three cases of symmetrical bicameralism that entered our analysis as relatively restrictive and incongruent—Finland, Victoria, and Western Australia—have all been substantially reformed to reduce symmetry and/or restrictiveness.[10] Given the historical origin of the respective institutional veto points, the reform processes also had a similar political component. Since the minority veto in Finland and the second chambers in the Australian states had been created as conservative brakes on popular majorities and the socialist movement, the political right had traditionally opposed constitutional reforms. Successful reforms thus required either favorable political conditions for the left or socioeconomic changes that made the constraint of the veto point felt more equally on both sides of the political spectrum.

Finland

In Finland, the relevant veto point was not a second chamber, and it was restrictive partly for this reason. A minority veto is unavoidably supermajoritarian, which makes issue-specific majority formation more difficult. It had originally been "enacted to protect the constitution from socialist takeover," but was later "used by the socialist block to protect the welfare state against the threat from the right" (Sundberg 1993: 420). Once both sides of the political spectrum felt the constraint of the veto, it was not difficult to achieve agreement on constitutional reform—despite the fact that constitutional amendment procedures are not particularly permissive in Finland (e.g. Tsebelis 2017, 2020). Since a minority veto is inherently restrictive, the reform implied its abolishment.

Western Australia

The second chamber in Western Australia was restrictive because it cannot be dissolved, had an absolute budget veto, and was elected under the same electoral system (alternative vote). Hence, it tended to become a rubber stamp when the same party controlled both chambers and created sharp partisan conflict when the second chamber was controlled by the opposition party (Black 1991; de Garis 2003; Phillips 1991). Moreover, massive vote weighting (malapportionment) in favor of rural areas meant that the problem was highly asymmetrical: conservative parties had a guaranteed second-chamber majority (Davies and Tonts 2007). A reform opportunity emerged in the 1980s, when a Labor government made a deal with the National Party holding the balance of power in the second chamber. The Labor Party's main interest was to abolish malapportionment in both chambers, but PR in the second chamber was what

[10] Sweden had abolished its upper chamber already by 1970. This reform was triggered, in part, by its restrictive effect on cabinet formation. However, the details are complex and summarized elsewhere (Eppner and Ganghof 2017: 182).

it could get (for details, see Pepperday 2002; Phillips 2013). The reform was also influenced by the previous introductions of PR in the second chambers of the Australian Federal Parliament (1949) and the parliaments of South Australia (1963) and New South Wales (1978). These had turned second chambers into more effective houses of review, while also making them more permissive. Additional reforms were considered at various points in time (including the abolishment of the budget veto), but second-chamber PR was sufficient to create an equilibrium (for details, see Pepperday 2002; Phillips 2013).

Victoria

The second chamber in Victoria had been restrictive in the same way as its Western Australian counterpart. Its ultimate reform came later, in 2003, but was more far-reaching. However, a first step towards greater permissiveness was already made in 1984. The Labor government had wanted to abolish the absolute budget veto completely but had to compromise with the Liberal and National Parties, which had a second-chamber majority. The opposition agreed to the compromise because (parts of) it agreed that the Council's indirect power over the survival of the government was "excessive," "undemocratic," and "indefensible," and because it feared that Labor would soon win a Council majority (Costar 2008: 204–206; Strangio 2004: 42). The reform provided a maximum four-year term for the Legislative Assembly, with the first three years being fixed. The Council was thus deprived of the ability to force an early Assembly election by blocking supply. In addition, and for the first time, the reform linked second and first chamber terms, with half the Councillors retiring at each Assembly election (Strangio 2004: 42).

A more far-reaching reform became possible when Labor won, in November 2002, a majority in both chambers. It could have abolished the second chamber altogether, as it had attempted many times in the past. By 2002, however, the party's position had changed to reducing second-chamber restrictiveness further. This was achieved in three main ways (compare Table 7.1): The absolute budget veto was now fully abolished, the dissolution of the entire second chamber (as part of a double dissolution) became possible, and—as in the other mainland states—PR was introduced (Costar 2008).

Victoria went further than Western Australia in that the reform also affected the symmetry of bicameralism, at least to some extent. When there is bicameral disagreement over a bill, it is designated a "Disputed Bill" and referred to a Dispute Resolution Committee comprising seven members of the Assembly and five of the Council. If the dispute resolution process fails to achieve an acceptable compromise, there are two options: (a) the premier may advise a dissolution of both chambers, following which the bill may be put before a joint sitting of the two chambers; or (b) the bill may be held over and placed before a joint sitting after the next scheduled election of both chambers. Since the joint sitting favors the larger chamber, it compromises the veto power of the second chamber.

Two points should be noted here. First, the power of the second chamber remains substantial because the premier will often be hesitant to go to an early election over a single bill and because, in the absence of dissolution, legislation can potentially be delayed for a long time. Since governments are unlikely to wait for several years, bicameral compromise will often be the more attractive option (Tsebelis and Money 1997). Second, and more importantly, there is no reason to believe that this reduction of symmetry was necessary; it reflected the power of Labor in the reform process. The reduced restrictiveness would, in all likelihood, have been sufficient to bring Victorian bicameralism into an equilibrium.

Summary and limits

The results of our qualitative explorations are in line with expectations. High congruence and low restrictiveness are alternative options for stabilizing powerful second chambers. When congruence decreases (increases), reform pressures tend to intensify (weaken). When low congruence and high restrictiveness come together, constitutional tensions tend to become high and may trigger reform. Finally, and most importantly, reforms do not need to reduce the legislative veto power or legitimacy of second chambers—it is sufficient to make them more permissive with respect to cabinet formation.

Our analysis has obvious limits, too. As the case discussions are highly condensed and do not systematically take other explanations into account, we cannot gauge the *relative* explanatory importance of second-chamber restrictiveness. For example, a standard explanation would be that the institutional difficulty of changing constitutions (sometimes called constitutional rigidity) helps to explain patterns of stability and change. Another, developed in detail by Katja Heeß (2017), focuses on whether second chambers or other veto points strengthen or weaken the democratic legitimacy of a constitution. We do not argue against these explanations but see them as potential complements to ours. Our focus was not on building a multifactor explanation of second-chamber reform or stability, but on exploring the causal effects of second-chamber restrictiveness.

Conclusion

We can firmly reject the idea that constitutional designers who prefer "strong" forms of bicameralism necessarily have to accept either a presidential system of government or oversized and ideologically heterogeneous cabinets. Strong bicameralism is fully compatible with parliamentarism in the first chamber, as long as the design of the second chamber is sufficiently permissive with respect to cabinet formation. The second chambers' lack of a no-confidence vote is not only one of the defining features of semi-parliamentarism (Chapter 3), but it is also a crucial feature of a second chamber that puts less constraint on cabinet formation. If strong bicameralism is semi-parliamentary and designed permissively, it does not require presidentialism but can be an alternative to it.

8
Designing semi-parliamentary democracy

Each basic form of government allows for a great variety of specific constitutional designs. This chapter explores some potential designs of semi-parliamentary government. The exploration serves three main purposes. First, it highlights how semi-parliamentarism could be flexibly adapted to different contexts and how its design could better mimic the potential advantages of presidentialism. Second, it will keep us from exaggerating the lessons of Chapter 6. While we have seen that semi-parliamentarism can mitigate the tension between different visions of democracy, between simple and complex majoritarianism, this tension resurfaces in the design of inter-branch relations. Third, the discussion suggests that semi-parliamentary government can mitigate the problem of legislative deadlock in ways that would be more problematic under presidentialism or other forms of bicameralism. Strengthening the *agenda and dissolution powers* of the government or the first chamber may be less dangerous than under presidentialism because this power is not given to a single human being. At the same time, the equal or higher democratic legitimacy of the second chamber makes it possible to weaken the *veto power* of the first chamber—thus making deadlock less likely.

I first discuss how the two parts of the assembly may be constituted in terms of their relative sizes and their electoral systems. This discussion begins with bicameral versions of semi-parliamentarism and then explores ways in which the chamber of confidence may be turned into a committee of confidence, whose relative size may even be determined endogenously by the behavior of parties and voters. Then I discuss some issues in the design of inter-branch relations, focusing first on assembly dissolution and popular referendums and then on the legislative veto power of the two parts of the assembly.

Constituting the two chambers

Let us begin with the bicameral version of semi-parliamentarism and specifically with the *relative size* of the two chambers. We have seen in Chapter 6 that

Beyond Presidentialism and Parliamentarism. Steffen Ganghof, Oxford University Press.
 DOI: 10.1093/oso/9780192897145.003.0008

in the existing cases of semi-parliamentarism the second chamber is invariably smaller. Through the conceptual lens of semi-parliamentarism, however, this arrangement can hardly be viewed as justified. If the first chamber is most of all a chamber of confidence, whereas the second chamber is the chamber of fair representation and deliberation, legislative scrutiny, and of controlling the government, the latter should arguably be larger than the former. The comparison to presidentialism is instructive here, as the relative sizes of the two branches are reversed. Presidents can be seen as a one-person confidence chamber (giving confidence to themselves), whereas assemblies are much larger. A larger second chamber would make the goals of complex majoritarianism and horizontal political accountability easier to achieve. It would increase mechanical proportionality, everything else being equal, and allow for a greater division of labor.

A second important issue is the way in which the chamber of confidence is elected. If our goal is to mimic presidentialism (i.e. to enable voters to directly legitimize a single political force as the government), single-seat districts are a liability, rather than an asset. A superior approach is to elect the chamber of confidence in a single at-large district. This solution is also fairer in that every vote counts equally for the election of the government, regardless of where it is located.

What electoral system should be used? One option, prevalent under presidentialism, is a two-round system with a run-off election between the two parties with the greatest number of first-round votes. The difference to presidentialism is that the party that loses the run-off would still get confidence seats in proportion to their vote share in the run-off election. It would become the official opposition party. Run-off elections have the advantage of being relatively simple, while requiring the winning party to gain support from an *absolute* majority of voters in the final round of voting. Spurious majorities are avoided.

A more complex but potentially fairer option would be a modified alternative vote (AV) system (Ganghof 2016a). In this system, voters can rank as many party lists as they like in order of preference and thereby determine the two parties with the greatest support. The parties with the least first-place votes are iteratively eliminated, and their votes transferred to each voter's second-most preferred party, third-most preferred party, and so on. In contrast with a normal AV system, the process does not stop when one party has received more than 50% of the votes, but it continues until all but two parties are eliminated. Only these two top parties receive seats in the chamber of confidence in proportion to their final vote shares in the AV contest. Based on voters' revealed preference rankings, a mandate to form the cabinet is conferred to the winner of the AV contest.[1]

Electing the chamber of confidence in a single at-large district might be considered problematic because it removes constituency interests as a concern of assembly members, thus making them more dependent on the centralized leadership within the party and/or the chamber. I want to make three observations in this regard. First, there is a basic tension in the kind of Westminster model logic defended by authors like Rosenbluth and Shapiro (2018), which is that "the principle of local accountability and national accountability are logically mutually exclusive" (McGann 2006: 148; see also Cox 1987; Shugart and Carey 1992). National accountability based on a party platform requires party discipline and thus must weaken accountability to the constituents of single-seat districts. Moreover, given that the candidate/party vote is fused in single-seat districts, voters cannot sanction the local candidate and the party separately (Rudolph and Däubler 2016). The point of a single, jurisdiction-wide district would be to strengthen the programmatic accountability of the government—just as it does under presidentialism.[2]

Second, proportional representation might, to some extent, be seen as an alternative counterweight to the centralized power of party elites. This power is of particular concern when a single government party dominates the entire assembly. Within the logic of the Westminster model, therefore, single-seat districts may be a potential safeguard against excessively centralized power. In a semi-parliamentary system, by contrast, this safeguard can take the form of multiple parties that are liberated from the task of keeping the cabinet in office. A potential advantage of this solution is that the institutional safeguard against centralized party power avoids the inherent tension of the Westminster model. If this tension is resolved in favor of the party elite, the safeguard becomes ineffective; if it is resolved in favor of individual assembly members, the programmatic discipline of parties suffers. Semi-parliamentarism may provide a safeguard against too much centralized power that is fully compatible with the ideal of programmatically principled parties.

[1] Some may argue that there would still be better options, such as Coombs rule or the Borda count (Grofman and Feld 2004). While I do not want to enter this debate, it is worth highlighting three attractive properties of AV: (a) a party with an absolute majority of first-preference votes will always be selected as the winner; (b) voters can submit incomplete preference rankings without being discriminated against (Emerson 2013); and (c) a manipulation of the outcome via strategic voting would require very sophisticated voters (Grofman and Feld 2004: 652).

[2] As discussed in Chapter 5, using absolute majority rule in a single at-large district allows many parties or candidates to participate. It therefore increases voters' cognitive burden and reduces identifiability.

Finally, if additional counterweights are considered necessary, they might be better placed in the separated part of the assembly, where they are less constrained by the logic of parliamentarism and may be combined with proportional representation. Examples include moderate district magnitudes combined with upper-tier compensation (as, for instance, in Denmark) or open party lists.

In sum, the goals of both visions of democratic majority formation—simple and complex majoritarianism—might be achieved to a greater extent if first-chamber elections are clearly designed as a vote for a government in a single at-large district, while the vote for the second chamber is a vote for a programmatic party (and perhaps also specific candidates of this party).

Semi-parliamentarism within a single chamber

Once we accept the rationale for making the second chamber the larger chamber, it is not clear why we need two entirely separate chambers in the first place. If most or all of the actual deliberation about and scrutiny of legislative proposals ought to happen in the—at least equally legitimate—second chamber, the bicameral structure seems inefficient. We might potentially improve upon it by systematically differentiating the right to a no-confidence vote within a single chamber.

Perhaps the simplest way to do so, already discussed in Chapters 3 and 4, would be a *legal threshold of confidence authority*. Parties with a vote share below the threshold would be denied participation in the vote-of-no-confidence procedure. Only the parties that pass the threshold would become members of the confidence committee. Such a threshold might be useful even if it does not reduce the number of parties with confidence authority to only two. When party fragmentation in parliament is very high, as, for example, in the Netherlands, a moderate legal threshold of confidence authority might facilitate cabinet formation and governance without requiring a higher threshold of parliamentary *representation*.

Any legal threshold is arbitrary, however. If it affects one side of the political spectrum more than the other, the legitimacy of the election results may become questionable. For example, after the 2013 federal elections in Germany, Social Democrats, Greens, and the Left Party held a majority of seats (50.7%), despite their combined vote share only being 42.7%. The main reason was that two parties on the right—the Liberals and the Alternative for Germany—had vote shares just below the legal threshold of 5%. Had it been possible to form a center-left government, its electorally "manufactured" nature could have undermined its legitimacy.

A more systematic way to differentiate confidence authority could build on the logic of mixed-member proportional (MMP) electoral systems in countries such as Germany or New Zealand. That is, participation in the confidence committee could be limited to those assembly members elected under plurality rule in single-seat districts, whereas those elected from party lists would be denied this right. As discussed above, however, this would leave it to the voters to decide whether they interpret the constituency vote as one for the government—which it would essentially become—or one for a constituency representative. Moreover, since single-seat districts are used, it is far from guaranteed that the individual district contests would aggregate to a two-party system with a clear one-party majority in the confidence committee. And even if it did, the determination of the government party could hardly be considered fair.

For these reasons we might prefer a mixed-member system, in which the members of the confidence committee are elected in one at-large district. This approach could also be applied to the potential democratization of the European Union, for example. There has long been a discussion about transnational lists for European elections (Leinen 2015). The basic idea is to elect a fixed number of members of the European Parliament (MEPs)—say 20 or 30%—in a single pan-European district. Voters would have two votes, one of which is truly Europeanized. This idea of transnational lists could be combined with semi-parliamentarism by giving only the Europeanized members of the European Parliament the right to participate in a no-confidence vote against the European Commission. The elections to this pan-European confidence committee or chamber could be based on absolute majority rule (e.g. a run-off system), thus giving all voters a clear choice between competing programmatic mandates. The election of the rest of the European Parliament could be based on proportional representation in national or local constituencies.

Semi-parliamentarism with a single vote

It would, of course, also be possible to elect both parts of the assembly in a single at-large district. If this option were chosen, semi-parliamentary government would not necessarily require voters to cast two separate votes. They could simply be asked about their ranking of parties for two different purposes:

(a) forming the government; and (b) representation in parliament. These different purposes can be taken into account by allowing voters to rank parties on the ballot or by deciding on the governing party in a run-off election. These options may have a number of potential advantages, such as reducing partisan fragmentation and allowing for pre-electoral alliances.

In the run-off variant of such a single-vote system, voters vote for their preferred party and thereby determine the proportional composition of parliament. The two parties with the highest vote shares then enter a run-off election to determine their relative vote shares in the confidence committee. In the AV variant, voters can rank party lists according to their preferences. Their first preferences determine the proportional composition of parliament (with or without a legal threshold of representation), whereas their rankings determine the two parties with the greatest overall support. Only these two top parties receive seats in the confidence committee in proportion to their final vote shares in the AV contest.

One might wonder why the runner-up should be represented in the confidence committee at all. The main answer is that without this representation, the power of the executive would probably be strengthened. With opposition party representation in the confidence committee, the defection of a few members of the majority party might be sufficient for a successful no-confidence vote. By contrast, if a majority within the majority party were needed, the threat of a no-confidence vote would be less credible. It would be easier for the prime minister and cabinet to secure their power—especially if a substantial share of the members of the confidence committee are ministers themselves.[3] Another rationale for representing the runner-up in the confidence committee is that this party can be recognized as the main opposition party, as determined by the voters' preference rankings.

Determining the size of the confidence committee endogenously

The size of the confidence committee could be fixed in advance, but it might also be determined by the election itself. One option would be to give one of

[3] As noted in Chapter 3, it is not necessary that the cabinet is drawn only from the part of the assembly with confidence authority (here, the confidence committee). A substantial share of second-chamber ministers is common in Australia, partly because a ministerial presence in the second chamber facilitates the successful conduct of the government's parliamentary business and legislative program.

Table 8.1 A single-vote, mixed-member, semi-parliamentary system

Party	Seats based on first-preference votes	Final top party vote share	Confidence seats	Legislative top-up seats
A	27	43%	17	10
B	23	57%	23	
C	18			18
D	12			12
E	10			10
F	5			5
G	3			3
H	2			2
Total	100	100%	40	60

Source: Ganghof (2016a).

the two parties in the committee all of the seats it receives, based on the proportional count, as "confidence seats," while all other parties get additional top-up seats to make the overall composition of parliament proportional. Table 8.1 illustrates the procedure with a fictitious example of a 100-member legislature. The first column shows eight parties A–H, the second column their proportionally allocated seats. We assume that after the elimination of all but the top two parties, the winning party B has gained 57% of the votes, the runner-up A 43%. Given its proportional vote share of first preferences, B gets 23 seats overall, all of which are confidence seats. A's confidence seats are determined based on its two-party vote share, so that it gets 17 seats (43/57 × 23 = 17.4). The confidence chamber thus comprises 40 members. In order to maintain proportionality in the legislature, parties receive top-up seats. For parties outside of the confidence committee (C–H), all seats are "top-up" seats. Party A, the official opposition party in the confidence committee, receives both confidence and top-up seats.[4]

The system would allow voters to confer two mandates: one for a party that represents them in the legislative and deliberative process and one for the party

[4] While, in this specific example, the government party B determines the size of the confidence committee, this is not necessarily the case. If the goal is to have one party without any top-up seats, the size of the confidence committee must be fixed by the party with the smaller ratio between its total seats and its vote share in the AV contest. In the table, the ratio is 0.4 for B (23/57) and 0.63 for A (27/43). Imagine that A wins the AV contest against B by 60 to 40 and the two parties get 30 and 18 seats, respectively, in the proportional count. The ratio would then be larger for the winning party A (30/60 or 0.5 versus 18/40 or 0.45). If A's seats fixed the size of the confidence committee in this case, B's number of confidence seats would be 20, which is greater than B's total seats. This is why B should get all of its 18 seats as confidence seats and A should get 27 confidence seats plus three top-up seats.

that is put in charge of forming a government—the "formateur" in political science jargon. Ideally, the formateur's policy position would be identical or close to that of the median party in the assembly on the most important issue dimensions. Absolute majority rule does not guarantee a centrist outcome, but it may make it more likely than plurality rule (first past the post), at least under some range of background conditions (Grofman and Feld 2004; McGann et al. 2002). A moderately non-centrist outcome might also be desirable because it gives voters a meaningful choice between programmatic alternatives. However, it might also increase the likelihood of inter-branch conflict, to be discussed below.

The single-vote version of semi-parliamentarism sketched in Table 8.1 may also help to contain the partisan fragmentation of the assembly because voters cannot engage in ticket-splitting. As Israel's experience with the direct election of the prime minister has shown, ticket-splitting can increase partisan fragmentation, as voters' separate vote for the government may prompt them to choose a different, smaller party in the assembly elections (Chapter 2). Under the AV or run-off systems described, ticket splitting is not possible. While voters can certainly rank a number of smaller parties highly, they must also worry that their preferred party of government is eliminated early in the process.

Allowing for pre-electoral coalitions

Finally, when the size of the confidence committee is determined by the election itself, parties may be allowed to form pre-electoral alliances for the purposes of the AV count. For example, a centrist party might worry that it will be eliminated early on, even though it would profit from vote transfers in later counting rounds. Parties might thus be allowed to form a joint list with other parties in order to increase their chances to gain representation in the confidence committee. This also implies that if most parties group into two competing pre-electoral alliances, the size of the confidence committee increases. Table 8.2 illustrates this by modifying the example of Table 8.1. We now assume that parties group into two competing pre-electoral coalitions: AEF and BCD. Only G and H compete independently. Assuming the same voter preferences as before, the size of the confidence committee now increases from 40 to 93 seats and the two pre-electoral blocs get all, or most, of their overall seats as confidence seats.

This scenario differs in important ways from the situation in presidential systems. While parties and presidential candidates often build pre-electoral

Table 8.2 A single-vote, mixed-member, semi-parliamentary system with alliances

Lists	Seats based on first-preference votes	Final top list vote share	Confidence seats	Legislative top-up seats
AEF	42	43%	40	2
BCD	53	57%	53	
G	3			3
H	2			2
Total	100	100%	93	7

Source: Adapted from Table 8.1.

alliances that carry over into post-electoral coalition cabinets, the allies of the elected president have relatively little control over the terms of the post-electoral cooperation (e.g. Borges et al. 2020; Freudenreich 2016; Kellam 2017). By contrast, alliance formation under the version of semi-parliamentarism sketched in Table 8.2 would give the prime minister's pre-electoral allies representation in the confidence committee and thus a powerful position after the election.

Designing inter-branch relations

In a separation-of-powers system, the design of inter-branch relations becomes crucial. There has been much debate about how best to design these relations under presidentialism (e.g. Cheibub 2007; Colomer and Negretto 2005; Shugart and Carey 1992). I cannot provide a systematic review of this debate here but pursue two more modest goals. First, I sketch how the tension between simple and complex majoritarianism described in Chapters 5 and 6 resurfaces in the design of inter-branch relations. Second, I explore the potential advantages that semi-parliamentary government may have over presidentialism and other forms of bicameralism with respect to institutional fine-tuning. Strengthening the agenda and dissolution *powers* of the government or the first chamber may be less dangerous than under presidentialism because this power is not given to a single human being. At the same time, the equal or higher democratic legitimacy of the second chamber makes it possible to avoid legislative deadlock by weakening the veto power of the first chamber.

As shown in Chapter 6, semi-parliamentary democracies can achieve the goals of simple majoritarianism, especially identifiability and cabinet stability, in the first chamber and the goals of complex majoritarianism in the second chamber. However, the tension between the two visions resurfaces when we think about the relative constitutional power of the two parts of the assembly. When we strengthen the chamber or committee of confidence, we strengthen the goals of simple majoritarianism, including clarity of responsibility; when we strengthen the second chamber or the assembly at large, we strengthen complex majoritarianism.

Finding the right balance of formal powers is not easy because these powers must be fixed in the constitution, whereas political constellations vary. It matters where parties' preferences are located relative to one another and to the status quo but also whether actors behave "responsibly" or "obstructively." For example, when the cabinet party is the median party on most dimensions, we might want it (or its first-chamber majority) to have certain institutional prerogatives in the legislative process. These prerogatives would not necessarily be used *against* the second chamber but could be seen as "mechanisms that help the majority to organize itself" (Cheibub and Limongi 2010: 46) by solving collective action problems, facilitating party discipline, counteracting obstructive behavior, or limiting the power of anti-system parties (see also Huber 1996; Koß 2019). Once the formal prerogatives are in place, however, an executive with non-centrist preferences can also use them as weapons against a second-chamber majority (see, e.g. Weale 2018: 239). The resulting dilemmas are well known from the literature on presidentialism (e.g. Alemán and Tsebelis 2016; Chaisty et al. 2018; Cheibub 2007; Cheibub and Limongi 2010; Colomer and Negretto 2005; Shugart and Carey 1992). Constitutional design becomes a balancing act, in which we must gauge the relative risks of different scenarios.

I cannot pretend to know what the optimal design of inter-branch relations looks like, but I want to emphasize once more the differences between presidentialism and semi-parliamentarism in this regard. Any perils of constitutionally powerful executives are likely compounded by executive personalism. Under semi-parliamentarism, by contrast, the prerogatives of the executive or the first chamber must ultimately be exercised in line with the preferences of the first-chamber majority. The extent to which the government accommodates the policy preferences of the second chamber is ultimately decided by the majority *party* in the first chamber and is less dependent on the idiosyncrasies of the chief executive. There is an additional layer of protection against chief executives that act on the basis of extreme preferences or fail to accommodate a constructive second-chamber majority. This point also matters in the resolution of legislative deadlock, to which we now turn.

Resolving conflict: assembly dissolution

Early elections are a common way to resolve legislative deadlock under pure parliamentarism. Importantly, this resolution is not predicated on the assembly actually being dissolved. It may be sufficient for the prime minister or the government to make a dissolution *threat* (Becher and Christiansen 2015). When public support for the prime minister and her policies are relatively high, coalition parties—or opposition parties in the case of minority governments—may make concessions in order to avoid an election. Denmark is an example of a country in which the prime minister enjoys wide discretion in calling early elections (Goplerud and Schleiter 2016) and there is clear evidence that Danish prime ministers use this prerogative to increase their bargaining power and avoid legislative deadlock (Becher and Christiansen 2015; Green-Pedersen et al. 2018).

It has long been noted that assembly dissolution could be used to resolve deadlock under presidentialism, too, especially when it also implied an early election of the president. While such a "double dissolution" election represents a deviation from ideal-typical presidentialism, which is defined by its fixed terms, the principle of the separation of powers is still retained in the sense that one branch cannot dismiss the other without standing for re-election itself (Mainwaring and Shugart 1997: 453). Yet, the problem under presidentialism is that any institutional prerogative given to the chief executive becomes the power of a single human being, which can have negative consequences.

Ecuador's 2008 constitution might serve as a case in point. Its so-called *muerte cruzada* ("mutual death") provision (Art. 148) allows presidents—once in the first three years of their term—to dissolve the assembly, force new legislative and presidential elections, and rule by decree on urgent economic matters in the interim. While this provision has been conceived as "quasi-parliamentary" and a way to "align the incentive structure of the Executive and the Legislative branches of government," Ecuador's president Rafael Correa "found a way to parlay his popularity into the threatened misapplication of the muerte cruzada provision with the aim to quell dissent" (Sanchez-Sibony 2018: 105). When the ruling party caucus engaged in actions that defied or contravened the wishes of the president, he threatened to issue the *muerte cruzada* coupled with harsh admonitions directed at nonconforming ruling party lawmakers. Hence, the provision has probably strengthened the presidentialization of the governing party in Ecuador (Samuels and Shugart 2010). The literature on authoritarian forms of presidential supremacy also highlights the dangers of dissolution power under presidentialism (Stykow 2019).

Under semi-parliamentarism, by contrast, any formal prerogatives of the prime minister are not personalized, which reduces their risks. Moreover, the right to initiate a double dissolution may be placed in the hands of the chamber or committee of confidence, rather than the chief executive. As suggested in Chapter 7, the possibility of a double dissolution may contribute to the willingness of the majority party in the first chamber to govern as a minority cabinet in the second chamber.

Resolving conflict: referendums

Assembly dissolution may be seen as too blunt an instrument for resolving deadlock. If legislative stalemate is restricted to a particular issue, a more limited way to resolve it would be to refer only this issue back to the voters and allow them to decide the issue in a deadlock-resolving referendum. Since both branches claim to represent "the" majority, it seems straightforward to let the voters decide which of these claims is (more) correct. As in the case of assembly dissolution, however, giving the power of initiating a deadlock referendum to the president may strengthen the personalization of power in a presidential system. This is true especially when the president controls the agenda in the referendum process (Durán-Martínez 2012; see also Tsebelis 2002: Chapter 5). Under semi-parliamentarism, by contrast, the dangers of executive personalism are avoided, as the party of the chief executive and the majority in the first chamber remain in charge.

A popular referendum to resolve legislative deadlock is provided for under section 5B of the New South Wales Constitution Act (Twomey 2004: 254–267). The full process involves a "free conference" between "managers" of the two chambers, a joint sitting with a debate but no vote, and finally the first chamber initiating a popular referendum on the disputed bill in the version it prefers. The first chamber is thus the sole agenda setter in the referendum. If a majority of voters support the bill, it can be presented to the Governor and become law. While it is true that the process in New South Wales is "long and arduous" and that few governments have even contemplated it (e.g. Smith 2018a: 259), it could be streamlined. Moreover, we must not forget that—as in the case of assembly dissolution—a popular referendum does not necessarily have to be initiated to have an effect. The *threat* of a referendum, or even the common knowledge that the path is available to the government and its first-chamber majority, might be sufficient to influence bargaining and make opposition parties in the second chamber more accommodating.

It is also not clear that the first chamber must necessarily be the agenda-setter in the referendum process. The power to control the referendum agenda cancels the second chamber as a veto player (see also Tsebelis 2002: 130). This is justifiable when the second chamber is democratically inferior. As we noted in Chapter 3, the second chamber in New South Wales can be seen as democratically inferior because its members serve longer terms (eight vs four years). The government's legislative program could thus be blocked by second-chamber members elected several years earlier. When the two chambers have equal terms and legitimacy, as they do in Victoria, other design solutions become possible. One is to let voters decide on competing proposals; another is to let the second chamber control the referendum agenda and thus cancel the veto power of the first chamber. To discuss the latter option, we need to consider the veto power of the first chamber in more general terms.

Does the chamber of confidence require veto power?

So far, I have focused on how the absence of executive personalism may allow semi-parliamentary systems to avoid deadlock in ways that would be more risky under presidentialism. Now I turn to the comparison of semi-parliamentarism and other forms of bicameralism. The literature on bicameralism generally presumes the veto power of the first chamber and asks whether and to what extent the veto power of the second chamber is compromised (see Chapter 3). This perspective is warranted in most cases because second chambers are democratically inferior to first chambers: they are not (fully) directly elected, more malapportioned, and/or have longer terms. Even in the minimally semi-parliamentary systems, the democratic legitimacy of the second chamber is usually compromised (see Chapter 3). The only exception is the post-2003 Legislative Council of Victoria, but this has not kept the Labor government from curbing its veto powers (Chapter 7).

Once we fully accept the logic of a semi-parliamentary system, though, it is not obvious that it is the second chamber whose veto power on ordinary legislation should be compromised. It is, after all, the chamber of legislation, deliberation, and control. By contrast, the chamber (or committee) of confidence can be compensated for weakened veto power by its power over the survival of the government, as well as its (formal or informal) role as the agenda-setter in the ordinary legislative process. Hence, if absolute veto power must be denied to one of the two parts of the assembly, it might well be the chamber or committee of confidence. An obvious example would be to allow a two-thirds majority in the second chamber (or the assembly at large) to override a veto of the first chamber (or the confidence committee), but also a veto override by a simple or absolute majority is conceivable. This would be comparable to presidential systems like those in Peru or Nicaragua, where the president's veto can be overridden by the majority of a unicameral assembly (Alemán 2020: 138). Regardless of the requirements for a veto override, the veto of the first chamber could also be combined with agenda-setting power, as is frequently the case for the veto power of presidents (Tsebelis and Alemán 2005).

A semi-parliamentary system in which the chamber or committee of confidence lacks absolute veto power can be seen as a solution to the problems of minority governments under pure parliamentarism outlined in Chapter 5. Following Tsebelis (2002), I argued that minority governments might be most attractive when a single party in the center of the policy space can build issue-specific legislative coalitions in a multidimensional and multiparty parliament, but that *single-party* minority cabinets are unlikely to form and difficult to legitimize under these conditions. A semi-parliamentary system provides a solution because it allows voters to directly authorize a single cabinet party in one part of the assembly that can govern as a (stable) minority government in the other part. From this perspective, the first chamber's lack of veto power would reflect the nature of the second chamber as the—proportionally constituted—chamber of deliberation, legislation, and control. The first chamber would not be an institutional veto player but a venue through which voters select the government party as the executive and legislative agenda-setter. The resulting institutional design would balance simple and complex majoritarianism by giving agenda and dissolution powers to the government and/or the first chamber but absolute veto power only to the second chamber.

A proper understanding of semi-parliamentarism should thus also lead us to question the widespread view that (strong) bicameralism is necessarily "a method for protecting the status quo" and that there is no "nonconservative defense of bicameralism" (Przeworski 2010: 142; see also McGann 2006: 184; Tsebelis and Money 1997: 217). I have already argued in Chapter 6 that the situation under Australian-style semi-parliamentarism is not so different to that of single-party minority cabinets in parliamentary systems (Tsebelis 2002: 97–99). The majority coalitions in the second chamber will usually include the government, so that the *first chamber* will often be "absorbed" by the second chamber, rather than the other way around.[5] This point is reinforced when the first chamber lacks veto power and ceases to be an institutional veto player. In addition, the semi-parliamentary separation of powers may reduce the number of *partisan* veto players in comparison to pure parliamentarism because the placement of proportional representation in the second chamber, combined with this chamber's lack of confidence power, makes the formation of a fixed-majority coalition less likely (Chapter 7). In sum, then, the logic of semi-parliamentarism helps us to see a nonconservative defense of bicameralism.

To be sure, a chamber or committee of confidence without absolute veto power is merely an option under semi-parliamentarism, rather than a requirement. Moreover, the veto power that the two parts of the assembly have over ordinary legislation must cohere with their power over the budget. Hence, if the second chamber (or the assembly at large) is the only institutional veto player on ordinary legislation, it should probably also be able to veto the budget.[6] Rather than discussing these issues further, I want to explore possible behavioral consequences of denying the chamber or committee of confidence absolute veto power.

Veto power and cabinet formation

When the chamber or committee of confidence lacks veto power or certain types of agenda control, the government might have to accept at least some changes of the status quo that it rejects and that go against its own agenda (Damgaard and Svensson 1989; Tsebelis 2002: 98–99). A proponent of complex majoritarianism might welcome this acceptance from a normative perspective, in the hope that the government and its first-chamber majority are forced to implement the preferences of the issue-specific median in parliament and in the electorate (Ward and Weale 2010; Weale 2018). Yet, strategic political actors in the real world may not behave accordingly.

In particular, studies of presidential systems suggest that when presidents lack veto power, they are more likely to build majority coalitions in order to protect their agenda and prevent alternative majorities (Chaisty and Power 2019; Cheibub-Figueiredo et al. 2012; Negretto 2006). Something similar may

[5] On the "absorption" of veto players, see Tsebelis (2002).

[6] While this would raise the possibility that the budget veto can be used as a de facto no-confidence vote, we have seen in Chapter 3 that country experts disagree on how likely this is. Whether or not a government that cannot ensure supply must resign also depends on the details of constitutional design (Bach 2003: 304–305).

happen under semi-parliamentarism, so that the lack of first-chamber veto power might increase the likelihood of coalition cabinets and reduce legislative flexibility. This possibility is another example of how the tension between simple and complex majoritarianism resurfaces under the separation of powers. It should not be exaggerated, however, for several reasons.

First, we must be mindful of the differences between presidentialism and semi-parliamentarism. Under presidentialism, majority cabinets might also form because of executive personalism and the constitutional attempts to contain it. In particular, they might provide a "legislative shield" (Pérez-Liñán 2007) against politically motivated impeachments. This is not necessary under semi-parliamentarism. In addition, I argued above that, under semi-parliamentarism, it is less risky to give the government strong dissolution power, which tends to increase its bargaining power (Becher and Christiansen 2015). Coalition governments might thus be less likely to emerge under well-designed semi-parliamentarism than under presidentialism, even if the first chamber lacks absolute veto power.

Second, even if the first chamber's lack of veto power did lead to fixed veto player coalitions—in the form of majority or "formal" minority cabinets—this outcome might still be normatively preferable to that under pure parliamentarism on the grounds that the selection of the formateur is fairer. As noted in Chapter 4, the formateur is selected by the assembly under parliamentarism, which tends to favor the largest party and may thus create a bias against whichever side of the political spectrum is fragmented into a greater number of parties (Döring and Manow 2015). Under semi-parliamentarism, by contrast, voters can determine the formateur through the first chamber, based on absolute majority rule. This may be fairer, all things considered.

Third, we also have to be mindful of the differences between parliamentary and semi-parliamentary government. Even if the majority party in the first chamber builds a majority coalition in order to achieve a second-chamber majority, the additional coalition parties would not be veto players in a strict sense. They could always be excluded from the legislative coalition without any consequence for the survival of the government. This fact changes the underlying bargaining situation and may lead to distinct behavioral equilibria. While these are difficult to anticipate, the experiences of countries like Denmark or New Zealand may fuel our imagination.

Denmark shows us that even when veto player coalitions are built under parliamentarism, these may vary across policy areas. Danish governments use an informal institution called *forlig*, political accommodations, or legislative agreements (Christiansen and Klemmensen 2015). Between one-fifth and one-third of all laws result from such agreements. While all parliamentary parties in Denmark participate in agreements, the legislative coalition differs from one agreement to the next. An agreement grants all participating parties a veto right over the legislation covered in it. The government is willing to extend veto rights to opposition parties because it is able to prevent alternative majorities in return (Klemmensen 2010: 226). Legislative agreements also allow for logrolling across different issues; for example, economic and immigration policies (Christiansen and Klemmensen 2015: 37). Some agreements can last a long time, enduring beyond general elections and potential shifts in government. In sum, Danish minority cabinets are able to maintain some degree of legislative flexibility while also reducing uncertainty and preventing alternative majorities.

Minority governments in New Zealand have also created a number of innovative solutions to coalition management in complex assemblies (Boston and Bullock 2010). First, even where formal coalition governments were built, coalition discipline was loosened somewhat by way of agree-to-disagree provisions. Second, enhanced cooperation agreements were made, with the parties agreeing to collaborate on issues of shared interest in return for the opposition party's pledge not to oppose the government on confidence and supply. "Enhanced" meant that they could nominate spokespersons to speak *for the government* in specified policy areas. Such spokespersons enjoyed direct access to departmental officials, were able to request reports, and could attend cabinet committees dealing with policy issues in their designated areas. Finally, minority cabinets also negotiated "enhanced" confidence and supply agreements that allowed support parties to receive ministerial positions, albeit *outside cabinet*. These ministers no longer required the cabinet's consent to oppose government policy, except on matters directly affecting their portfolios or issues identified as matters of confidence. They were able to speak freely as assembly members or leaders of their party on any matter outside their portfolio areas. The agree-to-disagree provision could also apply to policies affecting their portfolios. Interestingly, this last innovation was continued even after the Labour Party won a parliamentary majority in October 2020. The party negotiated a "cooperation agreement" with the Greens, offering two ministries outside cabinet plus some shared policy priorities for the legislative term.

These examples suggest that when, in a semi-parliamentary system, the chamber or committee of confidence lacks veto power, the majority party does not necessarily have to build a rigid veto-player coalition in the second chamber. It can, rather, use its institutional advantage of not needing confidence (and possibly supply) from the second chamber to build more flexible arrangements, along the lines of Danish legislative agreements. In addition, it might negotiate enhanced cooperation agreements with some parties; for example, those that occupy the median position in the second chamber on specific issue dimensions. These parties might also receive ministerial positions but without becoming fully fledged veto players.

In sum, denying the chamber or committee of confidence veto power in a semi-parliamentary system may well be a workable solution, especially when this denial is compensated with some degree of agenda and/or dissolution power.

Conclusion

This chapter considered some of the constitutional fine print in potential semi-parliamentary systems. The discussion was necessarily explorative, selective, and preliminary. My goal was not to suggest an optimal semi-parliamentary democracy but to highlight the potential of the semi-parliamentary constitution. I emphasized how this constitution could be flexibly adapted to different contexts, how its design could be improved as an alternative to the presidential separation of powers, how the tensions between different visions of democracy might resurface in inter-branch relations, and how semi-parliamentarism could deal with the problem of legislative deadlock in ways that would be more problematic under presidentialism or other forms of bicameralism. Much more empirical and theoretical work remains to be done to understand the interactive effects of institutional rules under different forms of government.

9
Against presidentialism

Arguing against presidential government may seem trite. Much of the debate in political science since Juan Linz's (1990a, 1994) famous critique has been about the "perils of presidentialism"—and, for many observers, the Trump Administration made these perils as apparent in the United States as they had already been in the rest of the world. At the same time, however, the debate about presidentialism has become increasingly sterile, and this book has offered an explanation for why this is the case. Neither Linz nor his critics have systematically distinguished between presidentialism's two central features: the branch-based separation of powers, on the one hand, and executive personalism, on the other.

This distinction is crucial because political scientists' verdict on their merits has been quite different. As to the perils of powers separation, many authors have qualified and pushed back against Linz's claims. They have convincingly argued that he exaggerated the dangers of legislative deadlock and dual legitimacy, partly due to an overly stylized understanding of parliamentary systems (Cheibub et al. 2004; Cheibub 2007; Cheibub and Limongi 2010), and they have highlighted the advantages of powers separation (e.g. Cheibub 2006; Mainwaring and Shugart 1997; Shugart and Carey 1992). As to executive personalism, by contrast, we will see that empirical studies have corroborated many Linzian concerns.

I have shown in the previous chapters that powers separation and executive personalism can be disentangled in practice, and that semi-parliamentary government is a proven way to do so. This final chapter therefore ends with a critique of presidentialism that is entirely focused on executive personalism, while accepting the potential benefits of the branch-based separation of powers. This critique will allow us to synthesize much of what we have learned about semi-parliamentary government in this book—and what the existing literature has learned about the perils of executive personalism.

I start by briefly recapping the similarities and differences between presidentialism and semi-parliamentarism and then go through all major justifications

Beyond Presidentialism and Parliamentarism. Steffen Ganghof, Oxford University Press.
 DOI: 10.1093/oso/9780192897145.003.0009

of presidentialism I could find in the literature. These justifications are based on antipartyism, elite and voter psychology, effects of constituency size, the perceived democratic legitimacy of direct election or recall, cabinet stability and legislative flexibility, identifiability and mandate representation, electoral accountability, democratic stability, and simplicity. My general argument will be that the potential advantages of presidentialism highlighted in these justifications are those of the separation of powers, while executive personalism often threatens to undermine these very advantages. While democrats may have good reasons for powers separation, they have no principled reason to choose or maintain presidential government.

Presidentialism versus semi-parliamentarism

To summarize the similarity and difference between the two forms of government, it is useful to review the stylized depictions introduced in Chapter 2. There, I emphasized how semi-parliamentarism mirrors semi-presidentialism; here, the focus is on how it compares to pure presidentialism. Figure 9.1 shows that both systems separate powers by allowing voters to directly elect two separated branches. They differ in that presidentialism concentrates executive power in a single person, the president, whereas semi-parliamentarism fuses executive power with one part of the assembly. This part—the chamber or committee of confidence—selects the prime minister and cabinet and can dismiss them in a vote of no confidence for purely political reasons.

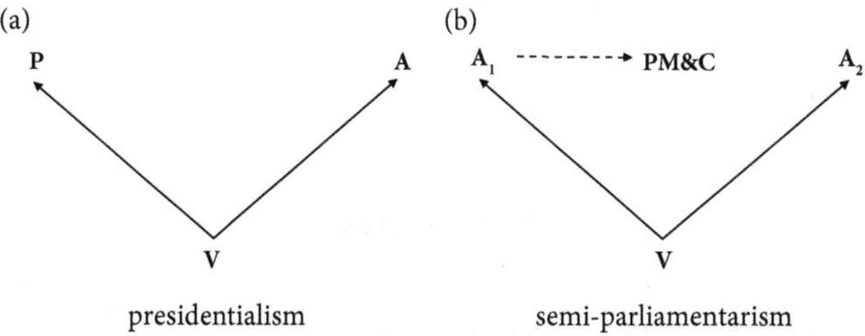

Fig. 9.1 Presidential and semi-parliamentary government: Fig. 9.1(a) presidential; Fig. 9.1(b) semi-parliamentary

Notes: V =voters, P = President, A = assembly, PM = Prime Minister, C = Cabinet, → = election, ⇢ = dismissal.

Figure 9.1 thus illustrates my core argument. Because both systems achieve a branch-based separation of powers, semi-parliamentarism can realize all of its potential benefits just as well as presidentialism. Chapter 6 has shown that the extent to which it does so depends on the design of the electoral systems of the two parts of the assembly. Moreover, Chapter 8 has shown how the election of the chamber or committee of confidence in a single jurisdiction-wide district could mimic direct presidential elections. That semi-parliamentarism avoids executive personalism is not only an advantage in its own right, but it also reinforces the potential benefits of the separation of powers. Under presidentialism, by contrast, many of these benefits tend to be undermined by executive personalism or by the constitutional efforts to contain its negative effects.

Antipartyism

The most direct way to justify executive personalism would be some form of "antipartyism" (Muirhead and Rosenblum 2020: 99). Rosenblum (2008) distinguishes two historically recurrent forms. One rejects political pluralism and thus sees political parties as disrupting some presumptive natural or aspirational unity, or holism. The other accepts some expressions of pluralism, such as a mixed constitution, but sees political parties as dangerously divisive.

While antipartyism has been historically important in defending presidentialism and semi-presidentialism (e.g. Muirhead and Rosenblum 2015: 222–225; Samuels and Shugart 2010: 39–40; Weber 1986), it is difficult to find an explicit and systematic articulation of this defense in the current academic literature. Elements of it arguably exist (e.g. Calabresi 2001; Lacerda 2020), but they remain implicit and are combined with other arguments, most notably those about human psychology, constituency effects, and democratic legitimacy.

Psychology

Executive personalism is sometimes justified in terms of the psychology of presidents and voters, but these arguments tend to be ad hoc and reflective of presidentialism's monarchical origins. This is most obvious for arguments about "charisma." Scheuerman (2005) interprets widespread public and academic concerns with executive charisma as an attempt to explain and justify the powers of the modern presidency. Since presidential executives were outfitted with some of the strong powers of European kingship, the focus on presidents' charisma is essentially an attempt to find a secularized version of the religiously grounded supernatural qualities once attributed to their royal predecessors. As Max Weber suggested, "the presidential version of liberal democracy appears adept at generating a necessary dose of executive charisma in an otherwise disenchanted universe" (Scheuerman 2005: 25).[1]

In this very vein, Calabresi (2001: 70), for example, claims that parliamentary systems tend to select leaders with less charisma than their presidential counterparts. He takes this to be "bad and dangerous" because, while compromise and logrolling are necessary, "it may be desirable for a democracy to showcase leaders who have a little more popular appeal." Charismatic leaders "fulfill the public's longing for that type of leadership, thus foreclosing the emergence of fascistic or communistic leaders who can campaign as charismatic alternatives to compromising democratic politicians."

Another psychological claim about presidents is that they care, to their very core, about their legacies. "They play to the ages. And because of this they are predisposed to seek coherent, durable policy solutions that will succeed in addressing the nation's key problems and enhancing social welfare" (Howell and Moe 2020: 161–162).

These types of psychological claims cannot justify executive personalism for two reasons. First, they are not systematically developed on the basis of psychological theory or empirical evidence. It is unclear to what extent the supposed psychological mechanisms exist, what their variability is, and how their putative benefits are to be weighed against their potential downsides (see also dos Santos 2020: 21–24; Serra 2018).

Second, we have to be careful about the actual comparisons being made. Howell and Moe (2016, 2020) use their claims about presidents' psychology merely to justify greater legislative powers for the presidency within the existing political system of the United States; they do not systematically compare different forms of government. Similarly, closer inspection shows that Calabresi's (2001: 70) argument is actually one about the party system, as he also claims that parliamentary systems with two or few parties can create charismatic leaders. Hence, even if his claims about charisma were supported by evidence, they would also apply to well-designed semi-parliamentarism with only two parties in the chamber or committee of confidence.

[1] On Weber's views, see Mommsen (1984), Weber (1986) and Baehr (1989).

Constituency size

One way to provide a systematic foundation for the psychological claims is to highlight the incentive effects of the size of constituencies. A common argument is that legislators are often elected in territorially bounded districts, whereas presidents usually have a national constituency. Hence, "they are held accountable by that constituency for embodying national values and national identities, pursuing the public interest, and addressing national problems" (Howell and Moe 2020: 161; see also Calabresi 2001: 71–72) .

This argument has the advantage of being partly grounded in systematic comparative research. In particular, Shugart's (1999) analysis of 21 countries measures how well different constitutional and electoral designs align the incentives of legislators with those of the president. He finds that the more divergent the constituencies are between the presidency and the assembly, the more constitutional (agenda, veto, and decree) powers the presidency tends to have. The suggested explanation for this finding is that presidents are granted constitutional powers to produce national collective goods and to compensate the constitutionally created propensity for deadlock and particularism. Howell and Moe's (2016, 2020) plea for giving the US presidency more proactive legislative powers is consistent with this explanation.

However, Shugart (1999) neither defends executive personalism nor claims that presidentialism is a good system; only that it might be the most feasible system under difficult societal conditions (i.e. in large, heterogeneous, and unequal societies). Moreover, his actual explanation merely highlights the desirability of a separate branch of government elected in a single constituency and manufacturing a single, jurisdiction-wide winner. It recognizes some of the same trade-offs we analyzed in Chapter 5: "parliamentary institutions would result in either highly unstable cabinets, due to multiple parties representing different occupational groups or regions, or else would shut out important societal interests, due to the manufacturing of majorities for one (minority) party" (Shugart 1999: 84). Shugart's point is that the separation of powers can mitigate these trade-offs, but we have seen in Chapter 6 that semi-parliamentarism can do the same. His explanation can help to justify the separation of powers, but not its presidential variant.

Another version of the constituency argument has played a role in the debate about democratizing the European Union (EU). A widely shared position is that a more democratic EU presupposes a demos based on a collective identity, a common public sphere, and an established political infrastructure. There is also broad agreement that a pan-European demos does not exist, but there is disagreement about whether and how it can be constructed. Proponents of EU-presidentialism, such as Sonnicksen (2017: 521), see it as a potential instrument of demos construction: "As a singular position elected by the European people, and not de-facto by Member State parties and national citizenries decoupled from one another, it would … incentivise precisely the kind of cross-national political organisation and mobilisation necessary for demos building."

Yet this, too, is merely an argument for the separation of powers and for electing one separated branch in a single pan-European district. It gives no reason for why the fully Europeanized part of the system ought to be a single human being, rather than a programmatic party. Indeed, if demos-building is the goal, it seems plausible that genuinely transnational parties have a greater capacity to credibly challenge "the national institutions and identities that play a significant role in preventing the emergence of a supranational demos in contemporary Europe" (Wolkenstein 2018: 297). Since semi-parliamentarism is more conducive to the development and flourishing of principled and programmatic political parties (Samuels and Shugart 2010), it may be a better structure for the creation of a European demos.

The legitimacy of direct election

Another way to justify executive personalism is to claim that the direct election of a fixed-term chief executive increases democratic legitimacy. As always, we have to be careful with the term "legitimacy." It can be understood normatively as a moral right to rule or empirically as the actual support by citizens. Chapter 4 has taken the normative perspective and shown that the direct election of the chief executive does not render presidentialism morally superior. Yet we might still hypothesize that direct election is *perceived* as being more legitimate by citizens. If this hypothesis were true, it might support an instrumental argument for the superiority of direct executive elections.[2]

The hypothesis faces two problems, though. First, to my knowledge there is no empirical evidence to suggest that support for, or satisfaction with, democracy is higher in democracies with directly elected chief executives. Studies on parliamentary and semi-presidential systems reject this hypothesis (Tavits 2009). Second, proponents of the hypothesis typically fail to specify a causal mechanism that separates executive personalism from the separation

[2] However, public opinion might be largely endogenous to the views and debates of political elites.

of powers without implicitly reverting to the kind of antipartyism discussed above. Lacerda's defense of semi-presidentialism, which draws heavily on Max Weber, is a good example:

> [A] popularly elected presidency can be mobilized as a counterpoint of national unity in relation to congressional, federal, and bureaucratic interests when these powers may contain features perceived as corrosive to the legitimate exercise of political power.... The plebiscitary element of semi-presidentialism is associated with the search for a core of legitimacy, protected against centrifugal tendencies in the political system, and the corrosion in public opinion caused by the establishment and maintenance of governing coalitions of sectoral interests.
>
> (Lacerda 2020: 25–26)

This quote conflates at least two distinct claims. Its second part highlights the benefits of having an executive branch that is dominated by a single political force and separated from the need to build coalition governments. We have seen in Chapter 6 that this can also be achieved by semi-parliamentarism in a party-based manner. By contrast, the first part hints at the idea that only a single human being can create the desired kind of unity. It piggybacks on anti-pluralist and quasi-monarchical ideas that are not spelled out and for which no empirical evidence is presented.

The legitimacy of direct recall

A more genuinely democratic argument for executive personalism highlights the possibility of direct *recall*. Pérez-Liñán (2020) suggests that procedures for deselecting chief executives should mirror those of selecting them—a feature he calls "symmetry"—and that among the symmetrical procedures, those involving voters directly are to be preferred. Selection and deselection by an assembly majority as under parliamentarism and semi-parliamentarism are also symmetrical but supposedly "lack the legitimacy granted by direct popular participation" (Pérez-Liñán 2020: 201). This argument has the great merit of giving the oft-neglected possibility of direct recall center stage (see also Albert 2009: 560–561). Yet it cannot justify presidentialism.

First, Pérez-Liñán's (2020) discussion seems to draw on both the empirical and normative meanings of the term legitimacy. To the extent that a normative use is intended, my arguments in Chapter 4 apply: A presidential system with direct recall is preferable on purely procedural grounds to one without it; but it does not follow that it is also preferable to other forms of government. The adequate comparison would be with those parliamentary or semi-parliamentary systems in which the members of the assembly could be recalled, either individually or as a group. And since we have to weigh the vertical and horizontal aspects of procedural equality against one another, the possibility of directly electing and recalling the chief executive does not render a presidential system morally superior.

Second, when "legitimacy" is understood in terms of the empirical support of democracy, this justification can apply only to those presidential systems that actually provide feasible ways of directly recalling presidents. Yet, we know that direct recall "is not commonly associated with a pure presidential system" (Alemán 2020: 135) and that, at the time of writing, no recall election has ever removed a national executive from office (Pérez-Liñán 2020: 202). Partly as a result, there is no systematic evidence that the direct recall of chief executives increases democratic legitimacy (Welp and Whitehead 2020b). Welp and Whitehead (2020a: 24) find "much evidence of recall procedures that are relatively unlikely to contain short-term tensions or to defuse longer-run threats to the credibility of the representative system."

Third, Pérez-Liñán conjectures that parliamentary no-confidence votes tend to be perceived negatively by the voters: "their elitist nature can haunt their legitimacy" (Pérez-Liñán 2020: 207). This conjecture not only lacks systematic empirical support,[3] but it is also based on a questionable causal model. Understood in empirical terms, democratic legitimacy is not a property of specific procedures but of a polity as a whole. And to the extent that the procedures for ousting the chief executives play a causal role for a polity's overall legitimacy, this role is likely to depend first and foremost on their feasibility, effectiveness, and what I will call political neutrality. Once we focus on these criteria, the advantages of no-confidence votes come to the fore.

[3] As empirical support, Pérez-Liñán cites Piersig (2016: 9–10), who discusses the constructive no-confidence vote in Germany and claims that "the demos views the mid-term transition as an usurpation of its ability to select the government." As a general statement about the no-confidence vote, however, this claim is false. The case Piersig discusses is the vote of no confidence in 1982, in which the Christian Democrats convinced the Liberals to leave their coalition with the Social Democrats. The subsequent early dissolution of parliament, which was supported by all parliamentary parties, was indeed preferred by a large majority of voters. However, this majority was mainly upset about the role of the Liberals. At the time, Germany followed an "alliance-centered" model of majority formation (see Chapter 5). The Liberals had committed themselves to the social–liberal coalition, thus turning the election into one of Chancellor Helmut Schmidt. Their mid-term switch was therefore widely perceived as "treason" (Kaase 1983: 159). Under semi-parliamentarism, the important scenario is one in which the no-confidence vote is used by a single majority party to replace the chief executive with another party agent. This may also upset some voters, but there is no systematic evidence that this implies a general negative effect on democratic legitimacy relative to removals by direct recall.

Given the direct power that modern chief executives have over their citizens, their dismissal should be feasible and effective. Direct recall and impeachment do not score highly on these criteria (e.g. Ginsburg et al. 2020; Pérez-Liñán 2020). The most fundamental reason is arguably the same for both procedures: they often lack what we might call political neutrality. That is, they are extraordinary procedures that tend to inexorably connect the ousting of the chief executive to the more general power struggle between competing political forces in society. They are, in fact, not just procedures for replacing the chief executive but potentially allow the losers of the last election to change the electoral outcome or, at least, to hurt the winners politically. This lack of neutrality can give rise to deeply divisive and traumatic struggles between the political forces that support presidents and those that oppose them.

The lack of political neutrality also leads to dilemmas in the design of recall and impeachment procedures. If the ousting of chief executives is made too easy, it is likely to be abused for political purposes by their political opponents; but if it is made too difficult, it is unlikely to happen at all—especially since presidents and their allies have strong incentives to obstruct and delay the process.[4] It is not surprising, therefore, that some reform proposals even envision the delegation of impeachment power to an independent, and thus supposedly neutral, Impeachment Agency (Prakash 2020: 270).

A lack of effectiveness and political neutrality is likely to affect the overall legitimacy of a polity. Pérez-Liñán (2020: 224–225) suggests this with respect to impeachment procedures. Following Kada (2003), he notes that two problems may undercut their legitimacy. If partisan allies shield the executive from an investigation when there is sufficient evidence to pursue it, they create impunity; but if partisan opponents remove the executive under false accusations or illegitimate proceedings, they undermine the rights of presidents and their voters. Yet the same basic tension arguably exists for direct recall procedures: if their use is made too difficult or actively prevented by the electoral bodies, their would-be users are likely to feel cheated; if not, they are likely to be used as a political weapon by the losers of the last election (e.g. Welp 2016).

No-confidence votes, by contrast, can be politically neutral in the sense that they need not affect the political balance of power established in the last election. The prime minister "can be changed without necessarily creating a regime crisis" (Linz 1990a: 55). This is especially true in the case of

[4] A related dilemma for impeachment procedures is that, when conviction results in the vice president taking office, the underlying political crisis may not be resolved; but if it triggers new elections, its lack of political neutrality becomes more obvious.

well-designed semi-parliamentarism. Under multiparty parliamentarism, no-confidence votes can certainly result from political conflicts within the governing coalition, and they can lead to a new round of cabinet formation or to new elections.[5] Under semi-parliamentarism, by contrast, and with a single majority party in the chamber or committee of confidence, the no-confidence vote becomes most of all an instrument for keeping chief executives accountable *to their party*.[6] The party can remove its chief executive without the risk of losing the office of the prime minister and without necessarily suffering a loss in the more general struggle between competing political forces in society. Indeed, it may use this removal to avoid the anticipated electoral losses of keeping a bad or dangerous incumbent in office (Samuels and Shugart 2010).

Cabinet stability and legislative flexibility

Two common arguments for presidentialism highlight two sides of the same coin: cabinet stability and legislative flexibility. Presidentialism stabilizes the executive by not allowing any assembly majority to dismiss the chief executive and cabinet in an ordinary political procedure (e.g. Calabresi 2001: 59–66). And since the assembly is thus liberated from the task of keeping the executive in office, specific policy issues can be considered on their merits, rather than as matters of confidence in the leadership of the ruling party or coalition: "If one desires the consensual and often painstaking task of coalition building to be undertaken on each major legislative initiative, rather than only on the formation of a government, then presidentialism has an advantage" (Mainwaring and Shugart 1997: 463). By contrast, we have seen in Chapter 5 that pure parliamentarism makes it very difficult to reconcile cabinet stability and legislative flexibility.

Under semi-parliamentarism, however, these two goals can also be reconciled (Chapter 6), and in a superior manner. As to cabinet stability, we have seen above that fixed terms are *too drastic a solution*: they require extraordinary procedures of impeachment and/or direct recall, as well as term limits as additional safeguards, with all the problematic downstream consequences. Semi-parliamentarism does not require these safeguards because the chamber

[5] Nevertheless, they are an ordinary political procedure that does not require any special political or judicial justification.

[6] In practice, the replacement may happen through intra-party institutions, rather than an explicit vote of no confidence.

or committee of confidence remains in control of the chief executive. What stabilizes cabinets under well-designed semi-parliamentarism is that the number of parties is manufactured to be low in the chamber or committee of confidence, whereas the proportionally elected chamber of legislation and control lacks the power of the no-confidence vote.

Semi-parliamentarism is also superior to presidentialism when it comes to issue-specific deliberation and decision-making in the assembly—at least, if we value programmatically disciplined parties. We have to distinguish between two types of legislative flexibility: between and within party groups. The presidential separation of powers tends to facilitate both.[7] Executive personalism tends to weaken party unity, especially within the party of the president. Carey (2007, 2009) argues that popularly elected presidents have this effect because they can become powerful *principals* of individual legislators: "they present a potentially competing source of directives against those of party leaders within the legislature" (Carey 2007: 106).

Moreover, this power of the president over individual legislators gives rise to a further design trade-off under presidentialism. While a "double dissolution" of the assembly and the presidency might be an attractive way to resolve deadlock, any power that the president has in making dissolution threats brings with it the danger that the *individual* power of the president is further increased. We have seen in Chapter 8 that this is what seems to have happened in Ecuador. Under semi-parliamentarism, by contrast, any dissolution power given to prime ministers can be balanced by the power of the chamber or committee of confidence to remove them. The threat of assembly dissolution can be granted as a weapon to the *government*—just as in a parliamentary system like Denmark—without becoming the weapon of a single human being. Semi-parliamentarism may therefore make it easier to reconcile flexible, issue-specific coalitions between parties with high unity within parties.

Identifiability and mandate representation

The argument that presidentialism is better at achieving identifiability of competing cabinet alternatives before the election is well established in the literature (Cheibub 2006; Mainwaring and Shugart 1997; Shugart and Carey

[7] Indeed, Alemán (2020: 132) formulates this advantage of presidentialism entirely in terms of within-party flexibility. Legislators' independence from party leaders under presidentialism is thought to increase opportunities for bargaining and compromise because "there are often a few legislators willing to cross the party line" (Alemán 2020: 132).

1992). As we have seen in Chapter 5, parliamentary systems can achieve this goal only under the restrictive conditions of pure two-party or two-bloc systems and must therefore be willing to give up other goals. By contrast, direct presidential elections can achieve identifiability independently from the party system in the assembly; this achievement is, to some extent, "institutionally guaranteed" (Cheibub 2006: 361).

This argument from identifiability is often combined with arguments about mandate representation, and it has been used in proposals for presidentialism in the EU. The popular election of the president of the European Commission would grant "citizens the opportunity to vote for a person and a political direction at the same time" (Decker and Sonnicksen 2011: 189) and thus create a stronger democratic mandate for governing (Hix 2014).

The arguments from identifiability and mandates cannot justify presidentialism for two reasons. First, I have shown in Chapters 6 and 8 that semi-parliamentary government can also be designed to achieve identifiability. The achievement of this goal does not require executive personalism. Second, by connecting identifiability to executive personalism, presidentialism tends to weaken mandate representation. The fundamental reason is that "[t]he identifiability in presidentialism is of *one* person" (Linz 1994: 12, emphasis in the original). While under parliamentarism an entire party or coalition has to switch its policy to betray its mandate, under presidentialism the president's switch may be sufficient.

Samuels and Shugart (2010) argue that this logic can be corroborated in a global study of 401 election campaigns between 1978 and 2002. Since under presidentialism parties cannot control their agents either on the campaign trail or in office, "they cannot hold them to the party's stated platform—and that's when you'll see switches" (Samuels and Shugart 2010: 248). More specifically, the authors show that policy switches in presidential systems occur in two situations: close presidential elections and minority government. In close presidential elections, parties give their candidates greater discretion to maximize the chances of winning; and under minority government, presidents have more freedom to choose coalition partners and push policy independently. For parliamentary systems, by contrast, the authors find that competitiveness has no effect on policy switching and that prime ministers were more likely to switch when they had a majority in parliament, suggesting that it was the party as a whole that switched. The results of other recent studies are at least consistent with these findings (Thomson et al. 2017).

In sum, the identifiability/mandate argument may give us a reason for the separation of powers—for allowing voters to directly elect two separate agents—but not for presidentialism. Semi-parliamentarism is better suited to translate identifiability into actual mandate representation because policy switches require a switch by the majority party in the chamber or committee of confidence.

Electoral accountability

It is also often postulated that presidentialism increases electoral accountability. In the context of the EU, for example, Sonnicksen (2017: 521) claims that the popular election of the Commission President would "establish a link of representation and accountability of the European government directly to the European citizenry ... ." This claim is closely related to the identifiability/mandate argument, but the focus is now on a retrospective, rather than prospective, conception of democratic representation.

Historically, the argument from accountability was indeed framed as an argument for executive personalism. The Framers of the United States Constitution disagreed strongly on the design of the executive. Critics of a single-person executive saw it as a "foetus of monarchy" and preferred a three-person executive; others wanted to attach some kind of council to the single-person executive (DiClerico 1987: 303). Influential figures such as James Wilson and Alexander Hamilton responded to these concerns with a quasi-monarchical version of the contemporary political science concept of clarity of responsibility. They argued that vesting executive power in a single person was crucial to this clarity (e.g. DiClerico 1987: 304; Scheuerman 2005: 42).

The modern political science literature, however, does not support this quasi-monarchical view. Clarity of responsibility is instead operationalized in terms of the *partisan* concentration of powers. Schwindt-Bayer and Tavits (2016: 18, 20) observe that single-party majority control of government is the "most widely accepted measure of the concept of clarity of responsibility" and that it "applies to both parliamentary and presidential systems." With respect to presidential systems, Powell (2000: 52) maintains that "clarity of responsibility is greatest when a single, unified political party controls both the national legislature and chief executive."

Hence, the goal of clarity of responsibility does not give us a reason for presidentialism. It may, at best, give us a reason for the separation of powers; that is, if we accept the need for proportional representation in the legislature but nevertheless want a single party to control the executive, the separation of powers is a way to achieve this. But a semi-parliamentary system can achieve this, too. Instead of majority party "control" of the presidency, there is majority party control of the chamber or committee of confidence.[8]

Moreover, when we compare presidentialism to semi-parliamentarism, we can see that executive personalism actually weakens or fully undermines electoral accountability. This is because it creates a deep dilemma in designing the rules for presidential re-election (Baturo and Elgie 2019; Carey 2003; Linz 1994: 16–18). On the one hand, electoral accountability logically requires the unrestricted possibility for presidents to be re-elected (Cheibub and Medina 2019: 531). If presidents cannot be re-elected, bad performers in office cannot be punished and good performers cannot be re-elected. At best, a very indirect form of accountability is possible, if one of the candidates is a close political ally of the outgoing president (De Ferrari 2015, 2017). Barack Obama might well have pursued a third term if that had been possible, and Donald Trump might never have been elected (Korzi 2019: 410). The absence of re-electability might also have negative incentive effects on incumbents in their last term (Baturo and Elgie 2019: 7).

On the other hand, there is much evidence that the absence of term limits can become a danger to democracy itself (Baturo and Elgie 2019). One reason is that they act as a check on presidents with authoritarian ambitions who might work to undermine democracy during their time in office. Another is that in the absence of term limits, different forms of incumbency advantage may make presidents very likely to win, which in turn increases the chances that a disgruntled opposition turns to "other strategies such as coups, revolutions or assassinations to provide alternation" (Baturo and Elgie 2019: 614; Marsteintredet 2019: 116). Based on data from 1820 to 1985, Marsteintredet (2019: 116) even suggests that the prohibition of consecutive presidential re-election was a *necessary condition* for any type of democracy in Latin America: "No country that allowed for consecutive re-election ever experienced a relatively long and stable democratic period before 1985." The international community, too, has embraced term limits as ways to prevent too strong a concentration of powers in the hands of the president (Murray et al. 2019).

The resulting dilemma is vexing—and ignored by many spirited defenses of presidentialism (e.g. Calabresi 2001; Sonnicksen 2017). Baturo's (2014: 45) pointed statement of the trade-off is worth reading twice, as it brings out a tragic irony: it is a "trade-off between the possibility of dictatorial takeover

[8] As I noted in Chapter 6, the separation of powers also tends to reduce clarity of responsibility by creating additional institutional veto players. Here, I am only concerned with the comparison between powers separation with and without executive personalism.

and a restriction of democratic choice." Ginsburg and Elkins (2019: 50) note that even well-meaning and seemingly independent courts have found that term limits violate democratic rights and thus wonder: "What is a committed democrat to do with term limits?" One answer under presidentialism is to replace term limits with institutional rules that would only eliminate outright manipulation and thus *undue* incumbency advantage: campaign finance regulation, free access to media, the design and strengthening of agencies that oversee electoral campaigns, and so on (Cheibub and Medina 2019: 533; Mainwaring and Shugart 1997: 452). Another answer is the search for some optimal balance between protecting democracy and enabling electoral accountability; for example, by only banning re-election for consecutive terms (Dixon and Landau 2020).

My view is that the stark trade-off between two evils is unnecessary and should be avoided altogether. As already explained, semi-parliamentary systems can do so by keeping the chief executive under the ongoing political control of the majority party in the chamber or committee of confidence. Based on the available empirical evidence, this renders term limits unnecessary without creating a fundamental danger to democracy.

There are two objections to this position that require discussion. On the one hand, Cheibub and Medina (2019: 520) insist that there is "no necessary connection between incumbency advantage and form of government" because prime ministers may also manipulate advantages from office. While this may be true in theory, the empirical fact remains that executive term limits have not generally been necessary to maintain democracy under parliamentarism and semi-parliamentarism (see also Ginsburg and Huq 2018: 181). This seems to support those who argue that the relevant political unit of analysis—party versus individual—is *endogenous* to the form of government (Samuels and Shugart 2010). In other words, it seems to be executive personalism that renders incumbency advantage particularly dangerous for democracy.

On the other hand, Landau (2020: 305–306) speculates that the rise of populist authoritarianism may render term limits necessary, even under parliamentarism (and presumably semi-parliamentarism, for that matter). The scenario he has in mind is one where—despite the confidence relationship—governing parties become dominated by their populist and authoritarian leaders. Yet, if an entire party becomes authoritarian in this way, it is hard to see how term limits for the leader can be much of a remedy. The party can either evade the term limits or choose an equally authoritarian successor. Indeed, Landau (2020: 305) notes that the president of the Polish Law and Justice Party, Jarosław Kaczynski, is the "de facto ruler despite not holding the post of prime minister." Hence, the better solution might be to limit the power of the would-be authoritarian *party* (through the semi-parliamentary separation of powers) and to create good conditions for its electoral containment or defeat (through unbiased electoral rules in both parts of the assembly). Landau's scenario gives us little reason to introduce term limits under parliamentarism, but it might give us one for preferring semi-parliamentarism over parliamentarism. I will elaborate on this point in the next section.

All in all, the argument that presidentialism strengthens electoral accountability is flawed. A concern for electoral accountability may provide an argument for the semi-parliamentary separation of powers, as I argued in Chapter 6, but not for presidentialism.

Democratic breakdown and backsliding

A branch-based separation of powers may help to stabilize democracies for two reasons. First, it may create checks and balances against legal forms of democratic backsliding, whereas the fusion of powers under parliamentarism may "allow for perfectly legal institutional transformations that gradually establish authoritarianism" (Weyland 2020: 393). Second, we have seen, in Chapters 5 and 6, that efforts to create normative balance under pure parliamentarism may require a greater degree of mechanical disproportionality. This can contribute to the political concentration of power in a single party and thereby facilitate authoritarian transformations.

The case of Hungary exemplifies both points. After the transition to democracy in 1990, Hungary had in many ways adopted Ackerman's (2000) model of constrained parliamentarism, with a unicameral parliament, but strong judicial review. However, it had also adopted a mixed electoral system that created substantial electoral disproportionality.[9] This disproportionality not only helped Fidesz become the hegemonic party of the center-right and gain an absolute majority of votes (53%) in 2010, but it also mechanically transformed this absolute majority into a supermajority of seats (68%). Given the absence of any political, branch-based separation of powers, the amendment rule of the Hungarian constitution allowed a single, two-thirds majority of parliament to alter any provision of the constitutional text. This, in turn, allowed Fidesz to dismantle the system of constitutional review, entrench its own electoral advantage, and transform Hungary's democracy into a form of electoral

[9] This was largely the result of strategic bargaining and compromise between self-interested parties (Benoit 2005; Schiemann 2004).

authoritarianism (Haggard and Kaufman 2021; Halmai 2019). A separation-of-powers system and greater mechanical proportionality in the legislative branch could have been important barriers to this development.

While this potential advantage of powers separation is shared by presidentialism and semi-parliamentarism, the former creates its own risks for the survival of democracy (Linz 1990a, 1994). As is well known, Cheibub (2007) finds no statistical evidence that presidentialism contributes to democratic breakdown, once the analysis controls for a country's military legacy (i.e. whether democracy emerged from a military dictatorship). This finding is challenged by Sing (2010) but confirmed, for full democracies, by Aydogan (2019).[10] Maeda (2010: 1141), however, argues that we need to distinguish military coups from executive takeovers and finds evidence that "presidents in presidential systems are more likely to become authoritarian than prime ministers in parliamentary systems." Svolik (2015), too, shows that presidentialism raises the risk of incumbent takeovers but not coups. The findings of Maeda and Svolik are important because, after the end of the Cold War, incumbent takeovers have become the greatest risk for democracies (Svolik 2019; see also Pérez-Liñán et al. 2019).

Maeda (2010: 1141) suggests that a president's greater likelihood of becoming authoritarian is caused by legislative deadlock: "Conflicts with other governmental institutions that may arise due to separation of powers may tempt presidents into seeking unconstitutional measures to achieve their goals." Yet, we have seen in Chapter 6 that it does not seem to be the separation of powers as such that causes presidentialism to have substantially lower legislative success rates than pure parliamentarism. Governments' legislative success in semi-parliamentary systems is only slightly below that of pure parliamentary systems, despite its branch-based separation of powers. The problem of legislative deadlock under presidentialism—to the extent that it exists—may rather result from the way that *powers separation is coupled with executive personalism*.

Regardless of whether the causal connection between executive personalism and incumbent takeovers runs through legislative deadlock, there are a number of causal mechanisms that establish this connection. One is just the flip side of the psychological arguments discussed above. The "plebiscitarian component" of the presidents' authority may foster "a certain populism," a conflation

[10] Aydogan (2019) also finds that if non-democracies with a modicum of multiparty competition are included in the analysis, parliamentary systems are indeed less likely to experience military coups, even when military legacy is controlled for. His proposed explanation is that in parliamentary systems, and especially those that allow for coalition governments, the military has other ways to influence politics.

of their supporters with "the people" as a whole, and a refusal to acknowledge the limits of their mandate (Linz 1990a: 53, 61–62; see also Serra 2018). This tendency may be reinforced by the exaggerated popular expectations that are often associated with a directly elected presidency.

A closely related causal mechanism, already discussed in Chapter 6, is that presidentialism contributes to the rise of outsiders or newcomers (Linz 1990a; see also Ginsburg and Huq 2018: 180–181). Empirical studies confirm that presidential systems facilitate this rise (Carreras 2017; Samuels and Shugart 2010) and that these outsiders or newcomers increase the likelihood of executive–legislative conflict and illegal attempts to dissolve the assembly (Carreras 2014).

The constitutional attempt to contain executive personalism through impeachment procedures also affects the dynamics of inter-branch conflict. Helmke (2017) argues that democracy-undermining presidential attacks on the legislature and the courts can often be understood as a "pre-emptive strike" from a position of political weakness, rather than strength. According to Helmke, this scenario is most likely when presidents have weak partisan support in the assembly and thus face a credible threat of removal. From this position of vulnerability, presidents become more likely to pre-emptively attack legislative and judicial independence.[11]

None of these causal mechanisms is operative, in the same way, under the semi-parliamentary separation of powers. Since chief executives emerge from the legislature and remain agents of their parties, the rise of outsiders or newcomers becomes less likely (Müller 2000; Samuels and Shugart 2010). Since chief executives are not "the voice of the nation or the tribune of the people" but rather a "spokesperson" (Linz 1990a: 56) for some temporary coalition within a party or between parties, their leadership style may be less likely to be, or to become, authoritarian. And since chief executives can be removed from office in an ordinary, politically neutral procedure, pre-emptive attacks on the legislature or the judiciary are less likely, especially in response to weakening support in their own party. Would-be authoritarians can be removed more swiftly and at relatively low political cost to the majority party.

[11] Helmke (2017) argues that this dynamic is amplified when the president is constitutionally powerful. The idea is that these powers allow the president to make policies unilaterally, rather than to cooperate with the assembly majority. However, whether and under what conditions presidents can truly make policies unilaterally is controversial (e.g. Cheibub and Limongi 2010). On the relationship between presidents' constitutional powers and democratic survival, see also Morgenstern et al. (2020). On the measurement of presidential powers, see also Fortin (2012).

Of course, no institutional structure is foolproof. It is certainly possible under semi-parliamentarism that an individual leader may come to dominate a party or that an entire party turns authoritarian. Yet, this arguably requires more specific circumstances and a more demanding coordination between a larger group of individuals. The collective political control over the chief executive does not render incumbent takeovers impossible, but it may provide an additional constitutional layer of protection. Ginsburg and Huq (2018: 184) suggest that "if the threat to democracy is from a charismatic populist, a parliamentary system may be better; if the threat is from partisan degradation, presidentialism might be a preferable option." Once we recognize semi-parliamentarism as a distinct form of government, we can see its potential to contain both threats simultaneously.

Simplicity

Let me finally discuss an advantage of presidentialism's executive personalism that is not typically highlighted but which comes to the fore in the comparison with semi-parliamentarism: simplicity. It is certainly prima facie simpler to concentrate executive power in a single human being, rather than to establish a chamber or committee of confidence. This simplicity is especially alluring in polities that are already complex; for example, due to their federal or quasi-federal structure. This may be part of the reason why presidentialism seems so attractive to many as a way to democratize the European Union (Calabresi and Bady 2010; Decker and Sonnicksen 2011; Hix 2014; Sonnicksen 2017).

I want to make two points here. First, simpler formal structures may be deceptive, as the behavioral patterns that emerge from them may well end up increasing complexity from the perspective of voters. As noted in Chapter 5, the United States is a good example. Its presidential system has contributed to the maintenance of two parties that not only tend to become "presidentialized" (Samuels and Shugart 2010) but are also extremely heterogeneous internally. This heterogeneity makes it very difficult for voters to understand what parties actually stand for, and it creates incentives for political "demonization" campaigns (Cox and Rodden 2019). That is, parties provide voters with targeted information about the *most extreme* positions within their competitor(s), rather than balanced information about their own platform. Hence, a constitutional design that avoids executive personalism and creates maximal incentives for the creation and maintenance of coherent programmatic parties may well lead to political processes that voters find easier to comprehend, all things considered.

Second, even if executive personalism were simpler overall, the value of this simplicity would still have to be weighed against the associated risks. For the reasons given above, these risks are generally not worth taking. Hence, if we truly believe that the complexity created by the branch-based separation of powers can only be reduced by concentrating executive power in a single person, this should lead us to question powers separation, rather than to embrace presidentialism.

A case like Germany is a good example. The Bundesrat, Germany's de facto second chamber, is one of the very few second chambers that actually succeeds in delivering effective territorial representation (e.g. Swenden 2004). Hence, any move towards semi-parliamentarism would probably have to complement the Bundesrat, rather than replace it. Most plausibly, it would require the creation of a confidence committee in the Bundestag along the lines discussed in Chapter 8. If this additional layer of powers separation is considered too complex, this is a reason for sticking to a pure parliamentary system, rather than moving to presidentialism.

Conclusion

This final chapter has focused on the instrumentalist comparison between presidentialism and semi-parliamentarism and argued that we do not have any principled reason to choose the former. When the full range of constitutional design options is considered, and when the justifications of presidentialism are stripped of their quasi-monarchical and antiparty presumptions, there is rather little left of them. If the benefits of presidentialism are grounded in the separation of powers, it is possible to reap them without accepting the perils of executive personalism.

Of course, this does not mean that it will be politically feasible to prevent the creation of new presidential systems or to replace existing ones. It does not even mean that constitutional reformers should attempt to replace presidentialism in a particular country. There may be strong context-dependent reasons against such an attempt; for example, concerns about the risks and opportunity costs of large-scale reforms. My arguments have not been about the politics or the costs and benefits of constitutional reform. They have been about whether the academic literature has produced a principled and cogent justification of presidentialism as a form of democracy. I think it has not.

APPENDIX

Appendix to Chapters 5 and 6

The sample includes 29 democracies (23 nation-states and 6 Australian states). Table A1 provides their values for simple and complex majoritarianism displayed in Chapters 5 and 6, as well as for the six variables on which these dimensions are based. The values are averages for the period from January 1993 to March 2018. The Australian state of Victoria has two separate values for the periods before and after the constitutional reform of 2003 (VIC1 and VIC2, respectively). The operationalization of the six constituent variables and the data sources are explained below.

Operationalization

Identifiability

The measure averages two variables. The first is the joint vote share of the two biggest electoral blocs. A bloc can be a single party or a pre-electoral coalition of several parties. The second is a dummy variable indicating whether the formed cabinet consists of a single bloc, so that no pre-electoral coalition is split up after the election and no additional parties were included in the government. Switzerland's value is set to zero, because the Magic Formula convention implies that there is no choice between alternative cabinets in an election (see Chapter 2). Since the focus is on party-based identifiability, the potential effects of direct presidential or prime-ministerial elections are neglected.

Clarity of responsibility

The measure is an index that ranks cabinet types according to the clarity they provide and averages the resulting scores for each country, weighed by the duration of the cabinets. The scores are as follows: 1 = single-party cabinet with a majority that controls all chambers of the assembly with robust veto power (i.e. all second chambers whose veto cannot be overridden with simple or absolute majorities in the first chamber); 0.75 = single-party cabinet with a majority in one of two chambers that have robust veto power; 0.5 = multiparty cabinet with majorities in all chambers that have robust veto power *or* single-party cabinets with minority status in all chambers with a robust veto; 0.25 = multiparty cabinet with majority in one of two chambers with robust veto power; 0 = multiparty cabinets with minority status in all chambers with robust veto power.

Some closely aligned parties are counted as single parties, most notably the Flemish and Wallonian sister parties in Belgium, the Liberal and National Parties in Australia (unless their non-cooperation is explicit in a particular polity), and the two Christian sister parties (CDU and CSU) in Germany.

Table A1 Country values for Chapters 5 and 6 (1993–2018)

Country	Majoritarianism		Identifiability	Clear responsibility	Cabinet stability	District magnitude	Effective dimensions	Legislative flexibility
	Simple	Complex						
AUS	1.3	0.6	0.92	0.75	0.97	6.0	1.9	0.60
AUT	−1.1	−0.3	0.35	0.46	0.78	18.5	1.7	0.02
BEL	−0.9	0.2	0.23	0.50	0.85	19.9	2.1	0
CAN	0.5	−1.4	0.83	0.87	0.74	1.0	1.5	0.20
CHE	−0.6	1.1	0	0.50	0.96	15.9	1.4	1.00
DEU	0.0	0.0	0.67	0.39	0.95	14.0	2.0	0
DNK	−1.7	2.0	0.56	0.03	0.77	36.5	2.6	0.42
ESP	1.0	−0.6	0.88	0.67	0.95	10.3	1.1	0.35
FIN	−0.7	0.7	0.32	0.50	0.87	17.6	2.5	0
FRA	0.0	−1.3	0.67	0.50	0.88	1.0	1.9	0.01
GBR	0.9	−2.3	0.76	0.89	0.86	1.0	1.1	0.01
GRC	0.4	0.0	0.77	0.87	0.73	20.2	1.9	0.01
IRL	−0.4	−0.2	0.58	0.40	0.89	4.0	2.2	0.11
ISL	−0.7	−0.8	0.29	0.48	0.91	10.7	1.5	0
ISR	−2.7	0.6	0.23	0.40	0.46	42.2	2.1	0.06
ITA	−0.9	0.7	0.70	0.40	0.70	36.5	2.2	0.10
JPN	−0.8	0.0	0.72	0.45	0.68	20.5	1.8	0.10
LUX	−0.4	0.4	0.29	0.50	0.97	18.3	2.3	0

Table A1 Country values for Chapters 5 and 6 (1993–2018)

Country	Majoritarianism		Identifiability	Clear responsibility	Cabinet stability	District magnitude	Effective dimensions	Legislative flexibility
	Simple	Complex						
NLD	−0.9	1.2	0.37	0.41	0.85	110.9	2.3	0.02
NOR	−0.2	1.0	0.67	0.28	0.94	17.5	2.2	0.40
NSW	1.4	1.1	0.92	0.73	1.00	20.5	1.6	0.75
NZL	−0.3	−0.1	0.57	0.37	0.93	12.0	1.7	0.26
PRT	0.5	0.3	0.83	0.65	0.86	22.8	1.7	0.27
QLD	1.3	−1.6	0.90	0.85	0.92	1.0	1.3	0.23
SA	0.1	0.4	0.67	0.47	0.93	11.0	1.5	0.64
SWE	0.2	0.9	0.75	0.32	1.00	17.8	2.2	0.30
TAS	0.8	−1.5	0.82	0.67	0.93	5.5	1.2	0
VIC1	1.2	−1.4	0.95	0.89	0.84	1.0	1.6	0.17
VIC2	1.6	−0.1	0.90	0.83	1.00	5.0	1.6	0.50
WA	0.8	0.2	0.73	0.66	0.98	5.8	1.9	0.43

Cabinet stability

The measure expresses each cabinet's length as the share of its maximal length, as defined by the constitutional maximum. A cabinet that starts at the beginning of a term and ends in the middle of the term has a length of 0.5. A cabinet that starts in the middle of a term and completes it, has a length of 1. The resulting values are averaged for each country, weighted by cabinet duration. A new cabinet is identified when elections take place or the party composition of the cabinet changes. No new cabinet is identified when only the prime minister is replaced or when a cabinet loses a vote of confidence but re-forms with the same composition of parties.

Mechanical proportionality

The measure is an "effective district magnitude" (Taagepera and Shugart 1989) on a logged scale. When a directly elected second chamber exists, the respective values (in each point in time) are those for the more proportional chamber. In single-tier systems without a legal threshold and parallel multi-tier systems, the measure gives the average district magnitude, with magnitudes weighted by the share of parliamentary seats provided by a district. Compensatory multi-tier systems are treated like parallel multi-tier systems if the compensatory tier is too small to effectively compensate for the disproportionalities of the first tier. The compensatory tier is considered big enough if its share of seats is bigger than $1/(2M + 1)$, with M being the (average) magnitude of the lower tier (Gallagher and Mitchell 2005b: 16). The effective district magnitude is then considered to be the magnitude of the compensatory tier. When formal thresholds exist, they are translated into district magnitudes via the formula $M = (75\%/T) - 1$ (Gallagher and Mitchell 2005a: 607; Lijphart 1997a: 74; Taagepera and Shugart 1989: 397). Some electoral systems are so complex that additional assumptions are necessary. Their specification is available upon request.

Dimensionality

Data from (time-invariant) expert surveys on parties' issue-specific policy positions is used to compute an effective number of dimensions. The number of factors identified in a factor analysis of these positions is weighted by the size of the factors' eigenvalues. Seat shares are used to weight parties. When a directly elected second chamber exists, the value is that for the chamber with higher dimensionality (for the entire period under consideration).

Legislative flexibility

The measure is an index that ranks cabinet types (under different forms of government) according to the potential for legislative flexibility they provide and averages the resulting scores for each country, weighted by the duration of the cabinets. The scores are as follows: 1 = assembly-independent government (Switzerland); 0.75 = one-party cabinet with "substantial" minority status; 0.5 = multiparty cabinet with "substantial" minority status; 0.25 = cabinet with "formal" minority status; 0 = majority cabinet. When a directly elected second chamber exists, the measure reflects the status in the chamber with greater flexibility. Since the focus is on party-based flexibility, the kind of flexibility possible in Tasmania's second chamber due to the dominance of independents is neglected.

The distinction between formal and substantive majority status was made as follows. Formal minority cabinets are those based on an explicit agreement—covering all relevant issues and allowing for only a few enumerated exceptions—with one or more opposition parties, so as to create majority support in the assembly. Substantive minority cabinets are those without an agreement, or with one that covers only a few issues, or an agreement that is not sufficient to create a majority in the relevant chamber of the assembly. Cabinets that grant support parties ministerial portfolios are treated as majority cabinets.

Data sources

The data set is a revised and extended version of that used in Ganghof et al. (2015) and Ganghof et al. (2018). The primary data source for elections, first chambers, and cabinets in the nation-states is the ParlGov 2018 stable version (Döring and Manow 2018). For some cases, corrections or additions were made, which are available upon request. In particular, we recoded all Italian cabinets since 1994. The primary data source on the composition of symmetrical and directly elected second chambers for the nation-states is Eppner and Ganghof (2017). The data has been updated to incorporate changes until March 2018. The primary data sources on elections, parliaments, and cabinets in the Australian states are Campbell Sharman's Australian Politics and Elections Archive at the University of Western Australia (https://elections.uwa.edu.au/), Adam Carr's Election Archive (http://psephos.adam-carr.net/) and the electoral commissions of the respective states.

For the variables that required specific coding decisions, further documentation is available upon request. Pre-electoral coalitions were coded with the help of existing data sets (Döring and Manow 2018; Golder 2006), the academic literature, and press reports. Effective district magnitudes were computed on the basis of data from the Electoral System Change in Europe (ESCE) Project (http://electoralsystemchanges.eu/) and the country-specific literature on electoral systems. The expert survey data for the nation-states comes from Benoit and Laver (2006) and that for the Australian states from an expert survey conducted by Alexander Pörschke in 2016 (Pörschke 2021) and first used in Ganghof et al. (2018). The minority status of cabinets in the relevant chambers of the assembly was coded on the basis of the general and country-specific literature, as well as press reports.

Appendix to Chapter 7

Details for the conditional logit analysis underlying Figure 7.2

Sample

Switzerland is excluded from the set of 29 democracies, as there is no confidence relationship between the government and any chamber of the assembly. The analysis is extended back to January 1975 to capture more temporal variation. As explained in Chapter 7, Victoria and Western Australia enter the analysis as three and two separate observations, respectively.

Data sources

The data sources are the same as for Chapters 5 and 6 (see "Appendix to Chapters 5 and 6").

Data construction

We identify a new government formation opportunity when (a) a first chamber election takes place; or (b) the party composition of the government changes. We exclude opportunities in which a single party won a majority of seats in both chambers (or in a unicameral system), as well as those that resulted in caretaker governments. In the case of Japan, we also exclude cases where a majority party in the first chamber controls more than two-thirds of the first chamber's seats (the quorum for overriding a second-chamber veto). We also exclude all government formations for which we were unable to assign policy positions to 15% or more of the parliamentary seats. In line with the general argument of this book, we do not treat replacements of the prime minister as a new government formation opportunity. While such replacements may sometimes result from coalition politics (i.e. a coalition party may demand the change of the prime minister of another party), they can also result from the fact that the party of the prime minister remains in control of the person that occupies the office and, thus, can replace it with another agent of the party. Finally, we drop all parties from the cabinet formation analysis that do not have at least two seats in at least one chamber of parliament. Altogether, 369 cabinet formations are included, with a total of 577,879 potential cabinets (see Table A2).

Main explanatory variables

Veto Control is a dummy variable that takes the value one if a potential cabinet holds a majority in the second chamber. Restrictiveness is our index of the design of second chambers (in versions I or II). By interacting it with Veto Control, we can test if a higher Restrictiveness goes hand in hand with greater influence of Veto Control on cabinet formation. Since Restrictiveness does not vary between potential cabinets of one formation opportunity, it drops out of the estimation. The same is true for Veto Control when no symmetrical second chamber exists. Government formations in the absence of relevant veto institutions thus affect the estimation for the control variables.

Control variables

We include the following control variables, all of which refer to certain features of a potential cabinet: (a) its first-chamber seat share; (b) its minority status in the first chamber; (c) an interaction of the two previous variables (see Druckman et al. 2005: 538); (d) its oversized status in the first chamber; (e) its number of parties; (f) whether the largest and (g) median parties in the first chamber are included; (h) its ideological range on the left–right dimension; and (i) a dummy that indicates if the potential cabinet would split a pre-electoral commitment of two parties (by leaving out at least one of the parties).

Results

Table A3 shows the regression results. The three columns are for the same causal model but different measures of restrictiveness (compare Table 7.1). The first column is for Restrictiveness II and the basis for Figure 7.2. The second column is for the same index but uses the budget veto, rather than the no-confidence vote to determine whether the second chamber has constitutional power over the survival of the cabinet. The third column uses the leaner index Restrictiveness I. With these alternative indices, the substantive results remain unchanged.

Table A2 Number of cabinet formations and potential cabinets per country

Country/ state (Australia)	Number of cabinet formations	Number of potential cabinets	First cabinet formation included	Last cabinet formation included
AUS	13	123	03 Nov. 1980	19 Jul. 2016
AUT	12	316	24 May 1983	18 Dec. 2017
BEL	17	4,623	06 Mar. 1977	11 Oct. 2014
CAN	4	60	04 Jun. 1979	30 Oct. 2008
DEU	13	315	15 Dec. 1976	14 Mar. 2018
DNK	21	20,075	13 Feb. 1975	28 Nov. 2016
ESP	7	5,241	05 Apr. 1979	29 Oct. 2016
FIN	21	5,867	30 Nov. 1975	13 Jun. 2017
FRA	11	8,965	17 Aug. 1976	18 Jun. 2012
GBR	2	382	11 May 2010	11 Jun. 2017
GRC	6	658	02 Jul. 1989	21 Sep. 2015
IRL	12	932	30 Jun. 1981	06 May 2016
ISL	15	1,073	01 Sep. 1978	30 Nov. 2017
ISR	38	286,554	20 Jun. 1977	30 May 2016
ITA	28	202,340	12 Feb. 1976	12 Dec. 2016
JPN	17	16,367	27 Dec. 1983	24 Dec. 2014
LUX	8	312	16 Jul. 1979	04 Dec. 2013
NLD	13	18,419	19 Dec. 1977	26 Oct. 2017
NOR	16	1,648	11 Sep. 1977	17 Jan. 2018
NSW	8	168	25 Mar. 1988	28 Mar. 2015
NZL	10	518	01 Mar. 1996	26 Oct. 2017
PRT	14	1,010	23 Jul. 1976	26 Nov. 2015
QLD	4	28	19 Aug. 1983	14 Feb. 2015
SA	15	165	12 Jul. 1975	17 Mar. 2018
SWE	15	1,457	07 Oct. 1976	02 Oct. 2014
TAS	14	82	11 Dec. 1976	03 Mar. 2018
VIC1	1	7	08 Apr. 1982	08 Apr. 1982
VIC1	2	10	01 Oct. 1988	21 Oct. 1999
VIC3	2	30	25 Nov. 2006	03 Dec. 2014
WA1	8	120	04 Feb. 1989	11 Mar. 2017
WA2	2	14	25 Feb. 1983	08 Feb. 1986
Total	**369**	**577,879**	**13 Feb. 1975**	**17 Mar. 2018**

Table A3 Conditional logit regression results

	(1)	(2)	(3)
	Restrictiveness II	**Restrictiveness II (using budget veto)**	**Restrictiveness I**
Veto Control	0.79***	0.54**	0.51**
	(0.26)	(0.25)	(0.26)
Veto Control x Restrictiveness	0.69***	0.64***	0.81**
	(0.21)	(0.22)	(0.32)
First-Chamber Seat Share of Coalition	−0.90	−0.99	−0.89
	(0.86)	(0.85)	(0.85)
Minority Coalition	−9.21***	−9.27***	−9.27***
	(0.79)	(0.78)	(0.78)
First-Chamber Seat Share of Minority Coalition	16.56***	16.63***	16.65***
	(1.61)	(1.61)	(1.60)
Oversized Coalition	−0.53***	−0.53***	−0.52***
	(0.20)	(0.20)	(0.20)
Number of Parties in the Coalition	−1.07***	−1.07***	−1.08***
	(0.09)	(0.09)	(0.09)
Largest Party in the Coalition	0.03	0.04	−0.00
	(0.19)	(0.19)	(0.19)
Median Party in the Coalition	0.95***	0.94***	0.96***
	(0.17)	(0.17)	(0.17)
Ideological Divisions in the Coalition	−0.60***	−0.59***	−0.59***
	(0.05)	(0.05)	(0.05)
Coalition splits Pre-Electoral Pact	−2.58***	−2.59***	−2.59***
	(0.27)	(0.27)	(0.27)
Observations	577,879	577,879	577,879
Countries	28	28	28
Cabinets	369	369	369
Ll	−1,052	−1,053	−1,054

Note: Standard errors in parentheses. $^{*}p < 0.1$; $^{**}p < 0.05$; $^{***}p < 0.01$.

References

Åberg, Jenny and Sedelius, Thomas (2020), 'A Structured Review of Semi-Presidential Studies: Debates, Results and Missing Pieces', *British Journal of Political Science*, 50 (3), 1111–1136.

Abizadeh, Arash (2020), 'Representation, Bicameralism, Political Equality, and Sortition: Reconstituting the Second Chamber as a Randomly Selected Assembly', *Perspectives on Politics*, 18 (1), 1059–1078.

Abizadeh, Arash (2021), 'Counter-Majoritarian Democracy: Persistent Minorities, Federalism, and the Power of Numbers', *American Political Science Review*, 115 (3), 742–756.

Ackerman, Bruce (2000), 'The New Separation of Powers', *Harvard Law Review*, 113 (3), 633–729.

Ajenjo, Natalia (2015), 'Why Minority Governments in Spain? How the Party System Undermines Investiture Rules', in Bjørn E. Rasch, Shane Martin, and José A. Cheibub (eds), *Parliaments and Government Formation: Unpacking Investiture Rules* (Oxford: Oxford University Press), pp. 153–164.

Albert, Richard (2009), 'The Fusion of Presidentialism and Parliamentarism', *The American Journal of Comparative Law*, 57 (3), 531–578.

Albert, Richard (2010), 'Presidential Values in Parliamentary Democracies', *International Journal of Constitutional Law*, 8 (2), 207–236.

Alemán, Eduardo (2020), *Latin American Politics* (London: SAGE Publications).

Alemán, Eduardo and Tsebelis, George (eds) (2016), *Legislative Institutions and Lawmaking in Latin America* (Oxford: Oxford University Press).

Altman, David (2008), 'Collegiate Executives and Direct Democracy in Switzerland and Uruguay: Similar Institutions, Opposite Political Goals, Distinct Results', *Swiss Political Science Review*, 14 (3), 483–520.

Altman, David (2020), 'Checking Executive Personalism: Collegial Governments and the Level of Democracy', *Swiss Political Science Review*, 26 (3), 316–338.

Andeweg, Rudy, Elgie, Robert, Helms, Ludger, Kaarbo, Juliet, and Müller-Rommel, Ferdinand (2020), 'The Political Executive Returns: Re-Empowerment and Rediscovery', in Rudy Andeweg, Robert Elgie, Ludger Helms, Juliet Kaarbo, and Ferdinand Müller-Rommel (eds), *The Oxford Handbook of Political Executives* (New York: Oxford University Press), pp. 1–22.

André, Audrey, Depauw, Sam, and Deschouwer, Kris (2015), 'Changing Investiture Rules in Belgium', in Bjørn E. Rasch, Shane Martin, and José A. Cheibub (eds), *Parliaments and Government Formation: Unpacking Investiture Rules* (Oxford: Oxford University Press), pp. 49–66.

Arato, Andrew (2000), 'The New Democracies and American Constitutional Design', *Constellations*, 7 (3), 316–340.

Aroney, Nicholas, Gerangelos, Peter, Murray, Sarah, and Stellios, James (2015), *The Constitution of the Commonwealth of Australia: History, Principle and Interpretation* (Port Melbourne: Cambridge University Press).

Aydogan, Abdullah (2019), 'Constitutional Foundations of Military Coups', *Political Science Quarterly*, 134 (1), 85–116.

Bach, Stanley (2003), *Platypus and Parliament: The Australian Senate in Theory and Practice* (Canberra: Department of the Senate).

Baehr, Peter (1989), 'Weber and Weimar: The 'Reich President' Proposals', *Politics*, 9 (1), 20–25.

Bagehot, Walter (1867), *The English Constitution* (London: Oxford University Press).

Bagg, Samuel (2018), 'The Power of the Multitude: Answering Epistemic Challenges to Democracy', *American Political Science Review*, 112 (4), 891–904.

Baldi, Brunetta (2018), 'Second Chamber Reform in Italy: Federalism Left Behind', *South European Society and Politics*, 23 (3), 387–403.

Barry, Nicholas and Miragliotta, Narelle (2015), 'Australia', in Brian Gilligan and Scott Breton (eds), *Constitutional Conventions in Westminster Systems: Controversies, Changes and Challenges* (Cambridge: Cambridge University Press), pp. 204–216.

Bastoni, Jordan (2012), 'The South Australian Legislative Council: Possibilities for Reform', *Australian Journal of Political Science*, 47 (2), 227–238.

Baturo, Alexander (2014), *Democracy, Dictatorship, and Term Limits* (Ann Arbor, MI: University of Michigan Press).

Baturo, Alexander and Elgie, Robert (eds) (2019), *The Politics of Presidential Term Limits* (Oxford: Oxford University Press).

Bawn, Kathleen and Rosenbluth, Frances (2006), 'Short versus Long Coalitions: Electoral Accountability and the Size of the Public Sector', *American Journal of Political Science*, 50 (2), 251–265.

Becher, Michael and Christiansen, Flemming J. (2015), 'Dissolution Threats and Legislative Bargaining', *American Journal of Political Science*, 59 (3), 641–655.

Bechtel, Michael M, Hangartner, Dominik, and Schmid, Lukas (2016), 'Does Compulsory Voting Increase Support for Leftist Policy?', *American Journal of Political Science*, 60 (3), 752–767.

Beitz, Charles R. (1989), *Political Equality* (Princeton, NJ: Princeton University Press).

Bellamy, Richard (2007), *Political Constitutionalism: A Republican Defence of the Constitutionality of Democracy* (Cambridge: Cambridge University Press).

Benoit, Kenneth (2005), 'Hungary: Holding Back the Tiers', in Michael Gallagher and Paul Mitchell (eds), *The Politics of Electoral Systems* (Oxford: Oxford University Press), pp. 231–252.

Benoit, Kenneth and Laver, Michael (2006), *Party Policy in Modern Democracies* (New York: Routledge).

Bergman, Matthew E. (2019), 'Rejecting Constitutional Reform in the 2016 Italian Referendum: Analysing the Effects of Perceived Discontent, Incumbent Performance and Referendum-Specific Factors', *Contemporary Italian Politics*, 11 (2), 177–191.

Bergman, Torbjörn (1993), 'Formation Rules and Minority Governments', *European Journal of Political Research*, 23 (1), 55–66.

Bergmann, Henning, Bäck, Hanna, and Saalfeld, Thomas (2021), 'Party–System Polarisation, Legislative Institutions and Cabinet Survival in 28 Parliamentary Democracies, 1945–2019', *West European Politics*, Forthcoming.

Bernauer, Julian and Vatter, Adrian (2019), *Power Diffusion and Democracy. Institutions, Deliberation and Outcomes* (Cambridge: Cambridge University Press).

Besselink, Leonard (2014), 'The Kingdom of the Netherlands', in Leonard Besselink, Paul Bovend'Eert, Hansko Broeksteeg, Roel de Lange, and Wim Voermans (eds), *Constitutional Law of the EU Member States* (Deventer: Kluwer), pp. 1187–1240.

Birch, Sarah (2018), 'Democratic Norms, Empirical Realities and Approaches to Improving Voter Turnout', *Res Publica*, 24 (1), 9–30.

Bishop, Matthew L., Corbett, Jack, and Veenedaal, Wouter (2020), 'Labor Movements and Party System Development: Why Does the Caribbean Have Stable Two-Party Systems, but the Pacific Does Not?', *World Development*, 126, 1–14.

Black, David (1991), 'Financial Relations between the Two Houses, 1890–1990', in David Black (ed.), *The House on the Hill: A History of the Parliament of Western Australia, 1832–1990* (Perth: Western Australian Parliamentary History Project), pp. 429–459.

Blais, André (2014), 'Why is Turnout So Low in Switzerland? Comparing the Attitudes of Swiss and German Citizens Towards Electoral Democracy', *Swiss Political Science Review*, 20 (4), 520–528.

Blais, André, Singh, Shane, and Dumitrescu, Delia (2014), 'Political Institutions, Perceptions of Representation, and the Turnout Decision', in Jacques Thomassen (ed.), *Elections and Representative Democracy: Representation and Accountability* (Oxford: Oxford University Press), pp. 99–112.

Bochsler, Daniel, Hänggli, Regula, and Häusermann, Silja (2015), 'Introduction: Consensus Lost? Disenchanted Democracy in Switzerland', *Swiss Political Science Review*, 21 (4), 475–490.

Bonotti, Matteo and Strangio, Paul (eds) (2021), *A Century of Compulsory Voting in Australia: Genesis, Impact and Future* (London: Palgrave Macmillan).

Borges, André, Turgeon, Mathieu, and Albala, Adrián (2020), 'Electoral Incentives to Coalition Formation in Multiparty Presidential Systems', *Party Politics*, Forthcoming.

Boston, Jonathan and Bullock, David (2010), 'Multi-Party Governance: Managing the Unity-Distinctiveness Dilemma in Executive Coalitions', *Party Politics*, 18 (3), 349–368.

Brennan, Jason (2016), *Against Democracy* (Princeton, NJ: Princeton University Press).

Brennan, Jason and Hill, Lisa (2014), *Compulsory Voting: For and Against* (Cambridge: Cambridge University Press).

Brenton, Scott and Pickering, Heath (2020), 'Trustworthiness, Stability and Productivity of Minority Governments in Australia', *Parliamentary Affairs*, Forthcoming.

Calabresi, Steven G. (2001), 'The Virtues of Presidential Government: Why Professor Ackerman is Wrong to Prefer the German to the US Constitution', *Constitutional Commentary*, 18 (1), 51–104.

Calabresi, Steven G. and Bady, Kyle (2010), 'Is the Separation of Powers Exportable?', *Harvard Journal of Law and Policy*, 33 (1), 5–16.

Carey, John M. (2003), 'The Reelection Debate in Latin America', *Latin American Politics and Society*, 45 (1), 119–133.

Carey, John M. (2007), 'Competing Principals, Political Institutions, and Party Unity in Legislative Voting', *American Journal of Political Science*, 51 (1), 92–107.

Carey, John M. (2009), *Legislative Voting and Accountability* (Cambridge: Cambridge University Press).

Carey, John M. and Hix, Simon (2011), 'The Electoral Sweet Spot: Low-Magnitude Proportional Electoral Systems', *American Journal of Political Science*, 55 (2), 383–397.

Carney, Gerard (2006), *The Constitutional Systems of the Australian States and Territories* (Cambridge: Cambridge University Press).

Carreras, Miguel (2014), 'Outsiders and Executive–Legislative Conflict in Latin America', *Latin American Politics and Society*, 56 (3), 70–92.

Carreras, Miguel (2017), 'Institutions, Governmental Performance and the Rise of Political Newcomers', *European Journal of Political Research*, 56 (2), 364–380.

Ceccarini, Luigi and Bordignon, Fabio (2017), 'Referendum on Renzi: The 2016 Vote on the Italian Constitutional Revision', *South European Society & Politics*, 22 (3), 281–302.

Chaisty, Paul, Cheeseman, Nic, and Power, Timothy J. (2018), *Coalitional Presidentialism in Comparative Perspective. Minority Presidents in Multiparty Systems* (Oxford: Oxford University Press).

Chaisty, Paul and Power, Timothy J. (2019), 'Flying Solo: Explaining Single-Party Cabinets under Minority Presidentialism', *European Journal of Political Research*, 58 (1), 163–183.

Chapman, Emilee B. (2019), 'The Distinctive Value of Elections and the Case for Compulsory Voting', *American Journal of Political Science*, 63 (1), 101–112.

Cheibub, José A. (2006), 'Presidentialism, Electoral Identifiability, and Budget Balances in Democratic Systems', *American Political Science Review*, 100 (3), 353–368.

Cheibub, José A. (2007), *Presidentialism, Parliamentarism, and Democracy* (New York: Cambridge University Press).

Cheibub, José A. and Limongi, Fernando (2010), 'From Conflict to Coordination: Perspectives on the Study of Executive–Legislative Relations', *Revista Ibero-Americana de Estudos Legislativos*, 1 (1), 38–53.

Cheibub, José A. and Medina, Alejandro (2019), 'The Politics of Presidential Term Limits in Latin America: From Re-Democratization to Today', in Alexander Baturo and Robert Elgie (eds), *The Politics of Presidential Term Limits* (Oxford: Oxford University Press), pp. 517–534.

Cheibub, José A., Przeworski, Adam, and Saiegh, Sebastián M. (2004), 'Government Coalitions and Legislative Success under Presidentialism and Parliamentarism', *British Journal of Political Science*, 34 (4), 565–587.

Cheibub, José A., Elkins, Zachary, and Ginsburg, Tom (2014), 'Beyond Presidentialism and Parliamentarism', *British Journal of Political Science*, 44 (3), 515–544.

Cheibub, José A., Martin, Shane, and Rasch, Bjørn E. (2021), 'Investiture Rules and Formation of Minority Governments in European Parliamentary Democracies', *Party Politics*, 27 (2), 351–362.

Cheibub-Figueiredo, Argelina, Canello, Júlio, and Vieira, Marcelo (2012), 'Governos Minoritários no Presidencialismo Latino-Americano: Determinantes Institucionais e Políticos', *Dados-Revista de Ciências Sociais*, 55 (4), 839–875.

Christiano, Thomas (1996), *The Rule of the Many. Fundamental Issues in Democratic Theory* (Boulder, CO: Westview Press).

Christiano, Thomas (2008), *The Constitution of Equality: Democratic Authority and Its Limits* (Oxford: Oxford University Press).

Christiano, Thomas (2015), 'Democracy, Public Equality and the Modern State: Replies to Baccarini, Cerovac, Ivanković, Mladenović, Prijić-Samaržija and Zelić', *Anali*, 12 (1), 99–111.

Christiansen, Flemming J. and Damgaard, Erik (2008), 'Parliamentary Opposition under Minority Parliamentarism: Scandinavia', *The Journal of Legislative Studies*, 14 (1), 46–76.

Christiansen, Flemming J. and Klemmensen, Robert (2015), 'Danish Experiences with Coalition Governments and Coalition Governance', in Hanne L. Madsen (ed.), *Coalition Building: Finding Solutions Together* (Copenhagen: Danish Institute for Parties and Democracy - DIPD), pp. 26–43.

Clune, David (2021), 'The Legislative Council of NSW: A Progressive Conservative Institution', in Henry Ergas, and Jonathan J. Pincus (eds), *Power, parliament and politics: Essays in honour of JR Nethercote*, Forthcoming.

Clune, David and Griffith, Gareth (2006), *Decision and Deliberation: The Parliament of New South Wales 1856–2003* (Leichhardt: The Federation Press).

Clune, David and Smith, Rodney (2019), 'New South Wales', in Peter J. Chen, Nicholas Barry, John R. Butcher, David Clune, Ian Cook, Adele Garnier, Yvonne Haigh, Sara C. Motta, and Marija Taflaga (eds), *Australian Politics and Policy: Senior Edition* (Sydney: Sydney University Press), pp. 212–232.

Colomer, Josep M. (2005), 'It's Parties that Choose Electoral Systems (or, Duverger's Laws Upside Down)', *Political Studies*, 53 (1), 1–21.

Colomer, Josep M. (2013), 'Elected Kings with the Name of Presidents. On the Origins of Presidentialism in the United States and Latin America', *Revista Lationamericana de Politica Comparada*, 7 (1), 79–97.

Colomer, Josep M. (2018), 'Party System Effects on Electoral Systems', in Erik S. Herron, Robert J. Pekkanen, and Matthew S. Shugart (eds), *The Oxford Handbook of Electoral Systems* (Oxford: Oxford University Press), pp. 69–84.

Colomer, Josep M. and Negretto, Gabriel L. (2005), 'Can Presidentialism Work Like Parliamentarism?', *Government and Opposition*, 40 (1), 60–89.

Constitutional Reform Committee (1992[1848]), 'Report on the 1848 Draft Constitution of Switzerland', in Arend Lijphart (ed.), *Parliamentary versus Presidential Government* (New York: Oxford University Press), pp. 173–174.

Costar, Brian (2008), 'Reformed Bicameralism? The Victorian Legislative Council in the Twenty-First Century', in Nicholas Aroney, Scott Prasser, and John R. Nethercote (eds), *Restraining Elective Dictatorship: The Upper House Solution?* (Crawley: University of Western Australia Press), pp. 196–211.

Cox, Gary W. (1987), *The Efficient Secret* (New York: Cambridge University Press).

Cox, Gary W. and Rodden, Jonathan A. (2019), 'Demonization', Preliminary draft prepared for PIEP Seminar (Stanford University).

Crombez, Christophe (1996), 'Minority Governments, Minimal Winning Coalitions and Surplus Majorities in Parliamentary Systems', *European Journal of Political Research*, 29 (1), 1–29.

Cunow, Saul, Desposato, Scott, Janusz, Andrew, and Sells, Cameron (2021), 'Less is More: The Paradox of Choice in Voting Behavior', *Electoral Studies*, 69 (1), 1–38.

D'Alimonte, Roberto (2015), 'The New Italian Electoral System: Majority-Assuring but Minority-Friendly', *Contemporary Italian Politics*, 7 (3), 286–292.

Damgaard, Erik and Svensson, Palle (1989), 'Who Governs? Parties and Policies in Denmark', *European Journal of Political Research*, 17 (6), 731–745.

Davies, Amanda and Tonts, Matthew (2007), 'Changing Electoral Structures and Regional Representation in Western Australia: From Countrymindedness to One Vote One Value', *Space and Polity*, 11 (3), 209–225.

De Ferrari, Ignazio (2015), 'The Successor Factor: Electoral Accountability in Presidential Democracies', *Comparative Political Studies*, 48 (2), 193–230.

De Ferrari, Ignazio (2017), 'The Accountability Effect of Endorsements: A Survey Experiment', *Electoral Studies*, 45, 1–13.

De Garis, Brian (2003), 'The History of Western Australia's Constitution and Attempts at Its Reform', *University of Western Australia Law Review*, 31 (2), 142–153.

De Marchi, Scott and Laver, Michael (2020), 'Government Formation as Logrolling in High-Dimensional Issue Spaces', *The Journal of Politics*, 82 (2), 543–558.

Debeljak, Julie and Grenfell, Laura (2020), 'Diverse Australian Landscapes of Law-Making and Human Rights: Contextualising Law-Making and Human Rights', in Julie Debeljak and Laura Grenfell (eds), *Law Making and Human Rights: Executive and Parliamentary Scrutiny Across Australian Jurisdictions* (Sydney: Thompson Reuters (Professional) Australia Limited), pp. 2–28.

Decker, Frank and Sonnicksen, Jared (2011), 'An Alternative Approach to European Union Democratization: Re-Examining the Direct Election of the Commission President', *Government and Opposition*, 46 (2), 168–191.

Di Mauro, Danilo and Memoli, Vincenzo (2018), 'Targeting the Government in the Referendum: The Aborted 2016 Italian Constitutional Reform', *Italian Political Science Review*, 48 (2), 133–154.

DiClerico, Robert E. (1987), 'James Wilson's Presidency', *Presidential Studies Quarterly*, 17 (2), 301–317.

Diermeier, Daniel, Eraslan, Hülya, and Merlo, Antonio (2007), 'Bicameralism and Government Formation', *Quarterly Journal of Political Science*, 2 (3), 227–252.

Dixon, Rosalind (2019), 'The Forms, Functions, and Varieties of Weak(ened) Judicial Review', *International Journal of Constitutional Law*, 17 (3), 904–930.

Dixon, Rosalind and Landau, David (2020), 'Constitutional End Games: Making Presidential Term Limits Stick', *Hastings Law Journal*, 71 (2), 359–418.

Döring, Holger and Manow, Philip (2015), 'Is Proportional Representation More Favourable to the Left? Electoral Rules and Their Impact on Elections, Parliaments and the Formation of Cabinets', *British Journal of Political Science*, 47 (1), 149–164.

Döring, Holger and Manow, Philip (2018), 'ParlGov 2018 Release', (V1 edn; Harvard Dataverse).

Dos Santos, Tiago R. (2020), *Why Not Parliamentarism?* (Tunbridge Wells: Wordzworth).

Druckman, James N. and Thies, Michael F. (2002), 'The Importance of Concurrence: The Impact of Bicameralism on Government Formation and Duration', *American Journal of Political Science*, 46 (4), 760–771.

Druckman, James N., Martin, Lanny, and Thies, Michael F. (2005), 'Influence without Confidence: Upper Chambers and Government Formation', *Legislative Studies Quarterly*, 30 (4), 529–548.

Drutman, Lee (2020), *Breaking the Two-Party Doom Loop: The Case for Multiparty Democracy in America* (Oxford: Oxford University Press).

Dunleavy, Patrick and Diwakar, Rekha (2013), 'Analysing Multiparty Competition in Plurality Rule Elections', *Party Politics*, 19 (6), 855–886.

Dunleavy, Patrick and Margetts, Helen (2004), 'The United Kingdom: Reforming the Westminster Model', in Josep M. Colomer (ed.), *The Handbook of Electoral System Choice* (London: Palgrave Macmillan, pp. 294–306.

Durán-Martínez, Angélica (2012), 'Presidents, Parties, and Referenda in Latin America', *Comparative Political Studies*, 45 (9), 1159–1187.

Duverger, Maurice (1980), 'A New Political System Model: Semi-Presidential Government', *European Journal of Political Research*, 8 (2), 165–187.

Duverger, Maurice (1997), 'The Political System of the European Union', *European Journal of Political Research*, 31 (1), 137–146.

Dworkin, Ronald (2000), *Sovereign Virtue: The Theory and Practice of Equality* (Cambridge: Harvard University Press).

Economou, Nick (2019), 'Victoria', in Peter J. Chen, Nicholas Barry, John R. Butcher, David Clune, Ian Cook, Adele Garnier, Yvonne Haigh, Sara C. Motta, and Marija Taflaga (eds), *Australian Politics and Policy: Senior Edition* (Sydney: Sydney University Press), pp. 296–313.

Edge, Peter W., Corrin, Jennifer, and Than, Claire de (2019), 'The Appointment and Removal of the Head of Government of the Kiribati Republic', *A Report for Daphne Caine MHK, October 2019* (Oxford: Oxford Brookes University).

Elgie, Robert (1999), 'The Politics of Semi-Presidentialism', in Robert Elgie (ed.), *Semi-Presidentialism in Europe* (New York: Oxford University Press), pp. 1–21.

Elgie, Robert (2011), *Semi-Presidentialism: Sub-Types and Democratic Performance* (Oxford: Oxford University Press).

Elgie, Robert (2016), 'Three Waves of Semi-Presidential Studies', *Democratization*, 23 (1), 49–70.

Elgie, Robert (2018), 'On New Forms of Government', *Australian Journal of Political Science*, 53 (2), 241–247.

Elgie, Robert and Passarelli, Gianluca (2019), 'Presidentialisation: One Term, Two Uses—between Deductive Exercise and Grand Historical Narrative', *Political Studies Review*, 17 (2), 115–123.

Elliott, Kevin J. (2017), 'Aid for Our Purposes: Mandatory Voting as Precommitment and Nudge', *The Journal of Politics*, 79 (2), 656–669.

Emerson, Peter (2013), 'The Original Borda Count and Partial Voting', *Social Choice and Welfare*, 40 (2), 353–358.

Eppner, Sebastian and Ganghof, Steffen (2015), 'Do (Weak) Upper Houses Matter for Cabinet Formation? A Replication and Correction', *Research & Politics*, 2 (1), 1–5.

Eppner, Sebastian and Ganghof, Steffen (2017), 'Institutional Veto Players and Cabinet Formation: The Veto Control Hypothesis Reconsidered', *European Journal of Political Research*, 56 (1), 169–186.

Estlund, David (2008), *Democratic Authority: A Philosophical Framework* (Princeton, NJ: Princeton University Press).

Estlund, David (2009), 'Debate: On Christiano's "The Constitution of Equality"', *Journal of Political Philosophy*, 17 (2), 241–252.

Fabbrini, Sergio (2001), 'Features and Implications of Semi-Parliamentarism: The Direct Election of Italian Mayors', *South European Society and Politics*, 6 (2), 47–70.

Farrell, David M. and McAllister, Ian (2006), *The Australian Electoral System: Origins, Variations, and Consequences* (Sydney: University of New South Wales Press).

Fewkes, Nathan (2011), 'Tasmania's Legislative Council Elections—Is Reform Needed?', *Australasian Parliamentary Review*, 26 (2), 87–98.

Field, Bonnie N. (2016), *Why Minority Governments Work: Multilevel Territorial Politics in Spain* (New York: Palgrave Macmillan US).

Field, Bonnie N. (2019), 'Is Something Wrong with Spain's Political Leaders?', Monkey Cage Blog, July 20, 2019.

Fortin, Jessica (2012), 'Measuring Presidential Powers: Some Pitfalls of Aggregate Measurement', *International Political Science Review*, 34 (1), 91–112.

Fortin-Rittberger, Jessica (2017), 'Strong Presidents for Weak States. How Weak State Capacity Fosters Vertically Concentrated Executives', in Philipp Harfst, Ina Kubbe, and Thomas Poguntke (eds), *Parties, Governments and Elites: The Comparative Study of Democracy* (Wiesbaden: Springer VS), pp. 205–226.

Fortunato, David, König, Thomas, and Proksch, Sven-Oliver (2013), 'Government Agenda-Setting and Bicameral Conflict Resolution', *Political Research Quarterly*, 66 (4), 938–951.

Fowler, Anthony (2013), 'Electoral and Policy Consequences of Voter Turnout: Evidence from Compulsory Voting in Australia', *Quarterly Journal of Political Science*, 8 (2), 159–182.

Franklin, Mark N. (2004), *Voter Turnout and the Dynamics of Electoral Competition in Established Democracies since 1945* (New York: Cambridge University Press).

Freiburghaus, Rahel and Vatter, Adrian (2019), 'The Political Side of Consociationalism Reconsidered: Switzerland between a Polarized Parliament and Delicate Government Collegiality', *Swiss Political Science Review*, 25 (4), 357–380.

Freudenreich, Johannes (2016), 'The Formation of Cabinet Coalitions in Presidential Systems', *Latin American Politics and Society*, 58 (4), 80–102.

Gallagher, Michael (1991), 'Proportionality, Disproportionality and Electoral Systems', *Electoral Studies*, 10 (1), 33–51.

Gallagher, Michael and Mitchell, Paul (2005a), 'Appendix C', in Michael Gallagher and Paul Mitchell (eds), *The Politics of Electoral Systems* (Oxford: Oxford University Press), pp. 607–620.

Gallagher, Michael and Mitchell, Paul (2005b), 'Introduction to Electoral Systems', in Michael Gallagher and Paul Mitchell (eds), *The Politics of Electoral Systems* (Oxford: Oxford University Press), pp. 3–23.

Ganghof, Steffen (2006), *The Politics of Income Taxation. A Comparative Analysis* (Colchester: ECPR).

Ganghof, Steffen (2010), 'Democratic Inclusiveness: A Reinterpretation of Lijphart's Patterns of Democracy', *British Journal of Political Science*, 40 (3), 679–692.

Ganghof, Steffen (2014), 'Bicameralism as a Form of Government (or: Why Australia and Japan Do Not Have a Parliamentary System)', *Parliamentary Affairs*, 67 (3), 647–663.

Ganghof, Steffen (2015a), 'Four Visions of Democracy: Powell's Elections as Instruments of Democracy and Beyond', *Political Studies Review*, 13 (1), 69–79.

Ganghof, Steffen (2015b), 'Is the "Constitution of Equality" Parliamentary, Presidential or Hybrid?', *Political Studies*, 63 (4), 814–829.

Ganghof, Steffen (2016a), 'Combining Proportional and Majoritarian Democracy: An Institutional Design Proposal', *Research & Politics*, 3 (3), 1–7.

Ganghof, Steffen (2016b), 'Reconciling Representation & Accountability: Three Visions of Democracy Compared', *Government and Opposition*, 52 (1), 209–233.

Ganghof, Steffen (2018a), 'A New Political System Model: Semi-Parliamentary Government', *European Journal of Political Research*, 57 (2), 261–281.

Ganghof, Steffen (2018b), 'On Consistently Defining Forms of Government: A Reply to Robert Elgie', *Presidential Power*, https://presidential-power.net/?p=8146 (accessed 20 October 2020).

Ganghof, Steffen and Bräuninger, Thomas (2006), 'Government Status and Legislative Behaviour: Partisan Veto Players in Australia, Denmark, Finland and Germany', *Party Politics*, 12 (4), 521–539.

Ganghof, Steffen and Eppner, Sebastian (2019), 'Patterns of Accountability and Representation: Why the Executive-Parties Dimension Cannot Explain Democratic Performance', *Politics*, 39 (1), 113–130.

Ganghof, Steffen, Eppner, Sebastian, and Heeß, Katja (2015), 'Normative Balance and Electoral Reform: A Finnish Puzzle and a Comparative Analysis', *West European Politics*, 38 (1), 53–72.

Ganghof, Steffen, Eppner, Sebastian, and Pörschke, Alexander (2018), 'Australian Bicameralism as Semi-Parliamentarism: Patterns of Majority Formation in 29 Democracies', *Australian Journal of Political Science*, 53 (2), 211–233.

Ganghof, Steffen, Eppner, Sebastian, Stecker, Christian, Heeß, Katja, and Schuhkraft, Stefan (2019), 'Do Minority Cabinets Govern More Flexibly and Inclusively? Evidence from Germany', *German Politics*, 28 (4), 541–561.

Gardbaum, Stephen (2014), 'Separation of Powers and the Growth of Judicial Review in Established Democracies (or Why Has the Model of Legislative Supremacy Mostly Been Withdrawn from Sale?)', *The American Journal of Comparative Law*, 62 (3), 613–640.

Gaus, Gerald F. (1996), *Justificatory Liberalism: An Essay on Epistemology and Political Theory* (New York: Oxford University Press).

Gerring, John and Thacker, Strom C. (2008), *A Centripetal Theory of Democratic Governance* (New York: Cambridge University Press).

Ginsberg, Benjamin (2016), *Presidential Government* (New Haven, NJ: Yale University Press).

Ginsburg, Tom (2003), *Judicial Review in New Democracies* (Cambridge: Cambridge University Press).

Ginsburg, Tom and Elkins, Zachary (2019), 'One Size Does Not Fit All: The Provision and Interpretation of Presidential Term Limits', in Alexander Baturo and Robert Elgie (eds), *The Politics of Presidential Term Limits* (Oxford: Oxford University Press), pp. 37-51.

Ginsburg, Tom and Huq, Aziz Z. (2018), *How to Save a Constitutional Democracy* (Chicago, IL: University of Chicago Press).

Ginsburg, Tom, Huq, Aziz Z., and Landau, David (2020), 'The Uses and Abuses of Presidential Impeachment', *88 University of Chicago Law Review*, Public Law Working Paper No. 731, Forthcoming.

Giudici, Anja and Stojanović, Nenad (2016), 'Die Zusammensetzung des Schweizerischen Bundesrates nach Partei, Region, Sprache und Religion, 1848–2015', *Swiss Political Science Review*, 22 (2), 288–307.

Golder, Sona N. (2006), *The Logic of Pre-Electoral Coalition Formation* (Columbus, OH: Ohio State University Press).

Goldoni, Marco (2012), 'Two Internal Critiques of Political Constitutionalism', *International Journal of Constitutional Law*, 10 (4), 926–949.

Goossens, Jurgen and Cannoot, Pieter (2015), 'Belgian Federalism after the Sixth State Reform', *Perspectives on Federalism*, 7 (2), 29–55.

Goplerud, Max and Schleiter, Petra (2016), 'An Index of Assembly Dissolution Powers', *Comparative Political Studies*, 49 (4), 427–456.

Graham, Matthew and Svolik, Milan W. (2020), 'Democracy in America? Partisanship, Polarization, and the Robustness of Support for Democracy in the United States', *American Political Science Review*, 114 (2), 392–409.

Green-Pedersen, Christoffer, Mortensen, Peter B., and So, Florence (2018), 'The Agenda-Setting Power of the Prime Minister Party in Coalition Governments', *Political Research Quarterly*, 7 (4), 743–756.

Grenfell, Laura (2020), 'South Australia: Ad Hoc and Unsystematic Rights Protection in Law Making', in Julie Debeljak and Laura Grenfell (eds), *Law Making and Human Rights: Executive and Parliamentary Scrutiny Across Australian Jurisdictions* (Sydney: Thompson Reuters (Professional) Australia Limited), pp. 499–527.

Griffith, Gareth and Srinivasan, Sharath (2001), *State Upper Houses in Australia* (Sydney: NSW Parliamentary Library Research Service).

Grofman, Bernard and Feld, Scott L. (2004), 'If You Like the Alternative Vote (a.k.a the Instant Runoff), Then You Ought to Know about the Coombs Rule', *Electoral Studies*, 23 (4), 641–659.

Guerrero, Alexander A. (2014), 'Against Elections: The Lottocratic Alternative', *Philosophy & Public Affairs*, 42 (2), 135–178.

Haggard, Stephan and Kaufman, Robert (2021), *Backsliding: Democratic Regress in the Contemporary World* (Cambridge: Cambridge University Press).

Halmai, Gábor (2019), 'The Rise and Fall of Constitutionalism in Hungary', in Paul Blokker (ed.), *Constitutional Acceleration within the European Union and Beyond* (London: Routledge), pp. 217–233.

Hamilton, Alexander, Madison, James, and Jay, John (1987), *The Federalist Papers* (London: Penguin).

Heeß, Katja (2017), *Einschränkung der Mehrheitsdemokratie?: Institutioneller Wandel und Stabilität von Vetopunkten* (Baden-Baden: Nomos).

Heller, William B. and Branduse, Diana M. (2014), 'The Politics of Bicameralism', in Shane Martin, Thomas Saalfeld, and Kaare Strøm (eds), *The Oxford Handbook of Legislative Studies* (Oxford: Oxford University Press), pp. 332–352.

Helmke, Gretchen (2017), *Institutions on the Edge: The Origins and Consequences of Inter-Branch Crises in Latin America* (Cambridge: Cambridge University Press).

Hirschl, Ran (2004), *Towards Juristocracy: The Origins and Consequences of the New Constitutionalism* (Cambridge: Harvard University Press).

Hix, Simon (2014), 'Democratizing a Macroeconomic Union in Europe', in Olaf Cramme and Sarah B. Hobolt (eds), *Democratic Politics in a European Union under Stress* (Oxford: Oxford University Press), pp. 180–198.

Howell, William G. and Moe, Terry M. (2016), *Relic: How Our Constitution Undermines Effective Government—And Why We Need a More Powerful Presidency* (New York: Basic Books).

Howell, William G. and Moe, Terry M. (2020), *Presidents, Populism, and the Crisis of Democracy* (Chicago, IL: University of Chicago Press).

Huber, John D. (1996), *Rationalizing Parliament: Legislative Institutions and Party Politics in France* (Cambridge: Cambridge University Press).

Huber, John D. and Powell, Bingham G. (1994), 'Congruence between Citizens and Policy-makers in Two Visions of Liberal Democracy', *World Politics*, 46 (3), 291–326.

Hyde, Sarah (2011), 'The Japanese 2009 House of Representatives Elections: The Beginning of Real Change and the End of One-Party Dominance in Japan?', *Japan Forum*, 23 (2), 157–183.

Jain, Purnendra (2020), 'Japan's 2019 Upper House Election: Solidifying Abe, the LDP, and Return to a One-Party Dominant Political System', *Asian Journal of Comparative Politics*, 5 (1), 23–37.

Kaase, Max (1983), 'The West German General Election of 6 March 1983', *Electoral Studies*, 2 (2), 158–166.

Kada, Naoko (2003), 'Impeachment as a Punishment for Corruption? The Cases of Brazil and Venezuela', in Jody C. Baumgartner and Naoko Kada (eds), *Checking Executive Power: Presidential Impeachment in Comparative Perspective* (London: Praeger), pp. 113–135.

Karvonen, Lauri (2014), *Parties, Governments and Voters in Finland: Politics under Fundamental Societal Transformation* (Colchester: ECPR Press).

Kellam, Marisa (2017), 'Why Pre-Electoral Coalitions in Presidential Systems?', *British Journal of Political Science*, 47 (2), 391–411.

Kenworthy, Lane and Pontusson, Jonas (2005), 'Rising Inequality and the Politics of Redistribution in Affluent Countries', *American Political Science Association*, 3 (3), 449–471.

Khaitan, Tarunabh (2020), 'Political Parties in Constitutional Theory', *Current Legal Problems*, 73 (1), 89–125.

Khaitan, Tarunabh (2021), 'Balancing Accountability and Effectiveness: A Case for Moderated Parliamentarism', *Canadian Journal of Comparative and Contemporary Law*, 7 (1), 81–155.

Klarman, Michael J. (2016), *The Framers' Coup: The Making of the United States Constitution* (Oxford: Oxford University Press).

Klemmensen, Robert (2010), 'Denmark: Agenda Control and Veto Rights to Opposition Parties', in Bjørn E. Rasch and George Tsebelis (eds), *The Role of Governments in Legislative Agenda Setting* (New York: Routledge), pp. 222–269.

Kollman, Ken (2018), 'Election Data and Levels of Analysis', in Erik S. Herron, Robert J. Pekkanen, and Mathew S. Shugart (eds), *The Oxford Handbook of Electoral Systems* (Oxford: Oxford University Press), pp. 405–424.

Kolodny, Niko (2014), 'Rule Over None II: Social Equality and the Justification of Democracy', *Philosophy & Public Affairs*, 42 (4), 287–336.

Korzi, Michael J. (2019), 'The Politics of Presidential Term Limits in the United States', in Alexander Baturo and Robert Elgie (eds), *The Politics of Presidential Term Limits* (Oxford: Oxford University Press), pp. 405–428.

Koß, Michael (2019), *Parliaments in Time: The Evolution of Legislative Democracy in Western Europe, 1866–2015* (Oxford: Oxford University Press).

Kotze, Dirk (2019), 'Election of the National President: South Africa's Approach and Its Implications for Presidentialism', *Politikon*, 46 (4), 443–461.

Krauss, Svenja and Thürk, Maria (2021), 'Stability of Minority Governments and the Role of Support Agreements', *West European Politics*, Forthcoming.

Lacerda, Alan Daniel Freire de (2020), 'The Normative Bases of Semi-Presidentialism: Max Weber and the Mitigation of Caesarism', *Brazilian Political Science Review*, 14 (1), 1–32.

Landa, Dimitri and Pevnick, Ryan (2020a), 'Is Random Selection a Cure for the Ills of Electoral Representation?', *Journal of Political Philosophy*, 29 (1), 46–72.

Landa, Dimitri and Pevnick, Ryan (2020b), 'Representative Democracy as Defensible Epistocracy', *American Political Science Review*, 114 (1), 1–13.

Landau, David (2020), 'Personalism and the Trajectories of Populist Constitutions', *Annual Review of Law and Social Science*, 16 (1), 239–309.

Landemore, Hélène (2017), 'Beyond the Fact of Disagreement? The Epistemic Turn in Deliberative Democracy', *Social Epistemology*, 31 (3), 277–295.

Landemore, Hélène (2020), *Open Democracy: Reinventing Popular Rule for the Twenty-First Century* (Princeton, NJ: Princeton University Press).

Laski, Harold J. (1940), *The American Presidency: An Interpretation* (New York: Harper & Brothers).

Lavapuro, Juha, Ojanen, Toumas, and Scheinin, Martin (2011), 'Rights-Based Constitutionalism in Finland and the Development of Pluralist Constitutional Review', *International Journal of Constitutional Law*, 9 (2), 505–531.

Laver, Michael and Schofield, Norman (1990), *Multiparty Government: The Politics of Coalition in Europe* (New York: Oxford University Press).

Laver, Michael and Shepsle, Kenneth (1996), *Making and Breaking Governments* (Cambridge: Cambridge University Press).

Leinen, Jo (2015), 'The European Electoral System. The Weak Link of Supranational Democracy', *The Federalist Debate*, 28 (1), 11–13.

Lento, Tal and Hazan, Reuven Y. (2021), 'The Vote of No Confidence: Towards a Framework for Analysis', *West European Politics*, Forthcoming.

Lever, Annabelle and Volacu, Alexandru (2018), 'Should Voting Be Compulsory? Democracy and the Ethics of Voting', in Annabelle Lever and Andrei Poama (eds), *The Routledge Handbook of Ethics and Public Policy* (Abingdon: Routledge), pp. 242–254.

Levinson, Daryl J. and Pildes, Richard H. (2006), 'Separation of Parties, Not Powers', *Harvard Law Review*, 119 (8), 2311–2386.

Li, Yuhui and Shugart, Matthew S. (2016), 'The Seat Product Model of the Effective Number of Parties: A Case for Applied Political Science', *Electoral Studies*, 41, 23–34.

Lijphart, Arend (1984), *Democracies. Patterns of Majoritarian and Consensus Government in Twenty-One Countries* (New Haven, CT: Yale University Press).

Lijphart, Arend (ed.) (1992a), *Parliamentary versus Presidential Government* (Oxford: Oxford University Press).

Lijphart, Arend (1992b), 'Introduction', in Arend Lijphart (ed.), *Parliamentary versus Presidential Government* (Oxford: Oxford University Press), pp. 1–27.

Lijphart, Arend (1997a), 'The Difficult Science of Electoral Systems: A Commentary on the Critique by Alberto Penades', *Electoral Studies*, 16 (1), 73–77.

Lijphart, Arend (1997b), 'Nomination: Trichotomy or Dichotomy?', *European Journal of Political Research*, 31 (1), 125–128.

Lijphart, Arend (1997c), 'Unequal Participation: Democracy's Unresolved Dilemma', *American Political Science Review*, 9 (1), 1–14.

Lijphart, Arend (2012), *Patterns of Democracy. Government Forms and Performance in Thirty-Six Countries* (2nd edn; New Haven, CT: Yale University Press).

Linder, Wolf and Mueller, Sean (2021), *Swiss Democracy: Possible Solutions to Conflict in Multicultural Societies* (4th edn; London: Palgrave Macmillan).

Linhart, Eric, Raabe, Johannes, and Statsch, Patrick (2018), 'Mixed-Member Proportional Electoral Systems—the Best of Both Worlds?', *Journal of Elections, Public Opinion and Parties*, 29 (1), 21–40.

Linz, Juan J. (1990a), 'The Perils of Presidentialism', *Journal of Democracy*, 1 (1), 51–69.

Linz, Juan J. (1990b), 'The Virtues of Parliamentarism', *Journal of Democracy*, 1 (4), 84–91.

Linz, Juan J. (1994), 'Presidential or Parliamentary Democracy: Does it Make a Difference?', in Juan J. Linz and Arturo Valenzuela (eds), *The Failure of Presidential Democracy: The Case of Latin America* (Baltimore, MD: Johns Hopkins University Press), pp. 3–90.

Llanos, Mariana and Nolte, Detlef (2003), 'Bicameralism in the Americas: Around the Extremes of Symmetry and Incongruence', *The Journal of Legislative Studies*, 9 (3), 54–86.

Lupia, Arthur and McCubbins, Mathew D. (2005), 'Lost in Translation: Social Choice Theory is Misapplied against Legislative Intent', *Journal of Contemporary Legal Issues*, 14 (2), 585–617.

Maeda, Ko (2010), 'Two Modes of Democratic Breakdown: A Competing Risks Analysis of Democratic Durability', *The Journal of Politics*, 72 (4), 1129–1143.

Mainwaring, Scott and Shugart, Matthew S. (1997), 'Juan Linz, Presidentialism, and Democracy', *Comparative Politics*, 29 (4), 449–471.

Manwaring, Rob, Dean, Mark, and Holloway, Josh (2019), 'South Australia', in Peter J. Chen, Nicholas Barry, John R. Butcher, David Clune, Ian Cook, Adele Garnier, Yvonne Haigh, Sara C. Motta, and Marija Taflaga (eds), *Australian Politics and Policy: Senior Edition* (Sydney: Sydney University Press), pp. 265–280.

Marsteintredet, Leiv (2019), 'Presidential Term Limits in Latin America: c. 1820–1985', in Alexander Baturo and Robert Elgie (eds), *The Politics of Presidential Term Limits* (Oxford: Oxford University Press), pp. 103–122.

Marti, Urs (2019), *Staat, Volk, Eidgenossen: Anmerkungen zum politischen System der Schweiz* (Zürich: Orell Füssli Verlag).

Martin, Lanny W. and Stevenson, Randolph T. (2001), 'Government Formation in Parliamentary Democracies', *American Journal of Political Science*, 45 (1), 33–50.

Martin, Lanny W. and Vanberg, Georg (2020), 'Coalition Government, Legislative Institutions, and Public Policy in Parliamentary Democracies', *American Journal of Political Science*, 64 (2), 325–340.

Martínez, Christopher A. (2021), 'Presidential Instability in Latin America: Why Institutionalized Parties Matter', *Government and Opposition*, 56 (4), 683–704.

Massetti, Emanuele and Farinelli, Arianna (2019), 'From the Porcellum to the Rosatellum: 'Political Elite–Judicial Interaction' in the Italian Laboratory of Electoral Reforms', *Contemporary Italian Politics*, 11 (2), 137–157.

Massicotte, Louis (2001), 'Legislative Unicameralism: A Global Survey and a Few Case Studies', *Journal of Legislative Studies*, 7 (1), 151–170.

McCargo, Duncan (2010), 'An Incomplete Change of Course: Japan's Landmark 2009 Lower-House Elections and Their Aftermath', *Representation*, 46 (4), 471–479.

McGann, Anthony J. (2006), *The Logic of Democracy. Reconciling Equality, Deliberation, and Minority Protection* (Ann Arbor, MI: University of Michigan Press).

McGann, Anthony J. (2013), 'Fairness and Bias in Electoral Systems', in Jack H. Nagel and Rogers M. Smith (eds), *Representation—Elections and Beyond* (Philadelphia, PA: University of Pennsylvania Press), pp. 90–113.

McGann, Anthony J., Smith, Charles A., Latner, Michael, and Keena, Alex (2016), *Gerrymandering in America: The House of Representatives, the Supreme Court, and the Future of Popular Sovereignty* (Cambridge: Cambridge University Press).

McGann, Anthony J., Koetzle, William, and Grofman, Bernard (2002), 'How an Ideologically Concentrated Minority Can Trump a Dispersed Majority: Nonmedian Voter Results for Plurality, Run-Off, and Sequential Elimination Elections', *American Journal of Political Science*, 46 (1), 134–148.

McKelvy, Andrew (2013), 'Variations in Legislative Success among Executives in Westminster Democracies', APSA 2013 Annual Meeting (Chicago, IL).

Medding, Peter Y. (1999), 'From Government by Party to Government Despite Party', *Israel Affairs*, 6 (2), 172–208.

Meinel, Florian (2019), *Vertrauensfrage: Zur Krise des heutigen Parlamentarismus* (Munich: Beck C. H.).

Meinel, Florian (2021), *Germany's Dual Constitution: Parliamentary Democracy in the Federal Republic* (Oxford: Hart Publishing).

Mitchell, Paul and Nyblade, Benjamin (2008), 'Government Formation and Cabinet Type', in Kaare Strøm, Wolfgang C. Müller, and Torbjörn Bergman (eds), *Cabinets and Coalition Bargaining: The Democratic Life Cycle in Western Europe* (Oxford: Oxford University Press), pp. 201–235.

Moe, Terry M. and Caldwell, Michael (1994), 'The Institutional Foundations of Democratic Government: A Comparison of Presidential and Parliamentary Systems', *Journal of Institutional and Theoretical Economics*, 150 (1), 171–195.

Mommsen, Wolfgang J. (1984), *Max Weber and German Politics* (Chicago, IL: University of Chicago Press).

Montesquieu, Charles-Louis de Secondat, Baron de (1977), *The Spirit of Laws*, ed. David Wallace Carrithers (Berkeley, CA: University of California Press).

Morgenstern, Scott, Perez, Amaury, and Peterson, Maxfield (2020), 'Revisiting Shugart and Carey's Relation of Executive Powers and Democratic Breakdown ', *Political Studies Review*, 18 (1), 125–144.

Moser, Robert, Scheiner, Ethan, and Stoll, Heather (2018), 'Social Diversity, Electoral Systems, and the Party System', in Erik S. Herron, Robert J. Pekkanen, and Mathew S. Shugart (eds), *The Oxford Handbook of Electoral Systems* (Oxford: Oxford University Press), pp. 135–158.

Muirhead, Russell (2006), 'A Defense of Party Spirit', *Perspectives on Politics*, 4 (4), 713–727.

Muirhead, Russell and Rosenblum, Nancy L. (2015), 'The Uneasy Place of Parties in the Constitutional Order', in Mark Tushnet, Mark A. Graber, and Sanford Levinson (eds), *The Oxford Handbook of the U.S. Constitution* (Oxford: Oxford University Press), pp. 217–240.

Muirhead, Russell and Rosenblum, Nancy L. (2020), 'The Political Theory of Parties and Partisanship: Catching Up', *Annual Review of Political Science*, 23 (1), 95–110.

Müller, Wolfgang C. (1999), 'Austria', in Robert Elgie (ed.), *Semi-Presidentialism in Europe* (Oxford: Oxford University Press), pp. 22–47.

Müller, Wolfgang C. (2000), 'Political Parties in Parliamentary Democracies: Making Delegation and Accountability Work', *European Journal of Political Research*, 37 (3), 309–333.

Murray, Christina, Alston, Eric, and Wiebusch, Micha (2019), 'Presidential Term Limits and the International Community', in Alexander Baturo and Robert Elgie (eds), *The Politics of Presidential Term Limits* (Oxford: Oxford University Press), pp. 557–584.

Nagel, Jack (1998), 'Social Choice in a Pluralitarian Democracy: The Politics of Market Liberalization in New Zealand', *British Journal of Political Science*, 28 (2), 223–267.

Nagel, Jack (2012), 'Evaluating Democracy in New Zealand under MMP', *Policy Quarterly*, 8 (2), 3–11.

Negretto, Gabriel L. (2006), 'Minority Presidents and Democratic Performance in Latin America', *Latin American Politics and Society*, 48 (3), 63–98.

Nelson, Eric (2014), *The Royalist Revolution: Monarchy and the American Founding* (Harvard, MA: Harvard University Press).

Nemoto, Kuniaki (2018), 'Electoral Systems in Context: Japan', in Erik S. Herron, Robert J. Pekkanen, and Mathew S. Shugart (eds), *The Oxford Handbook of Electoral Systems* (Oxford: Oxford University Press), pp. 825–850.

Orentlicher, David (2013), *Two Presidents Are Better Than One: The Case for a Bipartisan Executive Branch* (New York: New York University Press).

Ottolenghi, Emanuele (2001), 'Why Direct Election Failed in Israel', *Journal of Democracy*, 12 (4), 109–122.

Park, Brandon B., Frantzeskakis, Nikolaos, and Shin, Jungsub (2019), 'Who Is Responsible? The Effect of Clarity of Responsibility on Voter Turnout', *West European Politics*, 42 (3), 464–494.

Pepperday, Michael (2002), *Improving Democracy through Elite Power Struggle: The Introduction of Proportional Representation in the Western Australian Legislative Council* (Crawley: University of Western Australia).

Pérez-Liñán, Aníbal (2007), *Presidential Impeachment and the New Political Instability in Latin America* (Cambridge: Cambridge University Press).

Pérez-Liñán, Aníbal (2020), 'Narratives of Executive Downfall: Recall, Impeachment, or Coup?', in Yanina Welp and Laurence Whitehead (eds), *The Politics of Recall Elections* (Basingstoke: Palgrave Macmillan), pp. 201–228.

Pérez-Liñán, Aníbal, Schmidt, Nicolás, and Vairo, Daniela (2019), 'Presidential Hegemony and Democratic Backsliding in Latin America, 1925–2016', *Democratization*, 26 (4), 606–625.

Phillips, Harry (1991), 'The Modern Parliament', in David Black (ed.), *The House on the Hill: A History of the Parliament of Western Australia, 1832–1990* (Perth: Western Australian Parliamentary History Project), pp. 185–251.

Phillips, Harry (2013), *Proportional Representation in Western Australia. Its Principles, History, Outcomes and Education* (Perth: Western Australian Electoral Commission).

Piersig, Elsa (2016), 'Reconsidering Constructive Non-Confidence for Canada: Experiences from Six European Countries', *Canadian Parliamentary Review*, 39 (3), 5–15.

Pörschke, Alexander (2021), *Koalitionsbildung und Gesetzgebung im Semi-Parlamentarismus: die australischen Parlamente im Vergleich* (Potsdam: University of Potsdam).

Posner, Eric A. (2016), 'Presidential Leadership and the Separation of Powers', *Daedalus*, 145 (3), 35–43.

Powell, Bingham G. (2000), *Elections as Instruments of Democracy. Majoritarian and Proportional Visions* (New Haven, CT: Yale University Press).

Powell, Bingham G. (2019), *Ideological Representation: Achieved and Astray: Elections, Institutions, and the Breakdown of Ideological Congruence in Parliamentary Democracies* (Cambridge: Cambridge University Press).

Prakash, Saikrishna Bangalore (2020), *The Living Presidency: An Originalist Argument against Its Ever-Expanding Powers* (Cambridge: The Belknap Press of Harvard University Press).

Proksch, Sven-Oliver and Slapin, Jonathan B. (2006), 'Institutions and Coalition Formation: The German Election of 2005', *West European Politics*, 29 (3), 540–559.

Przeworski, Adam (2003), 'Freedom to Choose and Democracy', *Economic and Philosophy*, 19 (2), 265–279.

Przeworski, Adam (2010), *Democracy and the Limits of Self-Government* (Cambridge: Cambridge University Press).

Przeworski, Adam (2020), *Krisen der Demokratie* (Berlin: Suhrkamp Verlag).

Qvortrup, Mads (2020), 'The Political Theory of the Recall. A Study in the History of the Ideas', in Yanina Welp and Laurence Whitehead (eds), *The Politics of Recall Elections* (Basingstoke: Palgrave Macmillan), pp. 29–48.

Raabe, Johannes and Linhart, Eric (2018), 'Which Electoral Systems Succeed at Providing Proportionality and Concentration? Promising Designs and Risky Tools', *European Political Science Review*, 10 (2), 167–190.

Rasch, Bjørn E., Martin, Shane, and Cheibub, José A. (2015), 'Introduction: Investiture Rules and Government Formation', in Bjørn E. Rasch, Shane Martin, and José A. Cheibub (eds), *Parliaments and Government Formation: Unpacking Investiture Rules* (Oxford: Oxford University Press), pp. 3–26.

Rehfeld, Andrew (2005), *The Concept of Constituency: Political Representation, Democratic Legitimacy, and Institutional Design* (New York: Cambridge University Press).

Reilly, Benjamin (2018), 'Centripetalism and Electoral Moderation in Established Democracies', *Nationalism and Ethnic Politics*, 24 (2), 201–221.

Renwick, Alan, Hanretty, Chris, and Hine, David (2009), 'Partisan Self-Interest and Electoral Reform: The New Italian Electoral Law of 2005', *Electoral Studies*, 28 (3), 437–447.

Rhodes-Purdy, Matthew and Madrid, Raúl L. (2020), 'The Perils of Personalism', *Democratization*, 27 (2), 321–339.

Roberts, Shane (2016), 'A Safeguard against Impetuosity: The Franchise of the Tasmanian Legislative Council, 1856', *Tasmanian Historical Studies*, 21 (1), 41–59.

Rodden, Jonathan A. (2019), *Why Cities Lose: The Deep Roots of the Urban–Rural Political Divide* (New York: Basic Books).

Rodden, Jonathan A. (2020), 'Keeping Your Enemies Close: Electoral Rules and Partisan Polarization', in Frances Rosenbluth and Margaret Weir (eds), *Who Gets What? The New Politics of Insecurity* (Cambridge: Cambridge University Press), pp. 129-160.

Romeo, Graziella (2017), 'The Italian Constitutional Reform of 2016: An 'Exercise' of Change at the Crossroad between Constitutional Maintenance and Innovation', *The Italian Law Journal*, 2017 (Special Issue), 31–48.

Rosenblum, Nancy L. (2008), *On the Side of the Angels: An Appreciation of Parties and Partisanship* (Princeton, NJ: Princeton University Press).

Rosenbluth, Frances McCall and Shapiro, Ian (2018), *Responsible Parties. Saving Democracy from Itself* (New Haven, CT: Yale University Press).

Rosenbluth, Frances McCall and Thies, Michael F. (2010), *Japan Transformed: Political Change and Economic Restructuring* (Princeton, NJ: Princeton University Press).

Rosenzweig, Beate (2010), 'Das Japanische Oberhaus–Die "Kammer der Berater"', in Gisela Riescher, Sabine Ruß, and Christoph M. Haas (eds), *Zweite Kammern* (2nd edn; Munich: R. Oldenbourg), pp. 291–309.

Rovny, Jan and Polk, Jonathan (2019), 'New Wine in Old Bottles: Explaining the Dimensional Structure of European Party Systems', *Party Politics*, 25 (1), 12–24.

Rudolph, Lukas and Däubler, Thomas (2016), 'Holding Individual Representatives Accountable: The Role of Electoral Systems', *Journal of Politics*, 78 (3), 746–762.

Russell, Meg and Sandford, Mark (2002), 'Why are Second Chambers so Difficult to Reform?', *Journal of Legislative Studies*, 8 (3), 79–89.

Russell, Meg and Serban, Ruxandra (2021), 'The Muddle of the 'Westminster Model': A Concept Stretched beyond Repair', *Government and Opposition*, 56 (4), 744–764.

Russo, Federico (2015), 'Government Formation in Italy: The Challenge of Bicameral Investiture', in Bjørn E. Rasch, Shane Martin, and José A. Cheibub (eds), *Parliaments and Government Formation: Unpacking Investiture Rules* (Oxford: Oxford University Press), pp. 136–152.

Sabl, Andrew (2015), 'The Two Cultures of Democratic Theory: Responsiveness, Democratic Quality, and the Empirical-Normative Divide', *Perspectives on Politics*, 13 (2), 345–365.

Saiegh, Sebastián M. (2009), 'Political Prowess or "Lady Luck"? Evaluating Chief Executives' Legislative Success Rates', *The Journal of Politics*, 71 (4), 1342–1356.

Saiegh, Sebastián M. (2011), *Ruling by Statute: How Uncertainty and Vote Buying Shape Lawmaking* (Cambridge: Cambridge University Press).

Samuels, David (2007), 'Separation of Powers', in Carles Boix and Susan Stokes (eds), *The Oxford Handbook of Comparative Politics* (Oxford: Oxford University Press), pp. 703–726.

Samuels, David J. and Shugart, Matthew S. (2010), *Presidents, Parties, and Prime Ministers —How the Separation of Powers Affects Party Organization and Behavior* (Cambridge: Cambridge University Press).

Samuels, David J. and Snyder, Richard (2001), 'The Value of a Vote: Malapportionment in Comparative Perspective', *British Journal of Political Science*, 31 (4), 651–671.

Sanchez-Sibony, Omar (2018), 'Competitive Authoritarianism in Ecuador under Correa', *Taiwan Journal of Democracy*, 14 (2), 97–120.

Santucci, Jack (2020), 'Multiparty America?', *The Journal of Politics*, 82 (4), 34–39.

Sartori, Giovanni (1994), 'Neither Presidentialism Nor Parliamentarism', in Juan J. Linz and Arturo Valenzuela (eds), *The Failure of Presidential Democracy* (London: Johns Hopkins University Press), pp. 106–118.

Sartori, Giovanni (1997), *Comparative Constitutional Engineering* (2nd edn; New York: New York University Press).

Saunders, Cheryl (2021), 'Constitutionalism in Australia', in Peter Cane, Lisa Ford, and Mark McMillan (eds), *The Cambridge Legal History of Australia*, (Cambridge: Cambridge University Press), Forthcoming.

Scheuerman, William E. (2005), 'American Kingship? Monarchical Origins of Modern Presidentialism', *Polity*, 37 (1), 24–53.

Schiemann, John W. (2004), 'Hungary: Compromising Midway on a Mixed System', in Josep M. Colomer (ed.), *Handbook of Electoral System Choice* (London: Palgrave Macmillan), pp. 359–368.

Schleiter, Petra and Voznaya, Alisa M. (2014), 'Party System Competitiveness and Corruption', *Party Politics*, 20 (5), 675–686.

Schwartzberg, Melissa (2013), *Counting the Many: The Origins and Limits of Supermajority Rule* (Cambridge: Cambridge University Press).

Schwarz, Daniel, Bächtiger, André, and Lutz, George (2011), 'Switzerland: Agenda Setting Power of Government In a Separation-of-Powers Framework', in Bjørn E. Rasch and George T. Sebelis (eds), *The Role of Governments in Legislative Agenda Setting* (London: Routledge), pp. 127–144.

Schwindt-Bayer, Leslie A. and Tavits, Margit (2016), *Clarity of Responsibility, Accountability, and Corruption* (New York: Cambridge University Press).

Serle, Geoffrey (1955), 'The Victorian Legislative Council 1856–1950', *Historical Studies: Australia and New Zealand*, 6 (22), 186–203.

Serra, Gilles (2018), 'The Electoral Strategies of a Populist Candidate: Does Charisma Discourage Experience and Encourage Extremism?', *Journal of Theoretical Politics*, 30 (1), 45–73.

Sharman, Campbell (2013), 'Limiting Party Representation: Evidence from a Small Parliamentary Chamber', *Legislative Studies Quarterly*, 38 (3), 327–348.

Sharman, Campbell (2015), 'Upper Houses', in Brian Galligan and Scott Brenton (eds), *Constitutional Conventions in Westminster Systems: Controversies, Changes and Challenges* (Cambridge: Cambridge University Press), pp. 157–172.

Shepsle, Kenneth A. (1979), 'Institutional Arrangements and Equilibrium in Multidimensional Voting Models', *American Journal of Political Science*, 23 (1), 27–59.

Shugart, Matthew S. (1999), 'Presidentialism, Parliamentarism, and the Provision of Collective Goods in Less-Developed Countries', *Constitutional Political Economy*, 10 (1), 53–88.

Shugart, Matthew S. (2001), 'Electoral "Efficiency" and the Move to Mixed-Member Systems', *Electoral Studies*, 20 (2), 173–193.

Shugart, Matthew S. (2005), 'Semi-Presidential Systems: Dual Executive and Mixed Authority Patterns', *French Politics*, 3 (3), 323–351.

Shugart, Matthew S. (2021), 'The Electoral System of Israel', in Reuven Y. Hazan, Alan Dowty, Menachem Hofnung, and Gideon Rahat (eds), *The Oxford Handbook of Israeli Politics and Society* (Oxford: Oxford University Press), pp. 331–350.

Shugart, Matthew S. and Carey, John M. (1992), *Presidents and Assemblies. Constitutional Design and Electoral Dynamics* (New York: Cambridge University Press).

Shugart, Matthew S. and Taagepera, Rein (2017), *Votes from Seats: Logical Models of Electoral Systems* (Cambridge: Cambridge University Press).

Shugart, Matthew S. and Wattenberg, Martin (eds) (2003), *Mixed-Member Electoral Systems: The Best of Both Worlds?* (Oxford: Oxford University Press).

Sieberer, Ulrich (2015), 'Hire or Fire?: The Link between Cabinet Investiture and Removal in Parliamentary Democracies', in Bjørn E. Rasch, Shane Martin, and José A. Cheibub (eds.), *Parliaments and Government Formation: Unpacking Investiture Rules* (Oxford: Oxford University Press), pp. 309–330.

Sing, Ming (2010), 'Explaining Democratic Survival Globally (1946–2002)', *The Journal of Politics*, 72 (2), 438–455.

Sjölin, Mats (1993), *Coalition Politics and Parliamentary Power* (Lund: Lund University Press).

Smith, Rodney (2006), *Against the Machines: Minor Parties and Independents in New South Wales, 1910–2006* (Leichhardt: The Federation Press).

Smith, Rodney (2012), 'Parliament', in David Clune and Rodney Smith (eds), *From Carr to Keneally: Labor in Office in NSW 1995–2011* (Sydney: Allen & Unwin), pp. 55–71.

Smith, Rodney (2018a), 'New South Wales: An Accidental Case of Semi-Parliamentarism?', *Australian Journal of Political Science*, 53 (2), 256–263.

Smith, Rodney (2018b), 'The Development of Semi-Parliamentarism in Australia', *Democratic Audit UK* https://www.democraticaudit.com/2018/04/20/the-development-of-semi-parliamentarism-in-australia/ (accessed 20 April 2018).

Sober, Elliot (2015), *Ockham's Razors: A User's Manual* (New York: Cambridge University Press).

Sonnicksen, Jared (2017), 'Democratising the Separation of Powers in the EU: The Case for Presidentialism', *European Law Journal*, 23 (6), 509–522.

State Commission (2017), 'Democracy and the Rule of Law in Equilibrium. Final Report of the State Commission on the Parliamentary System in the Netherlands', https://www.staatscommissieparlementairstelsel.nl/documenten/rapporten/samenvattingen/072019/18/download-the-english-translation-of-the-final-report-of-the-state-commission, accessed 22 November 2020.

Stecker, Christian (2016), 'The Effects of Federalism Reform on the Legislative Process in Germany', *Regional and Federal Studies*, 26 (5), 603–624.

Stecker, Christian and Tausendpfund, Markus (2016), 'Multidimensional Government–Citizen Congruence and Satisfaction with Democracy', *European Journal of Political Research*, 55 (3), 492–511.

Stephenson, Scott (2013), 'Constitutional Reengineering: Dialogue's Migration from Canada to Australia', *International Journal of Constitutional Law*, 11 (4), 870–897.

Stephenson, Scott (2019), 'Is the Commonwealth's Approach to Rights Constitutionalism Exportable?', *International Journal of Constitutional Law*, 17 (3), 884–903.

Stojanović, Nenad (2016), 'Party, Regional and Linguistic Proportionality under Majoritarian Rules: Swiss Federal Council Elections', *Swiss Political Science Review*, 22 (1), 41–58.

Stojanović, Nenad (2020), 'Democracy, Ethnoicracy and Consociational Demoicracy', *International Political Science Review*, 41 (1), 30–43.

Stone, Bruce (2002), 'Bicameralism and Democracy: The Transformation of Australian State Upper Houses', *Australian Journal of Political Science*, 37 (2), 267–281.

Stone, Bruce (2008), 'State Legislative Councils: Designing for Accountability', in Nicholas Aroney, Scott Prasser, and John R. Nethercote (eds), *Restraining Elective Dictatorship: The Upper House Solution?* (Perth: University of West Australia Press), pp. 175–195.

Strangio, Paul (2004), 'Labor and Reform of the Victorian Legislative Council, 1950–2003', *Labour History*, 86 (1), 33–52.

Strøm, Kaare (1990), *Minority Government and Majority Rule* (Cambridge: Cambridge University Press).

Strøm, Kaare (2000), 'Delegation and Accountability in Parliamentary Democracies', *European Journal of Political Research*, 37 (3), 261–289.

St-Vincent, Simon Labbé, Blais, André, and Pilet, Jean-Benoit (2016), 'The Electoral Sweet Spot in the Lab', *Journal of Experimental Political Science*, 3 (1), 75–83.

Stykow, Petra (2019), 'The Devil in the Details: Constitutional Regime Types in Post-Soviet Eurasia', *Post-Soviet Affairs*, 35 (2), 122–139.

Sundberg, Jan (1993), 'Finland', *European Journal of Political Research*, 24 (4), 419–423.

Svolik, Milan W. (2015), 'Which Democracies Will Last? Coups, Incumbent Takeovers, and the Dynamic of Democratic Consolidation', *British Journal of Political Science*, 45 (4), 715–738.

Svolik, Milan W. (2019), 'Polarization versus Democracy', *Journal of Democracy*, 30 (3), 20–32.

Swenden, Wilfried (2004), *Federalism and Second Chambers: Regional Representation in Parliamentary Federations: The Australian Senate and German Bundesrat Compared* (New York: Peter Lang B.).

Taagepera, Rein (2007), *Predicting Party Sizes: The Logic of Simple Electoral Systems* (New York: Oxford University Press).

Taagepera, Rein and Shugart, Matthew S. (1989), *Seats and Votes. The Effects and Determinants of Electoral Systems* (New Haven, CT: Yale University Press).

Taflaga, Marija (2018), 'What's In a Name? Semi-Parliamentarism and Australian Commonwealth Executive–Legislative Relations', *Australian Journal of Political Science*, 53 (2), 248–255.

Takayasu, Kensuke (2015), 'Is The Japanese Prime Minister Too Weak or Too Strong?: An Institutional Analysis', 成蹊法学, (83), 147–169.

Takenaka, Harukata (2012), 'Why Japanese Politics Is at a Standstill',
http://www.nippon.com/en/currents/d00038/ (accessed 12 October 2020).

Takeshi, Sasaki (2005), 'The Dissolution of Parliament and Japan's Bicameral System', *Japan Spotlight*, November/December, 38–39.

Tavits, Margit (2009), *Presidents with Prime Ministers. Do Direct Elections Matter?* (New York: Oxford University Press).

Taylor, Greg (2006), *The Constitution of Victoria* (Sydney: The Federation Press).

Thies, Michael F. and Yanai, Yuki (2014), 'Bicameralism vs Parliamentarism: Lessons from Japan's Twisted Diet', *Japanese Journal of Electoral Studies*, 30 (2), 60–74.

Thomson, Robert, Royed, Terry, Naurin, Ellin, Artés, Joaquín, Costello, Rory, Ennser-Jedenastik, Laurenz, Ferguson, Mark, Kostadinova, Petia, Moury, Catherine, Pétry, François, and Praprotnik, Katrin (2017), 'The Fulfillment of Parties' Election Pledges: A Comparative Study on the Impact of Power Sharing', *American Journal of Political Science*, 61 (3), 527–542.

Thürk, Maria (2020), *Policy-Making under Minority Governments: How Minority Cabinet Parties Influence and Pass Public Policies* (Berlin: Humboldt-Universität).

Thürk, Maria (2021), 'Small in Size but Powerful in Parliament? The Legislative Performance of Minority Governments', *Legislative Studies Quarterly*, Forthcoming.

Thürk, Maria, Hellstrom, Johan, and Döring, Holger (2021), 'Institutional Constraints on Cabinet Formation: Veto Points and Party System Dynamics', *European Journal of Political Research*, 60 (2), 295–316.

Tillman, Erik R. (2015), 'Pre-Electoral Coalitions and Voter Turnout', *Party Politics*, 21 (5), 726–737.

Tokatlı, M. (2020), *Auf dem Weg zum »Präsidialsystem alla Turca?« Eine Analyse unterschiedlicher Regierungsformen in der Türkei seit 1921* (Baden-Baden: Nomos).

Toshkov, Dimiter (2016), *Research Design in Political Science* (London: Palgrave).

Traber, Denise (2015), 'Disenchanted Swiss Parliament? Electoral Strategies and Coalition Formation', *Swiss Political Science Review*, 21 (4), 702–723.

Tsebelis, George (2002), *Veto Players. How Political Institutions Work* (Princeton, NJ: Princeton University Press).

Tsebelis, George (2017), 'The Time Inconsistency of Long Constitutions: Evidence from the World', *European Journal of Political Research*, 56 (4), 820–845.

Tsebelis, George (2020), 'Constitutional Rigidity Matters: A Veto Players Approach', *British Journal of Political Science*, Forthcoming.

Tsebelis, George and Alemán, Eduardo (2005), 'Presidential Conditional Agenda Setting in Latin America', *World Politics*, 58 (3), 396–420.

Tsebelis, George and Money, Jeannette (1997), *Bicameralism* (Cambridge: Cambridge University Press).

Turner, Ken (1969), *House of Review? The New South Wales Legislative Council, 1934–1968* (Sydney: University of Sydney Press).

Twomey, Anne (2004), *The Constitution of New South Wales* (Leichhardt: The Federation Press).

Umbers, Lachlan M. (2020), 'Compulsory Voting: A Defence', *British Journal of Political Science*, 50 (4), 1307–1324.

Van Trease, Howard (1993), 'From Colony to Independence', in Howard Van Trease (ed.), *Atoll Politics: The Republic of Kiribati* (Christchurch: University of the South Pacific Press), pp. 3–22.

Vatter, Adrian (2016), 'Switzerland on the Road from a Consociational to a Centrifugal Democracy?', *Swiss Political Science Review*, 22 (1), 59–74.

Vercesi, Michelangelo (2017), 'What Kind of Veto Player Is the Italian Senate? A Comparative Analysis of European Second Chambers', *Journal of Modern Italian Studies*, 22 (5), 604–623.

Vercesi, Michelangelo (2019), 'Democratic Stress and Political Institutions: Drives of Reforms of Bicameralism in Times of Crisis', *Representation*, 1–18.

Viehoff, Daniel (2017), 'XIV—The Truth in Political Instrumentalism', *Proceedings of the Aristotelian Society*, 117 (3), 273–295.

Viehoff, Daniel (2019), 'Power and Equality', in David Sobel, Peter Vallentyne, and Steven Wall (eds), *Oxford Studies in Political Philosophy* (Oxford: Oxford University Press), pp. 3–38.

Volden, Craig and Carrubba, Clifford J. (2004), 'The Formation of Oversized Coalitions in Parliamentary Democracies', *American Journal of Political Science*, 48 (3), 521–537.

Von Mettenheim, Kurt (1997), 'Introduction', in Kurt von Mettenheim (ed.), *Presidential Institutions and Democratic Politics* (Baltimore, MD: Johns Hopkins University Press), pp. 1–15.

Waldron, Jeremy (1999), *Law and Disagreement* (Oxford: Oxford University Press).

Waldron, Jeremy (2006), 'The Core of the Case against Judicial Review', *The Yale Law Journal*, 115 (6), 1346–1406.

Waldron, Jeremy (2012), 'Bicameralism and the Separation of Powers', *Current Legal Problems*, 65 (1), 31–57.

Wall, Steven (2007), 'Democracy and Equality', *The Philosophical Quarterly*, 57 (228), 416–438.

Ward, Alan J. (2012), *Parliamentary Government in Australia* (North Melbourne: Australian Scholarly Publishing Pty Ltd).

Ward, Hugh and Weale, Albert (2010), 'Is Rule by Majorities Special?', *Political Studies*, 58 (1), 26–46.

Watkins, David and Lemieux, Scott (2015), 'Compared to What? Judicial Review and Other Veto Points in Contemporary Democratic Theory', *Perspectives on Politics*, 13 (2), 312–326.

Waugh, John (1997), 'Framing the First Victorian Constitution, 1853–5', *Monash University Law Review*, 23 (2), 331–361.

Weale, Albert (2018), 'What's So Good about Parliamentary Hybrids? Comment on 'Australian Bicameralism as Semiparliamentarianism: Patterns of Majority formation in 29 Democracies', *Australian Journal of Political Science*, 53 (2), 234–240.

Weale, Albert (2019), 'Three Types of Majority Rule', *The Political Quarterly*, 90 (1), 62–76.

Weber, Max (1986), 'The Reich President', *Social Research*, 53 (1), 128–132, transl. Gordon Wells.

Welp, Yanina (2016), 'Recall Referendums in Peruvian Municipalities: A Political Weapon for Bad Losers or an Instrument of Accountability?', *Democratization*, 23 (7), 1162–1179.

Welp, Yanina and Whitehead, Laurence (2020a), 'Recall: Democratic Advance, Safety Valve or Risky Adventure?', in Yanina Welp and Laurence Whitehead (eds), *The Politics of Recall Elections* (Basingstoke: Palgrave Macmillan), pp. 9–27.

Welp, Yanina and Whitehead, Laurence (eds) (2020b), *The Politics of Recall Elections* (Basingstoke: Palgrave Macmillan).

Weyland, Kurt (2020), 'Populism's Threat to Democracy: Comparative Lessons for the United States', *Perspectives on Politics*, 18 (2), 389–406.

Whitehead, Laurence (2018), 'The Recall of Elected Officeholders: The Growing Incidence of a Venerable, but Overlooked, Democratic Institution', *Democratization*, 25 (8), 1341–1357.

Wiens, David (2012), 'Prescribing Institutions without Ideal Theory*', *Journal of Political Philosophy*, 20 (1), 45–70.

Wilson, James Lindley (2019), *Democratic Equality* (Princeton, NJ: Princeton University Press).

Wilson, Wodrow (1844), 'Committee or Cabinet Government?', *Overland Monthly*, 3, 17–33.

Wolkenstein, Fabio (2018), 'Demoicracy, Transnational Partisanship and the EU', *Journal of Common Market Studies*, 56 (2), 284–299.

Index